sfergusen
@ciot-og.
UK

Media Relations for Lawyers

Related titles by Law Society Publishing

Marketing Your Law Firm
Lucy Adam
1 85328 745 8

Marketing, Management and Motivation
Dianne Bown-Wilson and Gail Courtney
1 85328 810 1

Excellent Client Service
Heather Stewart
1 85328 777 6

Internet Marketing: Strategies for Law Firms
Edited by Nicola Webb
1 85328 870 5

Titles from Law Society Publishing can be ordered from all good legal bookshops or direct from our distributors, Marston Book Services (tel. 01235 465656 or e-mail law.society@marston.co.uk). For further information or a catalogue, call our editorial and marketing office on 020 7320 5878.

Media Relations for Lawyers

2nd edition

Sue Stapely

The Law Society

ISBN 1 85328 857 8

Published in 2003 by the Law Society
113 Chancery Lane, London WC2A 1PL

Typeset by J&L Composition, Filey, North Yorkshire
Printed by Antony Rowe Ltd, Chippenham, Wilts

Contents

Ackowledgements		x
About the author		xi
Abbreviations		xii

	Introduction	**1**

1	**Why bother to spend time acquiring media relations skills?**	**5**
	The legal marketplace	6
	The modern media	7
	Responding to demand	8
	Gaining recognition for your expertise	8
	Marketing through the media	8
	Harnessing the media to support your client's case	9
	Enhancing the image of the profession	10
	The media's role when campaigning	11
	Crisis avoidance and limitation	13
	The philosophy of this book	13
	Your own media relations policy	13
	How to use this book	14

2	**Setting the rules: what you can and cannot do**	**15**
	Rules for solicitors	16
	Rules for barristers	25
	Advice to legal executives	28
	Lawyers employed in commerce and industry	28
	Legal and court constraints on media relations	28
	Reporting restrictions	41
	Family cases	46
	Tape-recording court proceedings	47
	Transcripts and skeleton arguments	47

3	**Defining and understanding today's media and handling online media**	**49**
	The print media	49
	Radio	55
	Television	57
	Alternative media	58

Online media   59
Understanding the media from a legal editor's perspective   66
Contacting the journalist   69

4   How to handle the print media   **71**

Getting going: dealing with journalists   71
Helpful props   72
Create one or more media lists   73
News agencies   74
Press cuttings and media monitoring   75
Active or reactive media relations   76
What is a journalist?   76
Myths exploded   77
Segmenting the media   79
Contacting journalists   84
What is your story?   87
Dealing with an unexpected approach from a journalist   90
On and off the record   91
Granting exclusive interviews   93
How you are described when being quoted   94
Can I ask to check the piece before it goes to print?   95
The press interview   96
When they get it wrong   99
Encouraging the journalist to contact you again   100
Journalistic rivalry   101
News releases   101
News on the wires   113
Profile pieces   113
Leader columns, opinion columnists and 'op ed' pieces   115
Use of photographs   115
What to do with research findings and other supporting documents   118
How to distribute your news release   118
Be prepared   121
Press conferences   122
Press briefings   124
Media lunches   124
Regular legal columns   125
Book reviews   125
Diary and gossip columns   126
Articles   126
Research-based stories   127
Keeping the story running   128
Bear-traps to avoid to achieve results   128
And if the piece never appears?   129
Litigation PR   129

5   How to handle radio   132

Preparing for radio communications   132
Questions to ask when approached by a radio programme   133
Preparing for the interview   133
In a radio discussion with others   147
Remote studios   148
Being a guest on a phone-in programme   149
'Fluffs' and 'dries'   151
Radio interviews conducted over the telephone   152
The end of the interview   153
Follow-up calls or correspondence   154
Some tips from a broadcaster   154

6   How to handle television   156

That first contact   156
Questions to ask before you appear   157
Familiarise yourself with the programme   158
Essential preparations   158
Pre-recorded or live?   159
Handling the pre-recorded interview   160
What if I grind to a complete halt on live television?   161
What shall I wear?   162
What about my nerves?   170
When should I get to the studio?   172
The 'hostility suite'   172
Microphones are there to help   173
Floor manager   174
What the studio looks like   174
On air   175
Evaluating your performance   178
Discussion and panel programmes   178
When the cameras come to you   180
The snatched interview   181
Down-the-line interviews   183
The aim of the game   183

7   Media relations for marketing   184

Marketing principles   184
Guidance from professional bodies   185
Have a strategy   187
Understanding the role of media relations in the marketing mix   188
Harnessing on the media for effective marketing   191

Regional media   192
Building relationships and knowing your sector   192
Planned media relations for marketing   194
Identifying and packaging stories and selling them in   194
Follow-up   199
Exploiting technology to promote your firm   200
Award-winning marketing   201
Marketing advice from a senior partner   203
Marketing advice from a legal editor   205
Finding and appointing a marketing or PR consultant   208

8   Litigation support   **219**

How to identify cases with potential media interest   220
The guiding principle   221
The practicalities   222
Trial by jury   222
The media as a litigation tool   224
The partner's experience   225
The client's perspective   227
High Court cases   229

9   Crisis management: not making a disaster out of a crisis   **230**

Risk analysis   231
Preparing by planning   231
First reaction   233
Speak up and speak up fast   234
When not to communicate   236
The rules of crisis management   236
A few negative principles   237
Who can I turn to for help?   239
The crisis toolkit   240
Preparing by questioning   241
Selecting your spokesperson   242
Things to avoid saying in a crisis   243
Actively managing the media   244
So what should you say?   244
Maintaining the media competence   245
The legal editor's viewpoint   246
The senior partner's viewpoint   252
Merger communications   252

Appendix 1 Solicitors' Publicity Code 2001   **258**

**Appendix 2 Guidance notes for branches of the Institute of
Legal Executives (ILEX)**   **262**

Appendix 3 Law Society's Commerce & Industry Group media relations guidelines **266**

Appendix 4 Campaigning on miscarriages of justice **267**

Appendix 5 Recommended additional reading **272**

Index 274

Acknowledgements

This book is the work of many not just of one.

If I attempted to list all those to whom I talked, from whom I have learnt, or whose wise counsel I have borrowed, I could fill the page and would still be bound to miss some out. You know who you are and I hope you know how grateful I am.

Some, however, deserve special mention: Geoffrey Robertson QC and Andrew Nicol QC have again allowed me to steal from their book; my colleagues at Quiller (Jonathan Hill, John Eisenhammer, George Bridges, Peter Barnes, Laura Montgomery and Petrina Gannon), and earlier those at Fishburn Hedges, have been endlessly patient and taught me a great deal; the members of the legal press corps remain a delight to work with – many have become good friends; my former PA, Angie Rossiter, who has gone on to grander things, has again held my hand when the technology threatened to defeat me; all of the clients, who over many years have sought my help have added to my knowledge; Jane Withey, my publisher, has provided encouragement when I flagged, Elizabeth Davison's editing was meticulous, Tim gently kept my nose to the grindstone, and my wonderful sons, Stuart and Shaw (now also a lawyer) have kept me sane throughout.

The help I have received from them all has been invaluable. Any errors are my own.

About the author

Sue Stapely's first career was with BBC Television. She then took a law degree and qualified as a solicitor while working as the manager of a Citizens' Advice Bureau and bringing up her two sons. During this period Sue stood as a parliamentary candidate for the SDP, chaired The 300 Group to bring more women into politics and public life and regularly appeared on radio and television programmes such as *Question Time*. After some years as a partner in a law firm, specialising in family law and public affairs, Sue was invited to head press and parliamentary affairs for the Law Society for five years. She then moved into issues management consultancy, first working with Fishburn Hedges and currently working mainly with Quiller Consultants. Her clients include major businesses and organisations of all kinds, law and accountancy firms and their clients and high-profile individuals. Most recently they have included solicitor, Sally Clark, for whom Sue mounted a media campaign pro bono alongside Sally's other lawyers to secure her release after she was wrongfully imprisoned.

Sue's extracurricular roles include membership of the Boards of the London Academy of Music and Dramatic Art, and the Spare Tyre Theatre Company, of the Advisory Councils of the National Consumer Council and the Solicitors' Pro Bono Group and the Development Council of the Royal Court Theatre. She is a Fellow of the Institute of Public Relations and of the Royal Society for the Arts and until recently a Board member of the Countryside Agency.

Abbreviations

APIL	Association of Personal Injury Lawyers
BMIF	Bar Mutual Insurance Fund
CFA	conditional fee agreement
ENG	electronic news gathering
FAQ	frequently asked question
FM	floor manager
ILEX	Institute of Legal Executives
IPR	Institute of Public Relations
LLP	limited liability partnership
MDP	multidisciplinary partnership
OFCOM	Office of Communications
PCC	Press Complaints Commission
PDF	portable document format
PRCA	Public Relations Consultants Association
PSMG	Professional Services Marketing Group
SME	small to medium-sized enterprise
URL	uniform resource locator

Introduction

What is this all about?

The first edition of this book, written in 1994, was the first aimed specifically to help lawyers – of all kinds – to communicate effectively through the media to the many audiences they seek to influence every day.

It was written during an uncomfortable period in my life, as head of public relations at the Law Society, spent trying to improve the reputation of all solicitors. As we know, lawyers are still almost universally disliked as a profession, though every client can tell a tale of how their own individual legal adviser must be the exception to the rule. Many politicians and company leaders initially qualified as lawyers. All businesses are reliant on legal advice for their existence. More and more young people elect to go into the law, despite the current downturn in the marketplace, with the gender balance completely changing. The first judge has sat wearing a turban instead of a wig and the numbers in the profession have risen in the nine years since 1994 from 70,000 to 113,372 solicitors on the Roll. Yet we remain the butt of cheap jibes and consistently near the bottom of popularity polls.

I hoped that by helping lawyers to communicate in a more straightforward, accessible way through the media, reports of our work might be more accurate and supportive and this might go some way to make us better advisers as well as to adjust public opinion – an ambitious project.

The trigger that galvanised me to write the first edition of this book was a piece of opinion research I commissioned, which involved stopping shoppers in a number of High Streets and asking them to say what the word 'solicitor' meant to them. The answers were depressing. The most common replies contained 'arrogant, expensive, aloof, elitist, in it for the money, stuck up, slow'. The numbers of complaints against our profession are at an all-time high, though we presumably do communicate better these days as most lawyers who are required to give interviews to the media or make presentations of any kind now undergo some form of media or skills training. So have things changed at all and is there any point in still trying to be more 'media savvy'?

The public certainly has a much more sophisticated understanding of the legal process and the part that lawyers play – at least as far as litigation goes. We watched the televised trials of O.J. Simpson and Louise Woodward from the United States. Judge Judy's show is screened in the United Kingdom and for two years now there has been talk of a British spin-off. We have had celebrities' difficulties with the law (Michael Barrymore, Jeffrey Archer, John Leslie) running for days on the front pages of the tabloid press. Ordinary people have the minutiae of their lives examined when they come to court (Barry George, Sally Clark). We follow with interest libel suits brought by stars against newspapers (Campbell versus *Daily Mirror*; Zeta Jones and Douglas versus *Hello*), and divorce and paternity suits (Countess Spencer; Prince of Wales; Bing versus Hurley) sell papers in enormous quantities. The *Daily Mirror*'s editor, Piers Morgan, reported with glee the increase in circulation after he bought Royal butler Paul Burrell's story after his trial collapsed. Police investigations, searches for missing people and hostage situations are conducted in front of cameras and searchlights (Soham; Millie Dowler; the Hackney hostage seige, which featured widely in the media at Christmas 2002), with the police carefully harnessing the media to support their work. The BBC devoted an entire day of broadcasting to crime last year and *Crime Watch* has attracted large audiences for 20 years.

In evidence to a Select Committee in March 2003, Rebekah Wade, the editor of the *Sun*, confirmed that her paper buys stories from police officers to supplement their incomes. Recent coverage of a celebrity's arrest and attendance at a police station could only have reached the press as a result of a phone call from the station. A standard tactic before making any allegations for police investigation is for the complainant to engage a publicist to assess the potential value of their story to the media.

On the other hand, submissions are now made to demonstrate that fair trials are impossible because of prejudicial media coverage and in a case in which I have been involved recently, it was clear that an individual's reputation had been ruined by rumour circulating on the Internet long before anything appeared in the print or broadcast media and some weeks before the police arrested or charged him.

We have, as was feared, become a more litigious country with most accident victims, no matter how minor the injury or loss, considering whether they can lodge a claim against someone for compensation. Anxiety about the risk of being sued has created defensive medical practice and a plethora of new 'nannyish' constraints on our daily lives.

'No win, no fee', conditional, contingency and success fees are all means for the impecunious to litigate and are now commonplace, yet when I was writing the first edition I was repeatedly told that it would never happen here and that the American style of litigation would always be regarded as unacceptable to the British. The advertisements now covering hoardings and filling our screens placed by claims handlers are far worse than any anticipated or permitted a decade ago, and for specialist solicitors trying to practise in the area of personal injury, competition with the unqualified is fierce and times are hard.

Harnessing media support for marketing activity is generally much more sophisticated now. We have Pro Bono Awards, flaunting the social conscience of lawyers in the way that the American firms have done for some time. League tables of the 'best' lawyers and firms are published annually with lavish celebrity-strewn dinners to hand out the prizes. For the first time, 2003 saw the Legal Aid Lawyer of the Year Award sponsored by *Independent Lawyer*. Few appointments of corporate lawyers are concluded without reference to the *Legal 500* or *Chambers* directories.

A whole parasitic industry, of which I admit I am part, has grown up to service these new needs. A major national firm I advised for some years had more than 70 marketing and communications professionals on its staff, and there is only one 'Magic Circle' firm (i.e. the five largest law firms: Clifford Chance, Linklaters, Allen & Overy, Freshfields and Slaughter & May) that does not have a marketing director or equivalent in post with a salary comparable to an experienced partner's equity share. A number of consultancies offer 'litigation support' among their public relations offerings.

The development of technology has also completely changed the way lawyers market and communicate. Virtually every firm and set of chambers now has a website. Almost every lawyer has a screen of some sort on their desk and many clients, themselves technically proficient, expect e-mail responses immediately, rather than careful letters some days later by 'snail mail', though I observe that lawyers are one of the only professionals still prone to dictating their own e-mails and refusing to be parted from a secretary. E-briefings are despatched in seconds to thousands, and the need for high-gloss marketing brochures has almost gone. Before instructing a solicitor, most clients will search the Web to research their options and client loyalty to a firm is decreasing as a result.

While revolutionising how businesses promote themselves, sophisticated technology can have a darker side in terms of reputational risk. Huge corporations are vulnerable to global discrediting by a few diligent campaigners harnessing the Internet, as was shown when McDonalds' reputation was substantially damaged by two young people skilfully using the Internet to publicise their disquiet about the company, even though McDonalds' action in court was largely successful. Incontinent use of e-mail during office hours is another worry.

In the first edition I suggested that effective and knowledgeable use of the media was a skill more lawyers should acquire if they were to provide their clients with a full professional service and defend them to those outside the courtroom as well as within. Some deprecated this view, but in the intervening years 'trial by media' has become commonplace, rumour runs for days on the Internet before it ever reaches newsprint, and fair trials unprejudiced by media activity are increasingly hard to achieve. The Attorney-General, on more than one occasion, has been obliged to issue a note to all editors warning them of prejudicial coverage, and has now started a consultation process to create new guidelines and a more rigorous regulatory environment to preserve the legal process from the worst excesses of public prurience. The Lord Chancellor's Department press office regularly issues briefings and sets up on-site press-handling facilities for major trials. We understand better the importance of perception as well as the impact of reality on the justice process.

But this is not a treatise or a political tome. This second edition (still, we believe, the only book in the UK on media relations targeted just at lawyers, their staff and clients) is simply designed to be a practical hand-book for solicitors representing clients on issues of interest. It is for bar-risters advocating high profile cases. It is for those in firms and chambers with marketing responsibilities, keen to publicise the respective merits of using their particular firm. It is for the politicians in the profession campaigning on fees, professional regulation and practice matters.

It will hopefully be useful to those in High Street practices doing largely publicly funded work, as well as those in the glamorous glass atri-ums of the cities, who while still lawyers have really become dealers and brokers and earn individually as much as many High Street firms make in a year.

It is based on personal experience – mine and others – written fast to be read fast and left nearby for when the need arises.

In the intervening years since leaving the Law Society, I have (as so many do) become a consultant. I retain my solicitor's practising certificate but now spend most of my professional time advising businesses, public organisations, professional firms and individuals of all kinds on how to preserve or enhance their reputations, build their businesses, get their messages across, succeed in their campaigns, remedy injustices or gener-ally operate more successfully in an environment where most of them are under continuous media scrutiny. I am often brought in by lawyers who generously recognise what I can bring to their work. I do not see myself as a 'spin doctor', as I always recommend truthfulness and candour to my clients, but I am very clear that skilful communications to all involved can often enhance the likelihood of a successful outcome in many cases.

Having been a partner in a law firm, and advised some 50 law firms and five sets of chambers, I know very well the time and budget pressures on most of those who will read this, but hopefully the indexing will route you fast to what you need and if questions remain unanswered I can always be reached at sue.stapely@ntlworld.com.

1

Why bother to spend time acquiring media relations skills?

If you and your firm are already in regular contact with the right media, receiving accurate and supportive coverage of your work and your clients, attracting more than enough of the right kind of clients, generating few if any complaints about your service, maintaining satisfied client referrals and staff retention levels, and you are all meeting or exceeding your billing targets, you probably have little need for this book, though you can clearly afford it.

There is usually, however, some room for improvement and acquiring new skills, as well as being sound in business terms, can be energising and enjoyable.

Every client relationship is influenced by the quality of the communications skills of the lawyer involved. Every group of professionals working together does so more effectively if the members communicate well with each other about their collective and individual objectives and concerns. The outside view of a person, a firm or an entire profession is strongly influenced by the way that individual, entity or profession communicates to all their various audiences. The Law Society's Clients' Charter is dedicated to clearer legal communications in the hope of reducing complaints about the profession, one-quarter of which are thought to have their basis in poor communications.

Communicating well with the media is a quite separate and particular skill, but increasingly the opinions of others are formed or affected by what they read or hear, through research on the Internet, reading newspapers and magazines, watching television or listening to the radio, or simply seeing advertisements and publicity materials.

Many chargeable hours in law firms are now invested in business development and marketing. Many people are employed by chambers and firms to help expand these businesses. All major firms pump out news releases every time a valuable deal is clinched for a client and an entire publishing industry specialises in legal reportage.

But from many years of working with lawyers, I am clear that much of this time and energy is still misdirected and fails to achieve all that is intended. The firms and chambers that communicate well to the media tend also to communicate impressively to their staff and clients and to flourish commercially. Some firms, small in size but big in ambition, have achieved entirely disproportionate media coverage for their size and as a result manage to attract clients, staff and work of a quality far higher than a modest-sized firm would otherwise acquire (e.g. H_2O, Fox Williams, Osborne Clarke). Huge firms, including the very largest in the world, have been rocked financially by gossipy internal communications that fell into the hands of journalists and received global exposure (e.g. Clifford Chance, Norton Rose).

Well-managed media relations can inform potential clients, reassure existing clients, raise internal morale, attract recruits, maximise the effectiveness of the organisation's marketing strategy and exclude and alarm commercial competitors. But when it goes wrong, it goes very wrong and its impact can linger for years.

The legal marketplace

Many of us trained in the expectation that we were entering a profession. We now find ourselves in a business, or even a trade, and one that is as commercially fierce and competitive as any other. Because of the argumentative personalities of most of those practising law, it is a business more sharp-elbowed than most.

Whenever the corporate world suffers a downturn, law firms and commercial chambers are also hit shortly afterwards. Firms may have to acknowledge publicly that they are obliged to encourage equity partners to take early retirement, or announce cuts in their profit shares, or that they are bribing trainees to defer the start of their training contracts. Those still doing publicly funded work struggle to meet their overheads and make a living, and are obliged each month to investigate new ways of generating and retaining profitable work.

Often, the first budget to be pared in a time of economic recession is that of the marketing team. It should be the last. If a firm stops marketing and begins to reduce its profile, it will not only confirm any suspicions that may exist about its stability, but it will provide opportunities for less well-known rivals to fill the vacuum to promote themselves.

Client loyalty still exists among many private clients and some commercial ones, but increasingly those who have big legal mandates in their gift are obliged to put the work out to competitive tender, and highly skilled specialist lawyers are required to present and pitch for work against several teams from other firms. This perhaps involves employing communications rather than legal skills, which they neither have nor wish to acquire.

The decision to invite a firm to pitch for work is based on a number of factors: personal knowledge of it, former or existing clients' comments, the word on the street, its position in the league tables and the comments in the legal directories. With monitoring systems like LexisNexis readily available, it is also the work of only seconds to pull all the relevant press coverage about the firm off the Web. Just searching on the name of a lead lawyer or firm can usually throw up all the deals with which he or she has been associated in the past few years, and more sophisticated search engines can tell the potential client much, much more.

The better established legal journalists working on the specialist publications or undertaking research for the directories are also often invited to contribute their views of firms and lawyers, as many have developed a highly sophisticated and knowledgeable understanding of some sectors in the legal marketplace.

As firms merge, acquire international partners, demerge, rebrand, disappear or expand, the perception of them usually lags some two to five years behind the reality. Some research I undertook into a medium-sized City practice with more than 50 partners revealed that the majority of its corporate clients believed there were between 20 and 30 partners in the firm and were unaware of the existence of at least three of the firm's most successful practice areas. Their perception of the firm had remained rooted in how it had been when the clients first instructed it and they were unaware of how it had developed and changed.

To build a positive and appropriate brand and profile for your firm takes time, requires expertise and energy, but is perfectly possible.

The modern media

The first edition of this book made only scant reference to the Internet as it was only just beginning to influence the way we all work and communicate.

This edition will focus more on the immediacy of modern media relations. While the construction of a speedy and practical website is a matter for the marketing professionals, the way in which you communicate with the media and the messages about your firm and its lawyers that appear on the Internet are very much your concern.

Many firms and chambers still send out news releases by fax to hundreds of outlets (there are at least 400 legal journalists on national and regional lists I maintain). Others e-mail them to the desks of individual journalists, and ensure they are available on the firm's or chambers' website. Others much more carefully target specific journalists on specific publications and, having established an easy, informal e-mailing relationship, just send them the bones of the story in an e-mail message and then sell the story in by phone or in greater detail electronically.

Some firms are still just faxing or even posting hard copy releases and remain surprised that they achieve scant take-up.

Responding to demand

Lawyers are easy to find. We are listed in innumerable directories, or a call to the Law Society, the Bar Council or the Institute will quickly track us down.

In-house lawyers are often the first the media approach when they require information about the employing company or organisation. When a local authority hits the headlines, it is often the senior solicitor who is expected to deal with the media enquiries.

When a matter comes to court, the solicitor rather than the barrister is invited to comment on their client's behalf, and if the client is prepared to make their own statement, it is often done after consultation with the lawyers and with them in attendance at the time.

Refusing to take a journalist's call, or responding with 'no comment' is not only rude and unhelpful, but is squandering an opportunity to promote your business or help your client.

Gaining recognition for your expertise

However superficial it may be of us all, we inevitably notice and usually respect those who are reported as expert in any field. We also all adore recognition of expertise. The more a lawyer appears on radio or television, or is quoted in the print media or on the Internet, the more likely it is that they will be presumed to be a skilled and professional operator. While a certain amount of envy may give rise to the odd snide remark by a professional rival, most clients are impressed and reassured to see the lawyer they are considering appointing, or have already instructed, reported. Obviously, the more credible the publication or programme, the more gravitas will attach to the lawyer. Standing alongside someone tacitly acknowledged to be – or even convicted of being – a rogue and a villain on the courtroom steps may not serve your professional profile as well as granting a thoughtful interview on the *Today* programme on the impact of the proposed changes to the Criminal Justice Act, or commenting knowledgeably in the *Financial Times* about the regulation of the financial services industry.

Marketing through the media

Media relations are obviously a vital part of the marketing mix. Lucy Adam, *Marketing Your Law Firm* (Law Society, 2002) is a good primer for all embarking on a marketing strategy. Chapter 7 covers this in detail.

Harnessing the media to support your client's case

An entirely different aspect is the duty owed by lawyers to their clients to utilise every possible means of achieving their desired results when the clients face the law. In 1994, when writing the first edition of this book, I suggested that many clients were seeking out lawyers whom they believed to be skilled media operators to represent them, sometimes in preference to a particular specialist. This was greeted by some with derision and I was told that many of the lawyers who were regularly quoted in or appeared on the media were not regarded highly by their peers and had unhealthy egos, combined with scant legal skills.

I remain unrepentant. The late Paula Yates went to a media lawyer for help with her divorce from Bob Geldof; Elizabeth Hurley sought advice on the paternity proceedings started by Steve Bing from a defamation specialist, not a family law firm; Steve Bing went to family law specialists, but I held their hand under the media spotlight. Most weeks I work alongside lawyers who are either out of their depth on the specific issue they have been asked to handle, but comfortable with the media's interest in it, or who are familiar with the legal work on which they have been instructed, but terrified of being wrong-footed by the media.

All the most interesting cases of litigation in the past decade, whether commercial, civil or criminal, have given rise to media interest and the usual description 'high profile' simply means they have been widely reported. Virtually every local paper has a court reporter and even most minor matters are dutifully written up. Phone-in programmes continue to have legal advice sessions. Legal developments in the many different business sectors are reported in their trade publications.

The 'media lawyers' appear to flourish and those in more invisible traditional practices are evidently struggling.

While there are strict rules that constrain what can and cannot be done to influence the outcome of the judicial process (all dealt with in Chapter 2), there is much that can be done to ensure that the climate of opinion surrounding a case is favourable to the client and the issues they want adjudicated. All of us in Sally Clark's legal defence team were clear that a carefully planned and executed media campaign was instrumental in alerting the widest audiences to the dreadful miscarriage of justice Sally had suffered.

With our prurient appetite for the least edifying aspects of human nature, however, it is often the case that the coverage has focused on the allegations and claims made against one party by another, and defence lawyers are forced to try to reduce the level of prejudice that has built up and counter misconceptions as well as facts. In the case of John Leslie, the 'disgraced' television presenter, John was dismissed from his job (about £350,000 a year), was vilified in all the media and faced a ruined career, long before he was even contacted by the police and advised if any charges were going to be laid. He had been condemned by rumour on a website called *popbitch* and by two inadvertent comments on television chat shows. A submission has been prepared by his lawyers, claiming that he can never face a fair trial because of the level of prejudicial media coverage he has received, which include some 80,000 mentions on websites and discussion groups, all entirely based on rumour and speculation. But he has now been charged with two charges of indecent assault and we wait to see if a fair trial is possible.

So clients, who are all the consumers of the media to a greater or lesser extent, increasingly expect that their legal advisers will be able to represent them before the court of public opinion as well as before the Crown Court or county court.

Enhancing the image of the profession

All of us who are lawyers are resigned to the fact that our profession is not loved. Despite most clients expressing gratitude to their own particular legal adviser, the profession as a whole is derided.

Much of that derision is fuelled by the way the media represent us. Nick Ross, the journalist and veteran presenter of BBC TV's *Crime Watch* and many other consumer programmes, has met many more lawyers, of all kinds, than most. He pulled no punches when asked for his views on the profession:

- Lawyers are the butt of so many jokes because they deserve to be: there is enough truth to complaints of prostituting themselves ('There are some things a shark just won't do') to make the gags ring true.
- When even senior judges concede that justice is a 'game' – yet do not resign – lay people should have doubts about their integrity.
- Lawyers, like most other white-collar professionals (doctors, accountants, politicians, journalists) have clung on to old practices while blue-collar workers have had to reform. Their power at the top of many establishments (and indeed the Establishment) has protected them, leading to smugness, sloth and arrogance.
- Even journalists are frightened of lawyers.
- Steelworkers, shipwrights, coalminers and others have gone to the wall, and car-makers have turned to automation, but the legal profession continues to swell. He suspects that if the Great Plague struck again, but targeted only lawyers, society would adjust very swiftly and relatively painlessly and injustice would not increase.
- Lawyers tend to be surpassingly conservative, especially those who consider themselves 'radical'. Usually this means they take an even more quaintly old-fashioned view than their peers. He has rarely met lawyers who challenge the very foundations of our legal system.

- Going to law is hugely expensive and cumbersome: avoiding litigation ought to be the aim, yet criminal proceedings are common. Indeed, 'prosecuting' criminals is the great purpose of the machine we have built to protect society from crime.
- His own experience leads him to the view that the criminal justice system is surprisingly tangential to crime. It rests on medieval concepts that are unsuited to solving today's problems.
- Criminal law, like religion, rests on faith – the intellectual rationalisations are often just window-dressing – and remains one of the few corners of human advance where 'precedence' is regarded as a virtue, rather than something likely to be old-fashioned and in need of iconoclastic reform.
- In the short term, if we are to cut crime we must keep the police and criminal out of court as much as possible – it is too time-consuming, resource-expensive and haphazard.
- In the long term, we need to see the criminal justice system as an engine for reducing crime rather than allocating blame. The change in emphasis would lead to a revolutionary change in perspective.
- Contracts have been revolutionised, but the 'red hand' principle should be extended to corporate law, i.e. if the terms of a contract are not clear and intuitive, attention must be drawn to any clauses that might prove unexpected to one of the signatories. If there is ever dispute about a contract, the lawyers who drew it up should be financially liable for the consequences of the ambiguity. Instead, the law machine parasitically feeds itself from the flesh of its own clients.
- Some of the brightest (and nicest) people he knows are lawyers. What a waste!

There is little we can do about the personalities and avarice of many in our profession, but accessible, truthful coverage of the work of lawyers can only serve to inform and educate the public, not only about just what lawyers do, but also the pressures they face and the constraints under which they operate. It will help to rebuild confidence in the legal system too.

Rumours often fester into facts, and there are many misconceptions about our work, our fees, our lifestyles, which good lawyers communicating well about our profession can correct.

The media's role when campaigning

Although the government, the House of Commons and the House of Lords all have alarming numbers of eminent lawyers in their midst, it is still fairly new for lawyers to be seen as campaigning political animals.

The professional bodies determinedly represented themselves as apolitical, and campaigning and lobbying were left to pressure groups, though many had radical lawyers in their ranks.

In the past decade or so, with major legislative changes imposed upon the legal profession, it has become essential for the professional bodies to become more vocal.

Both the Law Society and the Bar Council use professional external advisers to support their public affairs and public relations. The Law Society has both a Parliamentary Officer, lobbying on behalf of the profession, and a network of solicitors in the local law societies who assume voluntary responsibility for liaising with their MPs on matters of professional concern. A parallel network of solicitors operates voluntarily as public relations officers, ensuring that the local media are alerted to matters of concern to both the providers of legal services and local consumers.

With self-regulation under real threat as the level of complaints against the profession escalates, and the extension of the Courts and Legal Services Act 1990 opens up the legal marketplace in which we once enjoyed monopolies to more unqualified operators and market forces, a good relationship with the national and local media is vital if the concerns of the profession are to be presented as more than protectionist and self-serving.

Careful messages in local papers, which all MPs assiduously read, can counter the more abrasive utterances from the Lord Chancellor and explain the impact that proposed changes to the provision of legal services could have on a local community. Most solicitors need to be reminded that the motto of the Law Society translates 'To serve law and justice', not 'To preserve the incomes of solicitors', but the role of the media in building an understanding of the lawyer's role in society is always valuable.

Media reaction can also be powerfully influential. At the time of writing, the Lord Chancellor is under fire, having announced that fewer first-time and second-time offender burglars are to be imprisoned in future. This was reported widely. A few days later a further statement from the Lord Chancellor indicated his belief that the majority of the public was entirely happy with this decision. This second report has given rise to innumerable angry letters, phone-in calls, articles and Internet messages all determined to demonstrate that the public is very far from happy with this decision and expects it to be reconsidered. It is hard to forecast how this will be resolved, but it demonstrates how important it now is to gauge public opinion accurately and how influential it can be. The proposed changes to the entire constitutional and legal system announced in the June 2003 cabinet re-shuffle have yet to be clarified and explained.

Crisis avoidance and limitation

In most cases, by the time an issue has found its way into the media, there is little that can be done to shift substantially the impression that has already been created. Ideally, of course, a full risk assessment exercise has been undertaken, a crisis plan has been formulated and full preparation has been made (see Chapter 9 for guidance). In reality, most of the times when people like me get a phone call the story has already broken and is on the front page, or the camera crew is in the reception area wanting an interview.

Helping you to understand how the media operates and how you can at least manage the situation to some extent, rather than have it overtake you or your client, is another objective of this book.

The philosophy of this book

My aim is to help you control and manage the media, so that you can be 'on the front foot', 'in the driving seat' or in whichever active (if clichéd) position puts you in charge of the process.

The vast majority of media relations undertaken by lawyers seems to be the reverse. The media drives the agenda and asks questions, prints responses, takes pictures and forces the lawyers into a passive, back foot, passenger seat role. We then become defensive and complain.

There will always be times when the unexpected occurs, a rumour gets out, a crisis happens, and then you will inevitably be in fire-fighting mode, and I will provide some guidance for when that happens (see Chapter 9).

There will also, however, be many stories you will have to tell, issues to publicise, causes to support and material that you can make available to the media to the benefit of yourself, your firm and others. This book aims to make this easier and help you gain and maintain control.

Your own media relations policy

This should be thought through, defined and committed to paper. Some take the approach that 'all publicity is good publicity', others that 'those who live by the word, die by the word'. You and your colleagues may take the robust view that broadly all publicity is beneficial and be prepared for the occasional negative story or misunderstanding with the press. Those who reject all co-operation with the media are adopting a safer strategy but may be missing out on valuable opportunities for profile-raising.

You and your colleagues should decide which stance you will adopt with the media and stick to it. It may help to nominate one or two people in the firm or chambers as media spokespeople and channel all media enquiries to them. As Kim Tasso, former marketing manager at Nabarro Nathanson and now a highly regarded professional services marketing consultant, says:

> Whatever your policy, ensure the appropriate people receive training. The best courses are those that include real journalists or broadcasters for taped and videoed simulated interviews. Even if only one or two people in the firm or chambers regularly deal with the press, training and practice should be provided to everyone who may deal with the media. Some people will have more natural media skills than others, but training will remove some of the fear and build confidence.

How to use this book

While I would love to think you will sit down and read this from start to finish, the reality is that you will dip in and out as and when the need arises and the mood moves you. The Index is, therefore, designed to route you around quickly.

I would recommend that you read Chapter 2 on the rules and then depending on your role and your need, you should be able to find what you require.

The comments that pepper each chapter are from real practitioners, journalists and editors who have generously given their time to help me and you. You will also find tips and tricks, based on hard-won personal experience, which are all designed to be useful and illuminating.

2

Setting the rules: what you can and cannot do

One of the many reasons that lawyers are reluctant to comment to the media is a fear of transgressing a complex range of professional and legal statutes, precedents, codes and guidelines.

This chapter will begin with some basic guidance on *sub judice*, privacy, avoiding being held in contempt and the impact of reporting restrictions, and will then look at the professional rules and guidance as they impact on solicitors, barristers, legal executives, and finally those employed in commerce, industry, local government and voluntary organisations, who are usually bound by the rules laid down by their employing organisation as well as by those of their professional body.

It is important to bear in mind that the major challenge is often not one resolved just by reference to statute, rule books and practice codes. It is often a very personal judgement call as to whether a matter is likely to have a media dimension, and, if so, whether the client or their lawyer should talk about it to a journalist or programme-maker. If so, it is then necessary to calculate not just what to say and when, but what impact, if any, it will have on the outcome of the matter in which you, your firm or your client is involved.

It is also obviously vital that all who are legally qualified or practising in a legal context are fully cognisant of the evidential rules, the Codes of Practice promulgated by their professional bodies and, perhaps most importantly, are mindful that all their activities must be informed by stringent adherence to the highest standards of personal ethics and probity and client confidentiality.

Many would say that the legal profession's reputation has suffered irreparable damage as a result of the activities of a few promoting their services as if marketing a commodity, selling their clients' stories to the highest bidder or becoming overly fond of their own face and voice on the media.

Despite the growth of cheque-book journalism, the comparative uncontrollability of the Internet as a grapevine and the readiness of some to cash in on the trend to scrutinise the minutiae of celebrities' private lives, it is increasingly the duty of all lawyers, and particularly those working in the fields of litigation and other areas where their work is of interest to those outside the firm and the sector, not just to acquire a real understanding of how the media operates, and how to publicise something effectively, but also to appreciate how intensive media interest in something can, sometimes only subliminally, influence the way that issue is perceived and understood by a wide number of people.

A high-profile advocate has said that he is very aware that by the second day of any newsworthy trial in which he is involved, the jurors all arrive at court with that day's papers under their arms. They – quite understandably – cannot resist seeing how the case in which they are involved is being reported. It must be true that the reports they read influence their judgement. In the Sally Clark case, which was a substantial miscarriage of justice case, one statistic, later exposed as false, remained embedded in the minds of the jurors and influenced their verdict, despite instructions from the judge to disregard it. The statistic still appears regularly – each time it is perceived by some as accurate.

While harnessing the media for marketing purposes seems to be universally, if belatedly, accepted by the legal profession (though still not enjoyed by many), some lawyers believe that a willingness to engage with the media, be accessible and brief journalists, advise clients and their legal advisers on how to present their cases to the world outside the courtroom, contributes to the current tendency for 'trial by media'. We probably all deplore the prurience of the general public and the invasions of privacy which occur daily, and many of us believe the media has reached unacceptable levels of intrusion. Yet when the parties are famous for being photogenic, our knowledge of the details of the case can be quite accurate: witness the Elizabeth Hurley versus Stephen Bing paternity dispute.

We are all nosey, and relish learning about the misfortunes of others. If we are professionally engaged to help people in difficulties resolve their problems and, in many cases, are hired to help them retain or defend their reputations, it is arguable that they are also entitled to expect us to provide some defence against the media. If we do not have the relevant experience ourselves – and this book will help you acquire it – then there are a small number of appropriately skilled advisers out there whom the lawyers, in their clients' and their own interests, should be prepared to consult.

Rules for solicitors

All that solicitors could possibly want to know about what is acceptable professional conduct in relation to publicity is contained in Practice Rule 2 of the Solicitors' Practice Rules 1990. This was last published in printed form in *The Guide to the Professional Conduct of Solicitors 1999* (published by the Law Society) with some amendments and is also available online (**www.guide-on-line.lawsociety.org.uk**). To be safe, always check online for the latest amended version.

Practice Rule 2 (Publicity) simply states:

> Solicitors may at their discretion publicise their practices, or permit other persons to do so, or publicise the businesses or activities of other persons, provided there is no breach of these rules and provided there is compliance with a Solicitors' Publicity Code promulgated from time to time by the Council of the Law Society with the concurrence of the Master of the Rolls.

Many will be relieved to know that the lengthy Publicity Code of 1990, which had detailed and specific rules about what could and couldn't be done has been replaced by a short, much more liberal and workable Code. In essence most marketing and publicity activities are permissible with the over-riding requirement that there should be no misleading or inaccurate advertising or publicity.

It is not proposed to reproduce the Solicitors' Publicity Code 2001 here (see Appendix 1), but it may help to set out the headings of its general principles:

(a) Misleading or inaccurate publicity: 'Publicity must not be misleading or inaccurate'.
(b) Clarity as to charges.
(c) Name of firm.
(d) Unsolicited visits or telephone calls.
(e) Addresses to the court.
(f) International aspects of publicity.
(g) Practitioners' responsibility for publicity.
(h) Application.

Quite apart from the Publicity Code that forms part of the Solicitors' Practice Rules, solicitors are offered additional guidance within the Solicitors' Introduction and Referral Code 1990, which has also been amended since the last printed version was published in the Guide. Again, it is advisable to check the online version to be sure you are up to date.

This Code provides guidance on the introduction of clients to solicitors and so is relevant to all those with marketing and business development responsibilities.

As far as media relations are concerned, if your firm handles conveyancing, you should particularly see section 3A(7) within the section on contractual referrals for conveyancing, where publicity for conveyancing services is covered, as follows:

(7) In publicity material of the introducer which includes reference to any service that may be provided by the solicitor, any reference to the charge for conveyancing service must be clearly expressed and must not be misleading. It must be clear whether disbursements and VAT are or are not included.

For press relations advice, the Press Office at Law Society Hall, 113 Chancery Lane, London can be contacted by phone: 020 7316 5527 between the hours of 8 a.m. and 6 p.m. any weekday. Outside office hours a duty press officer can be contacted by phone: 07659 128500, whose details are also on the answerphone on the main press office number.

All press releases issued by the Law Society's Press Office are on the Society's website and worth checking if you are proposing issuing something or commenting on a specific issue.

A few issues are regularly raised however, and it may help to provide brief guidance here.

Mentioning your firm by name in interviews

There is sometimes some disquiet about the permissibility of mentioning the name of your firm when giving an interview, yet the justification for giving up chargeable time to the media is the expectation it will help to build the profile of you and your firm. Broadly, it is now entirely acceptable for solicitors to give the firm's name at every suitable opportunity, provided it is not done in such a way as to breach the Publicity Code, transgress good taste, or bring the profession into disrepute. However, bear in mind that to do this with too great frequency can be counter-productive and indicate a worrying degree of desperation on the part of the promoting lawyer, may well be edited out of any pre-recorded interview, will not endear you to the interviewer and will almost certainly give rise to irritated correspondence from other lawyers who heard the broadcast or read the interview.

It is necessary to be clear whether the interview has been triggered because of some media interest in your firm itself, in you or in a case or client with which you are involved. If the first, then it is entirely appropriate for the name of the firm to crop up on more than one occasion during the interview. You may, however, be confronted with an uncomfortable issue and prefer to try to distance your firm from it, when as few 'name-checks' as possible would be better. In one recent feature about a solicitor's practice that achieved Investors in People accreditation, there were 10 name-checks in a short article, which is a marketing director's dream. But when Norton Rose found that one of its assistants had forwarded an indiscreet and rather candid e-mail from his girlfriend to friends outside the firm, they clearly wished that their name was not at the bottom of the original e-mail doing the rounds, and therefore so inexorably associated with the issue in every subsequent piece of copy filed.

If you are a specialist in an area of law or on a topic, it is likely you will be introduced in print or on air with the name of your firm or chambers and that any further name-checks will be at your or the journalist's discretion. This is less certain to happen if the case or client is the reason for media interest, when you may well just be introduced as 'Jane Smith's solicitor' and may find it harder to get recognition for your firm.

Chapter 6 on using television will go into this in greater detail, but you should never forget the value of having your firm's name visible in the background of any photograph taken of an interviewee representing the firm, and of providing the journalist with a pen or notepad on which your name and logo appear prominently.

Reference to other lawyers

Lawyers are sometimes asked to comment on the transgressions of their peers. One of the least comfortable roles I had as a Law Society spokesperson was to be obliged to undergo media interviews when a wayward solicitor had been found to have had their hand in the client account. I always called it 'having to defend the indefensible'.

It would probably be a breach of the Publicity Code to use an interview about a negligent or incompetent fellow practitioner smugly to say, 'But clients are safe instructing me/my firm, because we do . . . to ensure that this problem doesn't arise' as it could run the risk of being misleading or inaccurate. It would be entirely acceptable, however, to take the opportunity to set out briefly Rule 15 and the client care procedures that you and all good firms adopt and the efforts made by the Law Society to promote these.

It is always attractive to recognise another's grievance and often helps to diffuse a confrontational interview. It is also recommended that a brief statement of sympathy should be made whenever someone believes that they have suffered at the hands of a lawyer, rather than a purely defensive response, seeking to distance yourself from the issues. All lawyers share some collective responsibility for the profession of which they are part, and it should be of concern to us all when anyone is ill-served by one of our number. Take care not to rubbish others in the profession, as each broadcasting solicitor is taken by some to be representative of us all. You may also find that many members of the public assume that any solicitor is speaking on behalf of the national or local law society rather than in a personal or firm-representative capacity.

Naming clients

This is another vexing issue. While there is no prohibition against naming clients, it would be wise to ensure that:

(1)   the client gives consent, and to protect yourself obtain this *in writing* (especially if the matter is being handled by unadmitted staff);

(2)   any such naming or identification of the client is not likely to prejudice that client's interests.

Therefore, before naming a client in a broadcast interview you should at the very least obtain their oral consent to do so on the phone, and clearly if time permits, consent in writing. Anything in print requires written authorisation.

Claims of specialism and expertise

Because of the requirements that publicity is not misleading or inaccurate, it would be unwise to claim expertise that could not withstand external scrutiny and challenge. But one man's 'expert' is another man's egocentric amateur. In recent years the issue of expertise has shifted more to third party endorsement. The two legal directories, *Chambers* and *Legal 500*, now list all the top lawyers, both solicitors and barristers, in all the main practice areas, and these classifications are carefully researched by teams of legal journalists, many of whom are themselves legally qualified, who seek the views of clients and use peer review. It is therefore safer to place reliance on the published league tables rather than just self-certify one's expertise and it is now common practice to make reference to one or other directory, perhaps with a quote, to authenticate any claim of excellence.

Referring to your success rate

The increasing trend for performance targets, external accreditation and best practice standards such as those enshrined in Investors in People or ISO kitemarks, make clients and recruits keener to find out what the track record is of a firm or lawyer before applying to join or appointing them.

The new more liberal Publicity Code only prohibits details of success rates if these are misleading or inaccurate, but I would recommend that great care is taken in giving statistics, for example of how many criminal clients are acquitted after instructing you, or of the number of your appeals that succeed, or the average amount of damages your personal injury clients receive. This is usually more of a problem with actual advertisements where statistics are sometimes quoted in the hope of attracting new business.

Commercial firms, are regularly reported as handling major corporate deals and there is no problem with recording or reporting the number of such deals, and with the clients' written consent, naming them and, often, the value of the transactions.

Being rude about judges, other lawyers and the courts

This is simply not acceptable, however tempting it may be on occasion. The Law Society's Code for Advocacy, effective from 1994, specifically deprecates any sideswipes at other lawyers, the judges or court personnel. The Advocacy Code also, at Part VI 6.3 states:

> Advocates must not in relation to any current matter in which they are or have been briefed offer their personal views or opinions to or in any news or current affairs media upon the facts of or issues arising in that matter.

This entirely reflects the guidance given to barristers, now that solicitor advocates are becoming more numerous. It should be perfectly safe, however, to preface remarks with e.g., 'My client believes that the prosecution counsel may not have read his papers', 'My client is concerned that the judge appears to be asleep' but as soon as you allow your own beliefs to surface you will be in breach of the Code.

It will sometimes be hard to remember this during a 'snatch' interview on the court steps after a verdict has gone against you and your client, and a judge has, perhaps, delivered himself of unhelpful observations, but you should restrain yourself if you want to avoid a charge of being in contempt of court. For this reason, among many others, it is wise always to prepare for all interviews – even those you are far from certain will take place.

Unadmitted staff

Your support staff – receptionists, telephonists, secretaries and assistants – will often be the first to have contact with the press and may, on occasion, be invited to comment to the media about a high-profile case or issue on behalf of their firm or chambers. Journalists are notoriously vague about the status of the person they are talking to and we do not make things easy for them with all the various titles we use: solicitor, lawyer, barrister, counsel, partner, silk, legal exec, paralegal, associate, professional support lawyer, assistant, trainee, PA. All of these may mean slightly different things to different people and the owners of the titles may like to enhance their own importance in the 'food chain' of life by implying that they are legally qualified when in reality they are not. Also, clients may sometimes just lump them all together as 'my lawyers'. Be careful how others introduce these people as it is easy for a broadcaster to say, 'And now Ms Bloggs of Pushface Simkins will explain just what has happened in court', or 'what this piece of legislation means to consumers . . .'. Ms Bloggs will be presented to listeners or viewers as a member of the firm and will probably be assumed to be a partner. The preferred introduction would be, 'Ms Bloggs, a trainee solicitor with . . .' or 'a member of staff of . . .'.

Ensure all staff who are even remotely likely to deal with telephone calls from the media are familiar with the professional guidelines that bind your firm and fully understand your firm's or chambers' stance on media enquiries. It always advisable to make absolutely clear to any PA who screens your calls before you receive them, that the media should be treated, *without fail*, with courtesy, speed and professionalism. The experience journalists receive at the hands of your staff could colour the way your firm is reported. A story currently doing the rounds concerns a major law firm whose switchboard operator uttered the memorable phrase to a journalist doing some research, 'We don't take calls from the public here'. I know of at least three sets of chambers where journalists have been told, 'Sorry, we don't talk to the media' despite the sets having marketing budgets. Firms that receive regular media exposure should consider training their support staff in media relations as well as their principals, since that first contact is crucial.

In the absence of formal training, at least instil in anyone fielding calls from the media the vital importance of the following:

- be charming and friendly, not defensive or guarded;
- don't be bounced into a comment or quote;
- find out who the caller is, which publication or programme they are from, what they want and what their deadline is;
- capture their contact details;
- ensure the call is returned, even if it is only to say, 'No, thank you';
- note the co-ordinates of the journalist somewhere safe for the future – you never know when they might come in useful.

Am I insured if what I say is wrong?

Solicitors speaking on behalf of the Law Society or their local law society have the security of special indemnity insurance cover. Local law societies are all able to take advantage of a special Professional Indemnity Insurance Scheme designed for them for a modest premium (contact the

Society's Information Services for more information by phone: 0870 606 2555 or at **www.lawsociety.org.uk**).

Any solicitor speaking in their capacity as a solicitor should also be covered by the indemnity cover taken out by their firm, but it is worth checking the extent of this cover and the fine print of the policy with your insurer. Interviews flowing directly from cases in which you are involved should logically be part of your legal work and covered. Interviews granted to promote yourself or your firm may fall outside the cover and you should check with the insurer or broker to clarify this.

Broadcasting that involves giving general legal advice or commenting on a case or legal issue, however, is arguably not part of a solicitor's job and it is therefore important to check the exact terms of your firm's or your personal indemnity insurance cover if you are likely to broadcast on a regular basis or to participate in radio phone-in programmes covering topics outside your own areas of expertise. You should consider taking out special insurance cover for this activity, and ensure that listeners know which areas are your areas of expertise, and those areas where you can only give basic advice.

I was always a little nervous when standing in for the 'legal beagles' on Jimmy Young's long-running radio programme, as the bulk of the callers seemed to have consumer complaints or neighbour disputes requiring resolution and my practice areas were quite different. I placed high reliance on the legal researchers who found other practitioners who did specialise in these areas and was reassured that I had special insurance cover to protect me from any errors. I was also always very careful to let the listeners know that some of the topics were ones in which I was in no way an expert and that while I could give them basic guidance, they should consult someone who specialised in the problem if it remained unresolved.

All national newspapers have 'night lawyers' who are responsible for checking the copy to ensure it is not defamatory and will not get the publishers into trouble. They are a shadowy breed who have encyclopaedic knowledge, but they have millions of words to check and tend to skim over copy provided by lawyers, so don't assume they will do the checking for you. The regional papers, as explained in Chapter 4, tend not to retain night lawyers but use local firms for guidance.

Charging for handling the media or negotiating fees for your clients' stories and interviews

As lawyers become more skilled at handling the media and more comfortable with this role, more clients are coming to rely on them to fend off media enquiries and to speak on their behalf to the media. This is a perfectly proper and appropriate role for a lawyer to fulfil, provided they are competent, have had some experience, preferably some training and can justify the trust placed in them by their client. It should not be necessary to say that a client's confidentiality should never be breached or exploited and no client should be exploited by the ego or ambitions of their lawyer.

Many lawyers, of course, go on to become the business managers of celebrities and others. Elton John has long been looked after by a former partner at Eversheds. Several boxers use their lawyers as managers and promoters. Footballers go to media lawyers to broker their contracts and all those in the ideas industries rely on lawyers to protect their intellectual property rights.

It can, however, be hard to remain as rigorous as one should when under siege by the media. The day that Sally Clark walked free from the Court of Appeal, I received bids from every one of the national newspapers, with offers of sums reaching the £250,000 mark, and editors ringing in person to request Sally's story on an exclusive basis. Journalists from Sunday papers turned up uninvited at my offices and one at my home. The phone rang non-stop and I received more than 500 e-mails on that first day. I was sent flowers, offered dinner at London's finest restaurant, invited to lunch with at least 10 newspapers and generally courted in the hope that I would persuade my client to sell her story to a particular publication. No matter how firmly I repeated that it was premature to consider this and most unlikely my client would be interested in selling her story anyway, the pressure continued for several months, as it was some 10 weeks after the Appeal Court had ordered Sally's release before the full judgment was handed down.

I have, on other cases, been offered large sums to tell the 'inside story', write the book or co-operate with those making the drama or film out of the case. It is heady stuff and could easily turn one's head. But unless you have real experience of withstanding this kind of pressure, I would recommend that you refer your client to an adviser, an agent, a broker or a manager to deal with this aspect on their behalf, as it is unlikely you will strike the best deal for them, if money is what they have decided they want. Nor will you be able to protect their interests securely if they have opted for privacy.

Lawyers are, however, the first point of contact. It is often the lawyer who has to announce redundancies on behalf of a company. It is the lawyers who are alongside the client as they go into and come out of court. It is often a lawyer who is also company secretary announcing interim results or a corporate merger. So we must accept we will continue to be the focus of media attention and try harder to handle it well.

Recording time for media-handling

The time involved representing a client's interests to the media should be recorded in the same way as you record the rest of your work for them. Where the lawyer is instructed by a private client to handle the media aspects of their matter as well, this time can normally be charged for in the usual way, at the usual hourly rate. Be transparent about how you propose to charge, particularly if the costs are likely to be recovered from public funds, or there is the remotest chance of the media ever enquiring about the legal costs of the case. Public relations consultants submit monthly or even fortnightly timesheets to clients to enable them to see precisely how the time is spent and we invariably notify them before we despatch an invoice so its contents are expected and not disputed.

When the media-handling is part of a high-profile case and particularly one that is publicly funded, it is much more complex to recover some of the time charges incurred. In a news-worthy child abduction case with which I was involved while still in private practice some years ago, the then Legal Aid Board, and subsequently a taxing master, both agreed that some 60 hours expended presenting my client's case to the media and to politicians at the highest level was justifiable in a last-ditch attempt to persuade the then Prime Minister to intervene with the Head of State of a country with whom the United Kingdom had no reciprocal legal arrangements. Alastair Logan advised me, however, that he was unable to recover much of the costs associated with representing the Guildford Four's case to the media prior to their release. Counsel has advised that at least some of my time alerting opinion formers and the public to Sally Clark's unsafe conviction may be recoverable, but this has yet to be decided. If any payment materialises it will go to the charity which studies sudden infant death.

Increasingly it will become accepted that specialist litigation PR becomes a recoverable expense, as it is in several American states, but it will require convincing credentials and a number of examples before a reliable precedent is established.

Rules for barristers

Unlike solicitors, barristers are quite tightly constrained from making personal media comment about cases in which they are involved, but can comment on behalf of their clients and put the clients' points of view.

The General Council of the Bar has a friendly website (**www.bar council.org.uk**). *Bar News*, published by the Bar Council, February 2003, contains guidance on media comments, as follows:

The rules on barristers providing comments to the media have changed substantially in recent years and it is hoped that this summary will assist barristers in understanding the present position.

The relevant paragraph of the Code is paragraph 709 which prohibits barristers from expressing a personal opinion to the press or other media about the facts of or issues arising out of any anticipated or current proceedings in which they are briefed, expect to appear or have appeared.

This says: 709.1: 'A barrister must not in relation to any anticipated or current proceedings in which he is briefed or expects to appear or has appeared as an advocate express a personal opinion to the press or other media, or in any other public statement upon the facts or issues arising in the proceedings'.

709.2: Paragraph 709.1 shall not prevent the expression of such an opinion on any issue in an educational or academic context.

This paragraph must, however, be read with paragraph 702 (the duty of confidentiality) and paragraph 301 (particularly the duty not to diminish public confidence in the legal profession or the administration of justice or otherwise bring the profession into disrepute).

The following points should be borne in mind:

Personal opinions: There is no longer anything to prevent barristers informing the press about their clients' view of the proceedings, or what their client is seeking to achieve. It is obviously essential that the client should agree to whatever is said on his or her behalf.

Similarly, there is nothing to prevent barristers informing the press of the facts of a particular case or of the particular legal issues that will be discussed. They should be careful, however, not to add any personal views about the merits of the case or the appropriate outcome.

Paragraph 709.2 allows barristers who are instructed in cases to express views on cases in an academic context. Thus a barrister could write an academic article about the likely impact of a case in which he or she has been involved and include their own views on this.

In all of these cases, barristers must bear in mind their duty of confidentiality, and the law of privilege. It is prudent to obtain the lay client's consent to anything that is said.

Current proceedings: The Professional Conduct and Complaints Committee takes the view that proceedings remain current during the period allowed for an appeal. Obviously in certain circumstances (for example, in a criminal trial where a client is acquitted) this will not be a relevant consideration, but barristers generally should not comment before the time-limit for an appeal has expired.

The prohibition does not cease if counsel is no longer instructed in the case but, nevertheless, it continues with other counsel. The duty of confidentiality is, of course, continuous.

The prohibition applies only in respect of existing or contemplated proceedings. The rule does not prevent barristers who have advised clients on matters that are not and have no prospect of becoming litigious from commenting on those matters. In doing so, of course, barristers must have an appropriate waiver of privilege and permission from the client.

Bringing the administration of justice into disrepute: Barristers should be careful to express themselves carefully if they are commenting on cases in which they have been involved. It will almost invariably be inappropriate to make allegations about the good faith of a judge or other judicial officer or to use inflammatory language.

The purpose of these rules is to protect the independence of barristers. While barristers owe strong duties to their lay clients, they also owe an overriding duty to the court and should be careful not to bring their independence into question.

Finally, it should be made clear that barristers are not required to speak to the press at all and are perfectly entitled to refuse to do so.

More information on all this can be obtained from the Bar Council's website or from Mark Stobbs, Head of Professional Standards and Legal Services Department at the General Council of the Bar, 3 Bedford Row, London WC1R 4DB, phone: 020 7242 0082; fax: 020 7405 7823; e-mail: markstobbs@barcouncil.org.uk

The Bar Council currently outsources its own public relations to Weber Shandwick, a public relations consultancy (see **www.webershand wick.com**). Jon McLeod there leads the team that advises the Bar Council and barristers, phone: 020 7222 2525. As a former legal journalist on the *Law Society's Gazette*, who has advised the Bar for many years, he is very experienced.

Insurance for barristers using the media

All barristers have to be insured with the Bar Mutual Insurance Fund for Professional Indemnity Insurance. Because barristers' rules are rather different from those relating to solicitors and restrict them from commenting on 'any current matter . . . upon the facts of or the issues arising in that matter' there is less likely to be the need to check insurance than there is for broadcasting solicitors.

The Bar Mutual Insurance Fund (BMIF) advises that the current position is:

- A barrister talking to the press in connection with a case in which he or she is instructed and in a way permitted by the Code of Conduct will be covered by the BMIF.
- Barristers dealing with the press in other ways (for example, writing articles of general legal interest or commenting on cases in which they were not involved) will not automatically be covered.

If in any doubt, barristers should contact either the Bar's PR advisers at Weber Shandwick, or Mark Stobbs at the Bar Council for guidance.

Advice to legal executives

Media Guidance Notes targeted at legal executives have been produced by the Institute of Legal Executives (ILEX) by its Head of Communications and PR, Irene Dodgson. They cover much of the same ground that is contained in this book. Relevant excerpts are set out in Appendix 2; copies and further information are available from Irene Dodgson, Head of Communications and PR, Institute of Legal Executives, Kempston Manor, Kempston, Bedford MK42 7AB, phone: 01234 845712; fax: 01234 853982; e-mail: idodgson@ilex.org.uk.

Lawyers employed in commerce and industry

The Law Society's Commerce and Industry Group does not issue a media relations policy for its members, but it does have a press adviser, Sue Blake, who has provided 10 basic guidelines, which employed lawyers dealing with the media are advised to follow (see Appendix 3). Sue can be contacted by phone: 020 8891 2203; e-mail: sue@sueblakemedia.co.uk.

Legal and court constraints on media relations

Apart from the constraints and guidelines imposed or provided by lawyers' professional bodies we are all, of course, subject primarily to the constraints of the law and court procedures.

Anyone intent on speaking to the media on behalf of cases, clients or causes should study the definitive text, *Media Law* by Geoffrey Robertson QC and Andrew Nicol QC, both of Doughty Street Chambers. This book has been my bible since it was first published in 1984 and the fourth edition (Sweet & Maxwell 1999) is the weightiest and most comprehensive yet. It is a book about the legal rights of journalists, broadcasters, authors, Internet providers, editors, dramatists, film-makers, photographers, e-mailers, website owners, producers and all who produce news or views through the communications media.

It describes in the clearest detail the common law safeguards of open justice, jury trial and the rule against prior restraint. It covers freedom of expression, the basic laws that apply to all publishing enterprises – libel, contempt, confidence, copyright and obscenity. There is a section examining the laws applicable to particular areas of reporting, the ground rules that open or close the doors of the courts, Whitehall, Parliament, local government and commercial enterprises. There is finally an account of the practices and procedures of the 'alphabet soup' of regulatory bodies: the British Broadcasting Corporation (BBC), the Independent Television Commission (ITC), the British Board of Film and Video Classification (BBFC), the Press Complaints Commission (PCC), the Broadcasting Standards Commission (BSC), the Advertising Standards Authority (ASA), the British Advertising Clearance Centre (BACC) and, finally, the big brother of them all, OFCOM.

The authors have generously agreed to the rewriting and reproduction of some of their text in this book. On any areas where you are uncertain, read their book and take counsel's opinion.

Freedom of expression

It is unsurprising that two barristers who are of independent and liberal minds, regularly represent the communications industry in pushing back the barriers, or advise campaigning individuals anxious to reduce institutional secrecy, are enthusiastic about fewer controls and greater freedom.

> The one and only proposition which is both absolute and undeniable in media law is that thought is free, and hence communicating with oneself via messages and images in the brain-pan cannot, however subversive or obscene, be interdicted. But communicate that message to anyone else, whether in a bottle cast onto the waves or an e-mail silently sliding from a computer on the other side of the world, and the thought, thus emitted, becomes subject to interception by a network of laws designed to jam or distort it in the interests of States or corporations or other persons or entities whom the thought disquietens.

Robertson and Nicol's approach to freedom of expression is that human beings have an absolute right to think and hence a presumptive right to put the information or opinion contained in that thought into the public domain. Others inevitably disagree with this libertarian stance, but their book covers in depth the advent of freedom of expression guaranteed in the Human Rights Act 1998, the impact of Article 10 of the European Convention on Human Rights, the development and impact of the criminal law on contempt, blasphemy, libel, sedition, obscenity and official secrecy.

But law does not exist in a political or social vacuum. The conclusion reached by these two specialist barristers is that the criminal law now impacts more harshly on editors and journalists than on burglars and rapists, as media offences do not require proof of a guilty mind, or any 'victim' damaged by the publication. They go on to argue that in civil cases, judges have routinely suppressed the publication of newsworthy information on the ground that it is a property that belongs in confidence to governments and corporations, and have constructed a vast libel industry on the illogical presumption that defamatory accusations are bound to be false. In Britain, they conclude, it may be said that speech is free, but often very expensive. Those horrified by 'trials by media' may disagree.

Media Law charts the development of defamation, which was initially part of the law of torts, and reminds us that breach of confidence was anchored in equity, official secrecy and contempt derived from specific statutes, while blasphemy and sedition were crimes at common law. There were no textbooks on media law until 1984 and yet now it is a distinct practice area, which develops daily. Much credit should go to Robertson and Nicol, who since their earliest edition have argued persuasively that all the disparate strands of the law should logically be brought within Article 10. While 'freedom of the press' remained a potent phrase, the fact that it was protected by an unwritten convention rather than a written constitution meant that there was in effect no external brake to stop Parliament and the courts moving to restrict it in particular ways, as the mood and temper of the times seemed to require. Britain remained a country where 'everything is permitted which is not specifically prohibited', but the specific prohibitions became much more numerous, because they never had to justify themselves against the standards set by Article 10. And, as Richard Crossman said, 'secrecy remained the British disease', because of the ingrained reluctance of government, national and local, and the civil service, to share information with the public.

Today, while we continue to have institutional conservatism and secrecy and members of the public are unable to obtain some basic information about how their country is governed, we have a level of media incontinence, as far as the private lives of individuals is concerned, that is causing widespread concern.

In newspapers 'free speech' these days is what is left in the papers after they have been checked by the 'night lawyers'. The array of media laws and regulations are formidable – it is a minefield that the communications professional treads through with caution. There are criminal laws (of contempt, official secrecy, sedition, obscenity and the like) which can be enforced by fines, or even imprisonment. Then there are civil laws, relating to libel and breaches of copyright and confidence, which can be used to injunct public interest stories and programmes before publication, or to extract heavy damages afterwards. And there are laws that permit regulatory bodies to censor films and television programmes and video and DVD cassettes. Our standards are odd: while our news channels are free to show extremes of violence, those seeking the most graphic sexual images are often required to pay for them or breach the law.

All the laws that constrain us, as Robertson and Nicol point out, have emanated from different sources at different times: statutory laws, imposed by Parliament and interpreted by the courts; common law, built up by judges with reference to precedents from centuries of case law; decisions of regulatory bodies based on broad duties to ensure 'good taste' and 'due impartiality', not to mention informal 'arrangements' such as the lobby and the D-notice system, which exert secret pressures and persuasion.

All newspapers and broadcasting companies employ teams of lawyers to advise on stories that might otherwise attract reprisals, and they inevitably tend to err on the side of caution. But most laws pertaining to the media are of 'vague and elastic' definition, and the working test of 'potential actionability' for critical comment is exceptionally wide. Journalists instead of asking 'what *should* I write?' are often obliged to ask themselves, 'what *can* I write that will get past the lawyers?' But the lawyers' caution is understandable as their employers, the proprietors and company directors will want to avoid high legal costs wherever possible.

This complexity can give rise to some depressingly feeble decisions. In 2001 Channel 4 broadcast *Brass Eye,* a savage and accurate satire about the tabloid treatment of paedophilia. Various government ministers (who had not actually seen the programme) led the protest against the programme having been made at all, let alone shown in a late-night slot. The tabloid press, against whom the satire was levelled, of course supported the protesters, and the regulators, the ITC and the Broadcasting Standards Commission upheld the complaints. In reality, Channel 4 had every right to make and broadcast the programme, it breached no law or regulation, and those of a thoughtful mind who work in the area of child abuse felt the programme made some telling points well.

A couple of years ago the BBC felt compelled to apologise, under pressure from newspapers and the government, for a *Question Time* programme that went out a few days after September 11, in which too many hostile questions were deemed to have been asked about American foreign policy, which visibly upset one of the panellists, the former American ambassador. *Question Time* should be a prime example of free speech but in these circumstances the constraints imposed are not legal ones, but those of the sensitivity of broadcasting executives to public opinion – known in the industry as 'fear of the fuss'.

But despite this, *Media Law* points out that the regime is not as oppressive as it may at first appear. When there is genuine public interest in publishing, legal snares can usually be side-stepped, and this book seeks to emphasise ways in which legal problems can be avoided in practice. Many laws that are restrictive in their letter are enforced in a liberal spirit or simply not enforced at all. Editors and broadcasters are familiar with the solicitor's 'letter before action' threatening proceedings in the event that matters unflattering to clients are published. Often such letters are bluffs, and it is important to know how and when that legal bluff should be used, or called.

On the public interest point, Robertson and Nicol argue compellingly for the publicly funded BBC and the wealthy ITV, which employ dozens of lawyers, to challenge more often the decisions that keep microphones and cameras out of the courts (even the appeal courts) and out of tribunals investigating matters of pure public concern, such as the 'Arms to Iraq' affair, and the Stephen Lawrence and 'Bloody Sunday' inquiries. The absurd result is unrealistic portraits of the participants by court artists and unconvincing dramatic reconstructions. My learned friends maintain that the Human Rights Act 1998 and the Freedom of Information Act 2000 will only work to public advantage if there is a determination on the part of the media to exploit them to the full.

But apart from the controls imposed by the law, communications are also restrained by shared ethical assumptions, by non-legal rules that find favour with the Press Complaints Commission and the Broadcasting Standards Commission, by pressure from advertisers, by the political predilections of proprietors and by the host of subjective considerations that make up 'editorial discretion'. Press monopolies inhibit those with different views from launching out on their own, and the law is often invoked by editors, executives or lawyers to support decisions to censor that are in reality taken on other grounds. Legal advice in this area is often convenient rather than correct.

The other force that is working to reshape media law in the United Kingdom is the revolution in information technology. This has produced genuinely international newspapers, instantaneous satellite communication, and contemporaneous book publishing. Commercial freedom in Europe, as the authors of *Media Law* point out, requires some degree of uniformity, and the European Commission and Council of Ministers and the European Court of Justice are issuing directives and rulings that affect media law in Britain. The human rights dimension of media law, informed by decisions of the European Court of Human Rights in Strasbourg, has become increasingly important, highlighting the various ways in which the existing law fails to comply with the great principle expressed in Article 19 of the Universal Declaration of Human Rights:

> Everyone has the right to freedom of opinion and expression; this right includes the freedom to hold opinions without interference and to seek,

receive and impart information and ideas through any media and regardless of frontiers.

But although the organisation of media law upon human rights principles is liberating, and technical advances (particularly of the Internet) are making it difficult for the 'nanny state' to censor, neither of these provide a one-way street for freedom to publish. The right to privacy and a fair trial must be taken into the equation and there are many who believe that the balance is grossly out of kilter at present.

Words can do damage – by betraying a military position, or by prejudicing a trial, or by inciting racial hatred, or by compromising a reputation.

While all of a liberal mind-set would wish journalists and broadcasters the right to have freedom to report and broadcast, we must acknowledge that others have valid rights to legal protection to lead a private life free from media harassment, to a fair trial free from sensational prejudice, and to have false accusations corrected swiftly and with the same prominence as they are made.

On balance, Robertson and Nicol believe that the legal rights of journalists and broadcasters are in many respects more secure now than they were when they last revised their book. For this they give credit to the impact of Article 10 of the European Convention and to the bold manner in which it was entrenched in the Human Rights Act 1998. They also applaud the liberal-mindedness of the current senior judiciary, who are more open than previous generations of Law Lords to strike down unconstitutional infringements of free speech. Judges used to regard the media with suspicion, and sometimes with contempt, but, they argue, this is being replaced by a grudging, but in some cases genuine, respect for the role of the media in a free and democratic society.

Lord Justice Kay opening Sally Clark's second appeal in January 2003 made the point that he was very well aware of the level of public interest in the case and the importance of ensuring that all that was said in the Appeal Court was communicated clearly and accurately by the media to the wider world outside the confines of the court. Throughout this ultimately successful appeal he was at great pains to ensure that this was the case and the clarity of the judgment and judicial comments were not only exemplary, but clearly made the task of all the journalists covering the case a great deal easier.

Sub judice and contempt of court

There are many misconceptions surrounding *sub judice* and contempt and the lawyers' innate cautiousness usually dictates that they often exercise a veto on all media comment citing these as their excuse. Cases have been cancelled midway because of media coverage deemed to be prejudicial and at the time of writing I am aware of at least two where there is real doubt if the matters will ever get to court because of the level of condemnatory comment in the press ahead of any trial, or in one case even charges.

In reality, there is a great deal that can be said, and often should be said, without risking a charge of contempt, but it is imperative to become conversant with the rules.

As legal commentator Marcel Berlins has said:

> Sub judice merely means that something is before the courts. It does not mean that no one can comment or write about the subject matter and be compelled to take Trappist orders. On the contrary, the law specifically says that to run the risk of contempt of court when there are legal proceedings about, there has to be a substantial risk of serious prejudice to those proceedings.

If in doubt, always consult an expert on media law – it is expensive and embarrassing if you get it wrong. As Robertson and Nicol point out:

> The power to punish for contempt of court is the means by which the legal system protects itself from publications that might unduly influence the result of litigation. The dilemmas caused by the conflict between the demands of a fair trial and the free press are real enough. We pin a certain faith on the ability of juries, judges and tribunals to resolve disputes, so we are justified in being concerned about the effect of outside influence on their deliberations, especially the sort of pressure generated by circulation-seeking sensationalism.

The Contempt of Court Act 1981, s.2(1) defines contempt as when the publication 'creates a substantial risk that the course of justice in particular proceedings will be seriously impeded or prejudiced'.

Liability is 'strict' in the sense that the prosecution does not have to prove that the publisher intended to prejudice legal proceedings. It is still necessary to show, beyond reasonable doubt, that the publication created *substantial risk of prejudice*.

The impediment or prejudice risked by the publication must itself be of a serious nature. In criminal cases, this means that it must be of a kind that could tip the final verdict one way or the other. A useful test of whether the prejudice is 'serious' is to consider whether it can readily be cured by the court itself, rather than by a prosecution or an injunction against publication. The simplest device is usually for the trial judge to ask jurors who have seen the prejudicial material to stand down from the panel, but increasingly it is hard to assess the impact of information communicated by the print and broadcast media and absorbed almost subliminally. In Sally Clark's case the judge, after hearing from defence witnesses, instructed the jury to discount a particular statistic that had been a crucial plank of the prosecution case. When the jury at the original trial reached their verdict, after six weeks of hearing complicated medical evidence debated by academic experts, it was clear that 10 of the 12 jurors were unable to forget the flawed statistic that had run as a headline in all the national newspapers and been repeated on the broadcast news for days.

The rationale behind the contempt law is an abiding British fear of 'trial by media' of the sort that we used smugly to consider disfigured major trials in the United States, where the First Amendment permits press, television and radio comment on a court case, and it is commonplace for high-profile trials to be televised throughout. When, in 1949, the *Daily Mirror* published sensational suggestions that a man arrested for one particularly foul murder was not only guilty, but guilty of other murders as well, its editor was gaoled for three months. The penalty for the massively prejudicial coverage of the arrest of the 'Yorkshire Ripper' Peter Sutcliffe was not the imprisonment of any editors, but Parliament's refusal to amend the Contempt of Court Bill, then under consideration, to make it easier for the press to report newsworthy developments in criminal investigations between the time of arrest and the time of charge.

Readers may recall that the Soham enquiry in 2002 into the disappearance of two young schoolgirls, subsequently found to have been murdered, involved continuous coverage on *Sky News* and other news channels from a team of journalists and programme-makers who just moved into the small Cambridgeshire village, befriended the family and their neighbours and observed and reported every stage of the investigations. I recall vividly sitting in a hotel in Marrakech and watching *Sky News* in which a young woman reporter did a piece to camera describing how she had gone into the home of the school caretaker subsequently charged with the girls' deaths, and used his video-recorder to play the latest tape produced by the police. The closeness of reporter to suspect was unnerving. Another report demonstrated that a male reporter was providing personal support to one of the bereaved mothers.

At that stage in the investigations no lawyers were involved, but once arrests had been made and charges laid, it would be an uphill struggle for the defence lawyers to ensure that the two young people charged had anything even approximating to a fair trial.

The twin burdens of the prosecution, under the Contempt of Court Act 1981, to prove both 'substantial risk' and 'serious prejudice' give a considerable latitude to the news media in reporting the background to a sensational case.

Contempt risks

The risk of contempt may arise in numerous situations. While it is impossible to lay down hard and fast rules, there are clear dangers in the following areas:

Criticising the decision to prosecute

The decision to prosecute involves the exercise of discretion and consideration of public interest, and as such can legitimately be the object of comment and criticism at the time when it is taken; objectors need not wait until the case is over. Consequently, much greater latitude is given to comments hostile to the prosecution than to those critical of the defendant.

Anti-prosecution commentaries are on more dangerous ground, however, if they attack witnesses or are likely to influence their evidence, but it seems to be accepted that the Director of Public Prosecutions and the police must tolerate a greater degree of criticism because of their public roles.

Anticipating the course of the trial

Predicting the outcome, or even giving odds on a particular jury verdict, would in most cases amount to contempt because it would be seen as creating a 'climate of expectation' that the jury might find difficult to resist. But much freedom is given to the media to publish informed speculation about the issues that are likely to be raised, as long as no opinion is expressed as to the way they should be resolved. It should be noted, however, that with the growth of contingency fees when solicitors will only be advised to accept cases where the odds for success can be specified, this area will need to be treated with special care.

Talking to the media before the trial

It is commonly – and wrongly – believed that a defendant must stay silent throughout the long period between arrest and trial. In cases where the arrest has been attended with publicity, invariably prejudicial to the defendant, there can be no objection to his/her repeated public assertion of innocence, which is after all echoing the law's most sacred presumption. Nor is it necessarily a contempt to publish a book by or about him or her. There is the risk that such a publication might be used in evidence against the defendant, but this is not a problem relevant to contempt of court.

Many of the recent 'miscarriages of justice' cases were clearly assisted by the work of campaigning journalists who took up the cases, and advocated them to the media in a way that the lawyers involved could not. Sally Clark is certainly indebted to the persistence of people like John Sweeney, whose BBC programmes alerted many to the injustice she had suffered.

Great caution is required with any reference to prosecution witnesses, and any comment on specific charges or issues that the jury will have to decide. Mere repetition of details already published should not be a problem, but overt attempts to elicit sympathy and support for a defendant must be avoided.

Contempt creates a difficult problem for individuals who are not witnesses, but who receive adverse publicity as a result of references to them at the trial or in pre-trial proceedings. From recent cases it seems that they are unlikely to be able to rebut false allegations while the trial is in progress, if by doing so they would suggest that a party to an action is a liar.

Defendants' convictions, bad character or admissions

Publishing derogatory information about a defendant's character, lifestyle or previous convictions *before* the verdict runs a very high risk of being contempt. This information will usually be kept from a jury so that they will not judge a defendant on his bad character in the past, rather than on the evidence of his involvement in the offence with which he has been charged, but this point is under consideration.

Not every adverse comment or description of a defendant will be contempt. It must be one that would be substantially likely to affect seriously the outcome of the case, but few journalists, editors or newspapers' lawyers can make these calls, and lapses occur regularly.

A similar type of contempt is exaggerating the charge against the defendant.

Particular care must be taken by the press when it publishes articles about criminal trials before they are concluded. These may unintentionally refer to matters that the jury is not permitted to hear in evidence.

Defendants' photographs

Publishing defendants' photographs can be contempt in criminal cases, where the correctness of identification is at issue. The danger is that eyewitnesses for the prosecution may then describe the person in the newspaper's picture, rather than the person they saw at the scene of the crime. It may be difficult for the media to know if identity is at issue. Defence solicitors may be willing to tell the press about their clients' defences, but they are under no obligation to assist the media. The problem can become acute when an arrest warrant has been issued for a suspect who is still at large. While the police might like the press to print photos to enable them to find a suspect, this could give rise to contempt. The Attorney-General, recognising this problem, has said that pictures of wanted persons issued by the police can be published by the media without risk of contempt and his assurance gives the media a practical immunity.

Witnesses

Many eyewitness accounts of crimes appear in the press without attracting contempt charges. Since strict liability contempt can be committed only when a prosecution is under way, there is not even this risk if a suspect has not been arrested, charged or been made the subject of a warrant. But any publication that seeks to deter or intimidate prospective witnesses will certainly be vulnerable to contempt charges.

Payment to witnesses for their stories before they give evidence is usually undesirable and will attract judicial criticism, but curiously no contempt charge has yet been brought to deter the practice. There is an obvious danger that bought witnesses will become sold on their stories, often ghosted by journalists. Having perhaps exaggerated evidence in order to increase a story's saleability, they may find the financial inducement makes them stick to the tale in the witness box.

At present payments to witnesses are contrary to the Press Council's declaration on 'cheque-book journalism', and on 19 March 2003 it was announced that, with immediate effect, the Press Complaints Commission issued new industry guidelines, after the Lord Chancellor, then Lord Irvine of Lairg, said he might ban such payments by law unless the voluntary code was tightened up. The changes were adopted by other media regulators: the ITC, the Radio Authority and the BBC.

Changes to the editors' code mean that no payments can be made to a witness in a criminal trial or a person who 'may reasonably be expected to be called as a witness' once proceedings are active under the Contempt of Court Act 1981.

If proceedings are not yet active, but are 'likely and foreseeable', payments can be made only where there is a 'demonstrable public interest'. Under no circumstances will journalists be able to offer payment that depends on the outcome of a trial.

The press has on many occasions aided the administration of justice by finding important witnesses. Sometimes witnesses have been jealously hidden from journalistic rivals. This is not in itself contempt, but it may sow suspicion that the witness's evidence has been affected. The line is crossed if the witness's evidence is tampered with or the witness is concealed from the police or prosecuting authorities.

Revealing a payment into court

'Payment into court' is a common tactical ploy by defendants in civil litigation – a formal offer to settle for the paid-in sum. Rules of court require such a payment to be kept secret, so any newspaper that disclosed the fact that a sum had been paid in would run a serious risk of contempt. This issue was under discussion at the time of writing, so check the latest position if it is relevant to your matter.

Television coverage of criminal trials

We are all familiar with television crews setting up outside courts to cover the entrances, exits and statements on the steps. So long as they are on public property and there is no element of harassment, there can be no question of contempt, unless members of the jury are deliberately pictured or otherwise identified. One difficulty yet to be resolved stems from the mass media coverage of security arrangements, especially at trials of alleged terrorists. Television news eagerly shows the marksmen on the court roof, the police helicopters circling overhead, and the sniffer dogs in the courtyard. The armoured van containing the defendants is filmed as it arrives and departs. The court artist portrays (albeit often rather badly) the defendant or appellant in the dock, behind bars and chained to a warder. All this undoubtedly contributes to the overall sense of the guilt of the defendants and, it can be argued, contributed to the convictions of the Irish defendants in the Guildford and Birmingham pub bombings.

The *sub judice* or 'active' period

The seriousness of the risk and the degree of prejudice will hinge, in the first place, on the nature of the tribunal that is to try the issue that is the subject of media treatment.

Trial by jury

The future of the jury is currently under some scrutiny. Jurors, drawn at random from the general public, are assumed to be the most susceptible to media influence. The publication of prejudicial information about any person awaiting jury trial is therefore dangerous, but increasingly commonplace.

The pool from which jurors are drawn is to be extended to include more professionals and people who have habitually structured good grounds for claiming exemption from service. This may mean that as juries become more sophisticated the influence of the media will wane, but it seems unlikely.

From the circulation figures achieved by the tabloid papers, it is clear that few people in the United Kingdom can be unaware of many details about defendants when their cases are of media interest. If the defendant is someone already in the public eye, it is increasingly hard to be confident that by the time they come to trial the jurors will not have formed some opinions, however incorrect, about the case and the defendant, informed solely by what they have read and heard in the media.

The law of contempt serves a valuable purpose in so far as its operation is confined to placing a temporary embargo on publication of information that would make a jury more likely to convict a person who is on trial, or shortly to face trial. Without such a law, the legal system would be forced to adopt the expensive, and not entirely successful, expedients used in notorious trials in the United States, where jurors are quizzed at length as to what they have seen in the press or on television and are then sequestered, under guard, in hotels, denied access to family, newspapers and television programmes for the duration of the case. For all the fuss made in the United Kingdom about 'trial by media' it is still very rare for convictions to be quashed because of adverse publicity, but in the last few years more cases have collapsed as a result of what is seen as media prejudice.

Trial by magistrates

Stipendiary magistrates, as professional full-time lawyers, are unlikely to be influenced by media reports. Greater care must be taken in cases decided by lay magistrates.

'Trial by media'

Striking a balance between the right of citizens to obtain information to which they are entitled, while preserving privacy, which they rightly value, will always be tricky. As lawyers, we are often required to come down on different sides of the debate, entirely influenced by who we are advising or representing at the time. The stance of lawyers defending the rights of editors to publish almost anything could not be further from that of lawyers seeking to protect a client protesting their innocence from having their private lives exposed prior to trial in those very papers.

The Attorney-General, Lord Goldsmith, announced in March 2003 that he was starting a consultation process expressly designed to find ways of limiting 'trial by media'.

At the same time, the new chief executive of OFCOM, Stephen Carter, the super-regulator of all communications regulators, signalled the stance that he intends to adopt. Shortly after his appointment, promising that OFCOM would be fully formed by the end of 2003, he wrote:

> there has been a vacuum of independent non-political thought, leadership and joined up thinking in this critical market and a lack of appreciation that the communications market demands investment, innovation and risk for sustained growth. OfCom will be a 'reach out' regulator that genuinely embraces consumer protection through the promotion of effective competition and choice, whilst being guided and informed by modern citizenship. There can be no role for punishing success, but equally, there is a clear need to effectively and speedily police abuse and for the rules to be clear.
>
> OfCom needs to be a powerhouse of intelligent, original and non-biased thinking across all the relevant media and communications markets.

For lawyers, the concept of 'consumers' and 'markets' is relevant when advising commercial clients and in the context of marketing and promoting their firms and expertise, but for litigators and clients facing claims and suits there are other concerns. We can only hope that as well as regulating the marketplace effectively, the Attorney-General, the legal professional bodies, Stephen Carter and the other regulators manage to find a way to ensure that the processes of the law become more open, accessible, and therefore better understood and trusted, while reducing the current concerns about 'trial by media', which can only prejudice the fair outcome of so many high-profile cases and undermine confidence in the entire legal system.

Reporting restrictions

We have covered some of the constraints that apply before a case ever gets to court, but attending court is merely the means to the end of publication. What takes place in open court 'is necessarily and legitimately made public and being public property may be republished'. Chapter 8 of *Media Law* (Robertson and Nicol) and the invaluable *McNae's Essential Law for Journalists* provide details of when reporters can and cannot be in court, and what they can report.

Remands and committal hearings

Up to 1967, committals could be reported in full. It was the 'Moors Murders' case that finally prompted the government to act, and then more to spare the public a double dose of grisly details than to avoid prejudice to defendants.

Reporting restrictions on committals are contained in the Magistrates' Courts Act 1980, s.8. Unless the restrictions are lifted a report in print or in a programme service about committal proceedings in Great Britain can only refer to:

(a)   the names of the examining justices and their court;
(b)   the names and addresses and occupations of the parties and witnesses, and the ages of the defendant and witnesses;
(c)   the charges;
(d)   the names of counsel and solicitors;
(e)   the decisions to commit or how the case was otherwise disposed of;
(f)   the charges on which each defendant was committed;
(g)   the date and place to which the hearing was adjourned;
(h)   arrangements for bail;
(i)   whether legal aid was granted or refused.

The reasons given by the police for opposing bail or by the magistrates for refusing it cannot be published. These restrictions apply only temporarily. Full details of the committal can be reported after the trial, but by then they are usually stale news and of little interest. All details can be reported if the magistrates decide not to commit or try the case themselves.

Breach of the restrictions can lead to a fine of up to £5,000. The editor and publisher of the *Gloucester Citizen* were fined £4,500 for an article they published about Fred West's first appearance at the magistrates' court in 1994, which reported that he had already admitted killing his daughter.

Lifting reporting restrictions

A defendant has the right to have restrictions lifted and must be advised or this right. It can be exercised on the first appearance and if the restrictions are to be lifted, the clerk must announce this when the hearing resumes.

Since the Criminal Justice (Amendment) Act 1981, if any defendant or a number of defendants objects to an application to lift reporting restrictions, the magistrates must refuse the application unless they are persuaded it would be in the interests of justice. Magistrates who wrongly refuse an application to lift restrictions are acting beyond their powers.

Newspapers and broadcasters can challenge the magistrates' refusal to lift restrictions by applying to the Administrative Court within the High Court for a mandatory order to compel the magistrates to follow the law. The court can act quickly. In one case the application was heard on one day's notice, but particularly for broadcasters this procedure can still take too long. If they are sure that the restrictions ought to be lifted (e.g.

because a lone defendant asked for them to be), and they broadcast a full account, they are most unlikely to be prosecuted for breach of a restriction order that was invalidly made or retained.

Transfers and preparatory hearings: fraud and other complex prosecutions

The length and complexity of some fraud trials has worried governments for many years. In 1986 the Roskill Committee recommended wide-ranging changes, and the Criminal Justice Act 1987 made substantial procedural alterations in the way that major fraud prosecutions are conducted.

In media relations terms, the most important concern is the 'preparatory hearing'. In serious fraud cases, the prosecution can now dispense with committal hearings by seeking a transfer order to an appropriate Crown Court. This in turn can order a preparatory hearing. This can be used by the defence to argue there is no case to answer, or it can be used by the judge as a pre-trial review, and he can compel both prosecution and defence to set out their respective cases in detail.

As the preparatory hearing is treated as part of the trial, the press and public have their common law right to attend, but reporting restrictions will apply in the same way as they do to committal hearings.

Children and the courts

This is a particularly tricky area, and requires extra care. The ITC's code requires broadcasters to have 'particular regard' to the potentially vulnerable position of child witnesses and victims before identifying them and that 'particular justification' is needed before child suspects are named.

Before criminal proceedings start, various restrictions are imposed on the identification of children involved. It used to be the case that restrictions only started once proceedings had begun. Parliament has now imposed new controls on the reporting of children involved in 'criminal investigation'. It should be noted that an 'investigation' can start much earlier than the period when a criminal case becomes 'active' for the purpose of strict liability contempt.

While the new regime currently only protects the alleged perpetrator of the offence, it will be extended to protect the alleged victim and possibly witnesses.

Where the protections apply, nothing must be published (so long as the person involved is under 18) that is likely to lead members of the public to identify him as the person involved in the offence.

No reference can be made to their name, address, school, place of work, and no still or moving picture or description of their appearance can be given if any of these would connect them with the offence.

Again, breach of the restrictions can give rise to a fine of up to £5,000 and prosecutions require the consent of the Attorney-General.

The media were very concerned that these restrictions would prevent the immediate reporting of tragedies involving children, such as the multiple murders at the school in Dunblane, or the killing of headmaster, Philip Lawrence, stabbed outside his West London school. So a defence was added to the main ones (*the defendant did not know or had no reason to suspect that the publication included the report or that a criminal investigation had begun*) and it is now possible for the media to argue that the inclusion of the identifying material was in the public interest on the ground that the suppressive effect of this law would have imposed a substantial and unreasonable restriction on reporting.

Section 52 directs the court to have particular regard to various matters when considering the public interest. They include the interest in the open reporting of crime, the open reporting of matters relating to human health and safety, the prevention and exposure of miscarriages of justice, the welfare of any protected person, the views of a protected person who is 16 or 17, or the views of an appropriate person if the protected person is under 16.

Youth courts

The general public is refused entry to youth courts, but journalists can attend and can report the proceedings, but must not publish anything relating to a person under 18 if it is likely to lead members of the public to identify him or her as someone concerned in the proceedings. Under the provisions of the Children and Young Persons Act 1933, as amended by the Youth Justice and Criminal Evidence Act 1999, Sched. 2, reporters must not reveal the young person's name, address, school, workplace or any particulars that can lead to their identification.

There are three situations where a court can give permission for a young person to be identified, even though he is involved in youth court proceedings:

- where identification is appropriate to avoid injustice to the child, such as to scotch rumours that he is a defendant, when in reality he is a witness;
- to assist in the arrest of a child or young person who is unlawfully at large and who is charged with, or convicted of, a violent, sexual or particularly serious offence;
- where, after conviction of the child or young person, the court considers that identification would be in the public interest.

The Crime and Disorder Act 1998 introduced 'anti-social behaviour orders', which are made by magistrates in civil proceedings, and the courts still have the power to require anonymity when reporting these proceedings.

Other criminal cases

Apart from youth courts and subsequent appeals from them, there is no automatic restriction on the coverage of criminal proceedings where children are involved, but there is a power to impose reporting restrictions, which is now found in the Youth Justice and Criminal Evidence Act 1999, s.45.

Notice of reporting restrictions concerning children

There should be no need for any notice of reporting restrictions in youth courts, since these apply automatically, but where an adult magistrates' court is being asked to vary or revoke a supervision order or an appeal from such an order, the court must draw specific attention to the application of the restrictions. If it does not, then the restrictions do not apply.

Rape and sexual offences

This is a vexing area under current review, as there are vocal advocates who support the anonymity of the accused as well as of the victim. In a recent case, the defence lawyers maintain that the career of the accused – a well-known personality – was irreparably damaged many months before he was brought to trial, and that even if vindicated by a court, the fact that his name had been reported in connection with the allegations would preclude his ever rebuilding his reputation.

We all observed how Matthew Kelly suffered in early 2003 while allegations against him of paedophilia were investigated and subsequently dropped. Though his employers, colleagues and fans supported him throughout, the damage done to him and his family psychologically is impossible to assess.

The complainants' anonymity is protected by the Sexual Offences (Amendment) Act 1976, which in turn was extended to a wider range of offences by the Sexual Offences (Amendment) Act 1992.

Reporting restrictions protecting witnesses in criminal proceedings

The Youth Justice and Criminal Evidence Act 1999 prohibits the identification of witnesses whose evidence (or co-operation with the case) is likely to be reduced through fear or distress at the prospect of being publicly identified as a witness in the proceedings. This power, however, does not extend to providing anonymity for the defendant.

Family cases

While family law cases remain the most fascinating to a prurient public and divorce scandals are particularly riveting, the press coverage of such matters has reduced, partly through reporting restrictions and partly because it is no longer necessary to prove cruelty or provide evidence of adultery to obtain a divorce. Even where evidence of newsworthy adultery is given and discovered by journalists, they must be circumspect in their reports. In all family law cases involving divorce, nullity, separation, financial provision, adoption or legitimacy, any coverage must be limited to:

- names, addresses and occupations of the parties and witnesses;
- a concise statement of the charges, defence and counter-charges, or of the declaration sought;
- submissions on points of law and rulings of the court;
- the judgment of the court and the judge's observations, if any.

Family Division: publicity injunctions

The courts have evolved special jurisdiction to grant injunctions precluding publicity in cases involving children, and if you find yourself involved in such a matter, reference to *Media Law* is advisable to ensure you are seized of the technical detail of such applications.

Children cases: automatic restrictions

The Children Act 1989 effectively extends the powers enjoyed by magistrates to the county court and the High Court. All courts can sit in private to exercise Children Act powers and it is an offence to publish anything that would identify any child involved in the proceedings.

Other topics covered in depth by Robertson and Nicol within the context of reporting the courts include:

- secrecy orders;
- indecent evidence;
- orders under s.11 of the Contempt of Court Act 1981 (prohibiting the publication of information);
- postponement orders.

Tape-recording court proceedings

The public – and therefore the journalist's – right to attend court includes the right to take notes of what is said there, although court officials will sometimes, wrongly, try to stop members of the public taking notes.

The Contempt of Court Act 1981 banned the use of tape-recorders, but the law has grudgingly recognised that fewer journalists write short-hand and that the interests of justice are probably better served by an accurate report. The judge, therefore, has discretion to give or withhold permission for proceedings to be taped, and this is increasingly granted. The tape, however, cannot be broadcast and if it were, it would be a contempt. The Civil Procedure Rules Practice Direction Part 39.6.1 recommends that when granting permission to tape-record, the user should be reminded of this.

Transcripts and skeleton arguments

There is a great deal more transparency about court deliberations and documentation than when the first edition of this book was published. Most judges now have reasonable computer skills. Some will always make copies of their judgment available to the media. In the commercial court both sides have immediate computer access to all that is said and simultaneously recorded on their screen.

All the law officers and several senior members of the judiciary have granted media interviews, which at one time was unheard of.

Whenever the High Court, Court of Appeal, Crown Court or county court is sitting, official shorthand writers will take a note of the proceedings. They have a statutory right to use tape-recorders, although the tapes are only transcribed on request. These tapes can be requested by others, including journalists, though there is no requirement for the court to agree to sell them.

Skeleton arguments are now lodged, not just in the Court of Appeal, but in other courts and the Court of Appeal now asks lawyers to produce an extra copy for the press, except when reporting is restricted. If a copy of the skeleton argument or opening speech is not provided, the reporters can apply to the judge. In the Sally Clark appeal, embargoed copies of the skilful 32-page skeleton prepared by Clare Montgomery QC were made available as if it were a news release; the team was gratified to see how faithfully its contents were reproduced by the large press corps in attendance at court.

Each judge has their own preferred way of operating and it is always worth checking with their clerk if your case is likely to attract media interest. It is also a courtesy to let the court listing office know if you are aware there may be many journalists wishing to attend, so that they can endeavour to arrange the hearing in a court large enough to accommodate them.

3

Defining and understanding today's media and handling online media

We are probably all quite clear what we mean by 'the media'. We mean the newspapers we read each day, the magazines we read each week or month, the radio we listen to in our kitchen and our car, and the television, which appears not just in our living rooms, but increasingly often in kitchens, bedrooms, children's rooms and now, in the back of cars to keep youngsters amused on long journeys.

There is a fourth medium and if we disregard it, we expose ourselves to risk, lose competitive advantage and miss many tricks. The single biggest change since the first edition of this book is the universal acceptance, use and growth of the Internet.

The collective output of the media is already enormous, and as new ways of communicating are developing, with online news, satellite relays, cable and digital television and radio, and cellphone technology, the capacity is expanding and the public's appetite for news, information and entertainment shows no signs of abating. The media's interest in legal matters has also clearly grown.

The print media

Lawyers are trained through reading and are naturally most comfortable with printed communications. Newspapers have been with us for more than 500 years, and in the past decades technological developments have made it possible for news to be gathered and spread literally at the speed of sound. While many in the communications game now read their daily papers online, most lawyers still seem to prefer the tactile experience of turning pages.

Ever since the stranglehold on the print unions was broken many years ago by Eddie Shah and later Rupert Murdoch, it has been possible for newspapers to be produced cheaply, providing the public with an increasingly wide choice of reading materials. Nearly 15 million people buy a newspaper every day and over 17 million buy one at the weekend. New national and regional papers are launched and others die. Colour and magazine supplements are now commonplace with almost all funded by increasing advertising space. A special trolley has had to be designed to enable newspaper boys and girls to deliver our Sunday papers as they can no longer be managed in a shoulder bag. My own daily paper, with never fewer than four supplements, is delivered by my newsagent by car.

There are over 2,000 trade and technical publications and around 600 consumer magazines. It is said that at least two new publications are launched in the United Kingdom every week, though the majority are ignored by lawyers. The health, beauty and diet field has expanded most dramatically and as there are always legal claims against cosmetic surgeons, hairdressers and therapists there may even be scope for legal publicity in some of these. Those read by people setting up small businesses, however, are ideal outlets for contributions from the law firms seeking to provide legal services to small to medium-sized enterprises (SMEs).

Women's magazines generally, of which there are far more than you imagine, have an insatiable appetite for material and often appreciate articles with a legal angle – cohabitation, living wills, property advice, financial advice, domestic violence, children's rights, divorce, consumer protection, all are topics of interest to their readers and worth a lawyer's time to promote.

No statistics seem to exist to give any idea of how many people read online versions of the various publications on a regular basis, but it must be millions more.

National newspapers

Unless you are based abroad, you will know that Britain's newspaper industry divides into two categories. The quality dailies are the *Daily Telegraph* (approx. circulation 970,000), *The Times* (670,000), *The Guardian* (420,000), *Financial Times* (440,000) and *The Independent* (203,000). Collectively these are all known as 'broadsheets', simply because their format is large unwieldy pages.

The daily tabloids (smaller size) are the *Sun* (3,450,000), *Daily Mail* (2,420,000), *Daily Mirror* (2,180,000), *Daily Express* (870,000), and *Daily Star* (720,000); the last three are also sometimes known as 'red tops' for no more imaginative reason than that their mastheads have red in them. Scotland has the *Daily Record* (560,000). They are the most populist and devote more space to sport and celebrity gossip than to hard news. More importantly, as you can see, five times as many people in the United Kingdom choose to read the *Sun* as read *The Times*. The tabloid readers, while largely loyal, can change. Piers Morgan, editor of the *Daily Mirror* boasted that when he secured the former Royal butler, Paul Burrell, to give his story exclusively to the *Mirror,* circulation rose by 150,000 a day. As a result of their popularity and volatility the red tops are the least rewarding for legal publicists, but sometimes the most dangerous if one is trying to manage a tricky issue or high profile case. Trickiest of all are those papers that are in one format but have the mind-set and style of another. Some, rather rudely, mutter these days that the venerable *Times* maintains its position in the circulation war by becoming a 'tabloid in broadsheet form'.

On Saturdays and Sundays millions of trees die in the cause of leisurely breakfast-time papers. The *News of the World* has the highest circulation (around 4,100,000 each Sunday), with *Mail on Sunday* (2,300,000) and *Sunday Mirror* (1,800,000) a long way behind. In order of popularity we then have *Sunday Times* (1,400,000), the *People* (1,350,000), *Sunday Mail* (Scottish, 700,000), *Sunday Express* (820,000), *Sunday Telegraph* (790,000), the *Observer* (450,000) and *Independent on Sunday* (230,000). These figures, of course, fluctuate wildly and are approximate only, but they give a sense of what our country chooses to read. If, therefore you are seeking to inform and influence large numbers, your targets must be the tabloids. If you are aiming to communicate with business people, high-net-worth individuals and those in positions of influence, your target will obviously be the broadsheets.

The real message from this, though, is that most people want their news served up simply. I am always very respectful of the professional journalists on the popular papers. They have the enviable ability to distil complex issues into short, punchy sentences. They use the plainest language and many lawyers would do well to emulate their style. Anyone serious about developing media-handling skills should ensure they read at least one tabloid paper every day as well as at least one broadsheet, and that they should not just stick to the same two papers each day. Observe how the same story can be covered quite differently in two papers, partially influenced by the political proclivities of its owner. While politics may play little part in a lawyer's guide, it should also be noted that newspapers are usually far less coy about declaring their political affiliations than the broadcast media. An awareness of a paper's political allegiance is relevant if you are trying to mobilise public sympathy on an issue, or influence opinion formers, for example, for realistic levels of funding for legal aid lawyers in the face of further government cuts, or to remedy a flawed judgment by a member of the judiciary.

Though papers are easy and cheap to read online, and cuttings may be obtained and circulated, hard copies should also be scanned, as the positioning and captioning of pieces influences their impact, and this can rarely be discerned when the copy is displayed on a computer screen or a cutting has been reduced on a copier and mounted.

If we are serious about effective communications at a national level, we should not just concentrate on the broadsheet newspapers, which many of us choose to read daily and which have legal editors or correspondents, contain regular law reports, and features on the profession and legal issues. *The Times'* Tuesday Law Supplement is the natural home for most of us; other legal journalists are Joshua Rozenberg in the *Daily Telegraph*, Robert Verkaik in *The Independent* and Clare Dyer and Marcel Berlins in *The Guardian*. But the people so many of our profession need to reach, to help understand how the law works, what their legal rights are and how lawyers can help them and their businesses, will be reading quite other publications. Also, never assume that income bracket, class or geography dictate which media outlets are preferred – the raciest papers often go to the classiest homes.

Regional newspapers

Never underestimate the importance of the regional press, which is often neglected, including the freesheets, which may litter your doormat but are often desperate for copy and widely read. A surprising number of people read their local paper more thoroughly and regularly than they read a national, and your chance of receiving coverage in your region is candidly considerably greater than your chance of achieving space in a national newspaper, unless you really have a newsworthy issue or firm.

Your firm or chambers is also frankly far more likely to be brought to the attention of potential clients in your local newspapers. So, get into the habit of reading all your local papers – they are a useful barometer not just of local issues, but also of what your publicity-aware competitors may be up to and developments in the business and property fields on which you might be able to capitalise.

More than two-thirds of the provincial press, including weekly papers, are owned by just four large companies. Some also have shares in local radio stations and are very powerful in the areas they serve.

Most big towns have an evening paper appearing six nights a week; in England and Wales there are about 75 of these at present. The readership profile for evening newspapers in the regions is predominantly in the social categories C1, C2 and D.

Most evening papers outside London have a monopoly and consequently considerable penetration. The expansion of the Metro series of urban free morning papers has probably eroded the monopoly enjoyed previously by some of the evening papers. But in Manchester, for example, with an adult population of about 950,000, the *Manchester Evening News* is still read by over a million people (which exceeds the less successful nationals). The Greater Manchester area has a population in excess of 2.6 million, and evening papers from Oldham, Bolton and Wigan also circulate in the area – that is a lot of people to get your messages to if you are practising in the North West. In addition, about 11 major cities have morning daily papers, but they generally do not sell as well as their evening counterparts. The decline in local morning paper sales is explained by the more efficient distribution of national newspapers in the regions, by the rising cost of the papers themselves and, perhaps, by the increasing popularity of television in the homes in the mornings.

There are still just three Sunday papers produced in the English provinces. But it is the weekly local papers that are most likely to be

profitable for the media-aware lawyer. These have a very different structure and rhythm from evening papers. They have much smaller staffs (for
example, just nine journalists produce the North London *Camden Journal,*
compared with 70 journalists who produce the medium-sized *Coventry
Evening Telegraph*).

Altogether there are 1,000 local weekly titles produced in Britain.
However, the word 'title' can be confusing as very often it is the same
paper being produced with a different front page and title, according to
where it is being sold, but with identical contents.

There are about 200 separate regional weekly newspaper newsrooms.
A few local weeklies come out two or three times a week. Local weekly
papers need the raw material of news more than any other news media.
They cannot rely on big national and foreign stories to fill up their pages.
The journalists on a local weekly paper are usually overstretched and
every week there is a hunt for local material.

If a story is presented to a local weekly paper already written out as a
news story, or statement or speech, or press release, it will almost certainly
be used, virtually unaltered, unless it is utterly awful and devoid of
interest. There is no such certainty with any of the national press.

To many lawyers, the local weekly paper is a bit of a joke, the 'rag',
not much better than a parish-pump magazine, full of news of jam-
making and leek competitions, letters from the local Wing Commander
Bufton Tufton (Retired) and lacking serious news and views. This is a mis-
taken attitude. Local weeklies are very important for the communities
they serve:

- They tend to be read for a longer period of time and are left lying
  around for the whole family to see.
- They are more carefully read and absorbed, because they are usually
  bought on a Saturday, a leisure day, and read over breakfast or a cup
  of tea, rather than scanned fast on a tube or bus.
- They relate as directly as is possible to the immediate life of the people in the circulation area – they cover people, places and events that
  they know.
- As life gets more pressured and anxiety about legal fees increases,
  people are likely to favour their local solicitor more.
- As home working extends through many sectors, workers whose
  offices are in cities may increasingly work at least some days a week
  from their homes, and read local papers and use local services more
  than they did.

What you can do for your local newspaper

While this book is mainly to help you work more effectively with the
media, it is also worth remembering that local lawyers are also regularly

needed to provide legal advice to their local newspapers. Andrew Smith is editorial director of NorthEast Press, part of the huge Johnston Press Group, which publishes some 230 regional papers. He is based in Sunderland and comments that:

> Night lawyers on the staff of newspapers are a luxury normally reserved for the national daily newspapers. Most regional publishers retain the services of local solicitors who can be contacted round the clock.
>
> While long-running investigations produce information that can be given a legal check well in advance of publication, it is often the case that lawyers, as well as editors, find themselves running to very tight deadlines in clearing reports for print. Solicitors acting for newspapers have to be prepared to drop everything to deal with stories that may be less than an hour from going to press.

The greatest call for pre-publication legal advice concerns either defamation or contempt. Journalists, Smith says, are usually fairly comfortable in determining for themselves the risks of being sued for defamation and they work by a very reliable rule of thumb – if it is true and can be proved, it can be published. Nevertheless, editors frequently will only feel confident if they have the support of a second opinion. He adds:

> Working reporters and editors are much more uncertain, however, about the risks of being held in contempt of court. Such is the myriad of reporting restrictions, many of which rely on test cases to determine, that legal advice is taken routinely. Editors also tend to take legal advice before publishing stories that may include general comment about issues that are the subject of high-profile court cases, either pending or in progress. As a rule, the regional press is much more likely to err on the side of caution than the nationals when the case law is undetermined.

While some newspaper companies have a policy of using the same legal advisers for both pre- and post-publication advice, others, including Johnston Press, allow editors the discretion to use approved local law firms for pre-publication advice, while (mainly to meet the demands of libel insurance) directing all post-publication legal complaints to their retained and frequently heavyweight (i.e. London-based) libel lawyers. This offers local firms with some expertise in libel and contempt the chance to seek to win the support of local editors as pre-publication legal advisers. Smith warns that a cold call to the editor is unlikely to succeed, but if firms already have established a relationship with the publishers (perhaps on property, employment or contract matters) they might find it possible to seek to meet the editors.

Radio

Daytime radio programmes are often overlooked by lawyers as most of us are at work while they are transmitted, unless we listen in our cars as we speed to appointments. It is easy to forget what a wide audience many of the national and regional programmes attract. Their presenters can be important opinion formers, though you should be aware of the dangers that the cult of personality can have for impartial coverage of the issues with which you are concerned. Devoted listeners place great reliance on the information they receive from the medium, partly because of the intimacy of having the voices in their kitchen or car. The proliferation of legal phone-ins and consumer programmes clearly indicates an increasing public interest in legal matters. Many housebound people, from all walks of life, and the rising numbers of those who live alone, have a radio permanently on in the background of their lives for company and information.

Since the late 1980s there has been a revival of radio with independent stations going public, others taking advantage of the split frequency (effectively the ability to run two radio stations for the price of one), and the increasing expansion of the network of regional stations. The latest development is the growth of digital radio, which is covered in a little more depth in Chapter 5. All these developments mean more opportunities for you to get your message across.

In 1972 the first five independent local radio contracts were granted. In 1998 alone, 219 new licences were issued. There are now hundreds of digital outlets and independent local radio stations and over 40 local BBC ones. National radio is covered by BBC Radios 1, 2, 3, 4 and Five Live. There is a growing number of specialist stations such as Classic FM and Jazz FM.

London, for example, has a station dedicated to broadcasting to women, several targeted at specific ethnic communities, and others catering to particular musical or sports interests and tastes. Twenty-four-hour rolling news has been with us for a few years now and continues to attract steadily increasing numbers, despite evidence that clinical depression can be caused by too much exposure to bad news.

Radio, unlike television, is often a supplementary medium. It does not require the listener's undivided attention. It can be absorbed, almost subliminally, while working, driving, jogging, doing the washing up, or performing leisure activities, and its enthusiasts have always maintained that it gives free rein to the imagination, and so is a superior medium to television, which provides its own images.

But with the voice as the only communications tool, hesitancy, lack of clarity, complex vocabulary all block the listeners' comprehension, and Chapter 5 offers some suggestions to ensure that a relationship with the listener is achieved.

There is a wealth of programmes that have a consumer or legal angle to them. Nationally, most tend to be on BBC Radio 4: Marcel Berlins continues to present *Law in Action*, the only programme that is devoted exclusively to legal topics. It airs in 10-week runs, and the current senior producer, Charlie Sigler, and researcher, Samantha McAllister, can be contacted by phone: 020 8752 6754. *Money Box* covers the whole range of financial issues, many with a legal dimension. Its current senior producer, Chris A'Court, can be reached by phone: 020 8752 5828. *Nice Work* and *Shop Talk* run 26 weeks a year, back-to-back in the same slot on Tuesday afternoons. Rosamund Jones is the senior producer, and can be reached by phone: 020 8752 7339.

But issues of interest and concern to lawyers and their clients are raised every day on many current affairs and news programmes as well as those with a consumer audience. Relevant topics crop up regularly on the *Today* programme (edited currently by Kevin Marsh), or in programmes with audience participation such as BBC Radio 4's *Any Questions?* and the follow-up *Any Answers?*. *You and Yours, PM, World Tonight* and others often make contact asking for lawyers to take part at short notice. Legal issues are covered in programmes targeted at women (*Woman's Hour*) or those with disabilities (*In Touch*) and daily at noon in the programme Jeremy Vine is now presenting on BBC Radio 2, which has filled the void left when Jimmy Young finally retired. As one of the solicitors who occasionally stood in for Jimmy's regular 'legal beagles' Andrew (now Lord) Phillips and Bill Thomas, I can testify that each broadcast gave rise to enormous interest from listeners. I contributed to one programme to alert the public to the Law Society's first 'Make A Will' campaign and chided Jimmy for having no will himself. It gave rise to requests for 100,000 leaflets – a great deal more than we ever anticipated.

On BBC Radio Five Live there is a weekly evening discussion programme, *Weekend News,* which is often looking for lawyers to contribute. Its assistant editor is Stephen Butterick, phone: 020 8752 7200. Five Live has a number of other opportunities to use legal contributors and the editors responsible for the various time slots are John Zilkha ('drivetime', i.e. rush hour), Richard Jackson (breakfast programmes), Louise Cotton (*Up All Night*).

Even soaps, like the durable *Archers*, have solicitors in the cast and legal quandaries befall the regular characters. While at the Law Society I worked with Vanessa Whitburn, the series editor, and Graham Harvey, one of its regular writers, on a storyline that involved sentencing Susan Carter to six months in prison. Listeners mounted a 'Free the Ambridge One' campaign, there was a leader in *The Times*, car stickers, letters in most national newspapers and correspondence to and from the Home Secretary. The purpose of our involvement with the programme-makers had been to alert the public to some concerns the Law Society had about sentencing policy, and the level of attention – albeit rather surreal – achieved this objective well.

Television

Ninety-eight per cent of homes in Britain have at least one television set. This was true in 1994, but the major difference now is the increase in the number of sets. It is now commonplace for a household of adults and children to have three or four sets on at any one time, with the family members watching different programmes in different rooms.

About 38 million of us watch television for an average of two or three hours every day; a sizeable number watch for more than five hours most days and in some homes all meals are consumed in front of the television.

Electronic news gathering (ENG) continues to revolutionise the way that television operates. Small portable cameras, like the home cam-corders you may use, with one- or two-person crews, cover up to three different news stories in a day. The immediacy of the medium means that technicians can respond instantly and broadcasters are often deprived of time for preparation or retakes. How many times have we seen the pre-senter in the studio cue some cold reporter standing disconsolately outside a building, with the line, 'Well, Charles, and what's happening now?' to have Charles bleakly reply words to the effect, 'Very little, James'.

News programmes are watched by at least 20 million people each day. Some London taxis have now been configured to provide television screens, albeit with limited news available; some petrol forecourts have screens to keep you amused while you put petrol in your car; most public areas where queues form or people have to wait are now equipped with television screens. If your personal computer is sophisticated enough, you can get television or video feeds, as well as Internet access and the usual suite of software. In 1993 research into the popularity of a national lottery revealed that the majority of respondents to a survey would rather keep their television sets than receive a million pounds!

The choice of channels continues to increase. We now have Channel 5, ITV 2, BBC 4 and others to add to BBC 1, BBC 2, ITV 1 (as it is now called) and Channel 4. After initial teething troubles, satellite and cable television is established, digital is expanding and many of us have access to more than 100 channels. Many of our handsets are interactive, allow-ing us to participate in national quizzes mounted by television pro-grammes, pledge money to fund-raising campaigns, or use our television sets to send e-mail without getting off the sofa.

Geographical boundaries are irrelevant. We can access CNN's reports from the United States just as easily as we can watch the deliberations in the House of Lords on the Parliamentary Channel or pick up a range of UK-generated news bulletins. The BBC's own News homepage is, as it boasts, 'updated every minute of the day' and I tend to use it as my Internet homepage in order to keep regularly abreast of news developments.

The proliferation and portability of the medium means that your chances of getting to appear on television in front of the passive millions or to work with programme-makers on an issue of concern and interest to you, your firm or your clients has tripled.

Research shows that television's impact is greater on its audience than all other media combined. But this impact is more to do with appearance, image and the picture than the content of the spoken word.

As our opinions about people are invariably fixed within the first 10 seconds of seeing them, television appearances are worryingly prone to superficial response. We notice what the presenter is wearing, what activity is going on behind them, the union leader's tie, the politician's hair, and whether the expressions match the words. We absorb these subconscious messages more readily than we do what is actually said. This can work to your advantage, or it can be your downfall. Chapter 6 details guidance on how to present yourself on television.

Televising the law

Dramatic representations of the legal profession and the law have always been popular. Many people absorb information about how the law operates and how lawyers work very readily from watching such programmes, but as they rarely distinguish fact from fiction it is vital that the programmes are as factually accurate as is possible within dramatic imperatives. The sequences in *Coronation Street* involving marital violence were carefully researched and helpline information was provided on air over the titles; when two characters divorce or a death occurs, care is usually taken to try to present the legal aspects of the situation correctly.

Alternative media

Probably of interest only to campaigning and radical lawyers, there are a number of 'alternative' media outlets, which are useful if you are involved with activism, civil liberties or human rights issues. Inevitably, these are mainly on the Internet and not available in any other form: we do not provide all the URLs but searching on their names will do the trick. They include:

- Undercurrents: video activism;
- SchNews: a weekly update on the 'real' news;
- Squall: an activists' news magazine, which provides an alternative take on events;

- Local Independent Television Network: LiTN is now part of Commedia and networks Britain's growing local TV broadcasters with a view to sharing programmes and resources;
- INK: Independent News Collective is a 'trade association' of independent periodicals that tackle issues of social, political and personal change, and helps its members in areas such as distribution and publicity;
- Indymedia UK: 'is a network of individuals, independent and alternative media activists and organisations, offering grassroots, non-corporate, non-commercial coverage of important social and political issues'; it has a good links page;
- Commedia: Community Media Association provides news, information services and a gateway to community media organisations in the United Kingdom and worldwide.

Online media

As noted above, the biggest single change since the first edition of this book is the online revolution. The Internet is accepted to be the most pervasive and immediate form of communication and the one that has changed legal communications most. Many legal transactions – the purchase of a new house, divorce and the administration of estates – can be conducted almost exclusively online, and for many the choice of solicitors is largely influenced by their willingness to work this way.

Communication with clients is frequently electronic, though you should also speak to them voice-to-voice, if not face-to-face, as nothing replaces that human interaction. Research into their businesses and communication with the media are also dependent on IT.

Modern viral marketing and Internet public relations require wholly new skills and while some lawyers and their firms are harnessing the technology very effectively, others have barely begun. Ideas can, as Michael Less of 'Reclaim the Streets' argues, spread like a virus and without hierarchy.

The speed and flexibility of the Internet are its major differences from other more traditional legal communications mechanisms. It can be used to communicate personally, one-to-one or organisation-to-organisation, globally and simultaneously. Because it routes messages on to the personal screens of individuals it is more intimate and compelling. The language and style is more informal and accessible. This tool can be used not only to 'push' messages from a communicating organisation to its audiences, but also to provide information to be 'pulled' off the Internet, when the audience knows it is there and has a need for it.

For many legal organisations, their website has replaced or complements the glossy brochures they lovingly created in the 1990s to tout their wares. It is the first impression of the firm or chambers. In these circumstances, it is surprising that so many are so dated and poor.

Most firms and chambers, and their corporate clients, tend apart from websites to use the Internet comprehensively for research and for e-mail, to send e-briefings to clients and others they wish to inform, and sometimes to hold online discussions, create Intranets to support complex pieces of litigation or provide a convenient and secure repository for information that has to be accessed by a group of lawyers. Thanks to the speed with which the technology develops, phones can also be used to send and receive messages and pictures, television can now be used interactively, and the wealth of information now available from around the world is literally limitless. The number of firms still producing high-quality brochures, carefully updated and reprinted regularly, will reduce. The number of firms texting their clients with short, abbreviated messages about changes in the law or new services the firm can provide will increase.

Now that the Internet is commonplace, we are increasingly turning to text messaging. *Mobile Commerce World* reported that in 2001 the total number of text messages sent in the United Kingdom alone was 12.2 billion – it has probably doubled or trebled since.

It is an essential skill to feel comfortable using this technology. When I took a short reporter's course many years ago, I never dreamt that the ability to type at 75 wpm would be about the most useful thing I ever learnt. I strongly recommend that all lawyers, regardless of age, should make time to go on a short typing course to get fast keyboard skills; increasingly those who refuse to acquire the expertise now commonplace for most 14-year-olds will be left behind.

You can easily spot the firms where senior lawyers still dictate their e-mails, just electronic versions of their standard hard copy letters – and those where the authors of the messages have created them themselves.

The five elements of the Internet are:

- its *reach*: from millions with one message, to just one person;
- its *speed*: instantaneous, global;
- its *transparency*: its availability to others who can gain competitive advantage by seeing it;
- it is *porous*: everyone can have access and its messages stay on hard drives and are accessible for years;
- the *lack of message control* because of the intermediary agency that provides the transmission.

While some information can remain on the Internet for years (I vividly recall being disconcerted when a senior lawyer in a City firm idly enquired at a presentation whether I still supported the legalisation of cannabis, as he had found on the Internet my support for the campaign in the 1960s), other messages can be, and frequently are, changed by others and by things. The messages that organisations so carefully craft can be changed by people on websites, in chatrooms, in e-mails, in discussion lists and even by the technologies themselves. Search engine rankings juxtapose good, bad, new and old messages and the Internet itself acts as an agent of change.

The consumers of your messages placed on the Internet may add to the information you provide, spread the word, change the content and all this will influence how organisations are managed, how they are perceived, how their services are delivered and even how the organisations are run. If the media is obtaining its view of you from the Internet, these changes could be crucial.

You should, therefore, never lose sight of the fact that the legal manager and their communications professionals lose control of their messages and the reach of the messages to selected audiences. This makes effective crisis management imperative; Chapter 9 covers this topic further.

I have neither the space nor the expertise to help you to become a truly effective public relations practitioner in cyberspace, but courses proliferate and the recommended reading list in Appendix 5 makes some suggestions. This is just a quick crash course in some basics to help lawyers keep up with the rest of the world.

David Phillips in his helpful book *Internet Strategies* outlines the four public relations disciplines to understand:

- richness;
- reach;
- constituency;
- empathy.

In his view, all organisations operating commercially compete to offer rich experiences. The Internet provides a means for people to see almost everything about a firm or chambers or individual lawyer, through their own websites and thousands of other websites. Your online publics are diverse. If you haven't yet done so, try putting your firm's or your own name into Google and wait to see what comes up. You may be surprised.

Richness

The Internet is an interactive resource that is millions of times larger than the global print and broadcast media. The massive amount of its content grows at an amazing rate and if your firm or organisation does not offer rich content to those you are seeking to reach, others will.

The ever-more interested and inquisitive online constituent seeks out the information and is getting very good at it. Two people, trying to persuade me to use their services, were able to drop into the conversation the names of my school and universities; a quick check on Friends Reunited had provided them with this information. My colleagues and I never embark on a conversation with a new client without having first done some speedy online research about them, both as people and as businesses – the wealth of information available in seconds never ceases to amaze me.

Search engines come in many forms (see **http://searchengine.watch. com**) and they provide a tool for all, from the almost computer illiterate, to the sophisticated search expert.

To use this tool, you must master the processes involved in creating content. As a starting point, once your homepage and core information is available online, all firms of more than a few partners should set up comprehensive, interactive and accessible virtual press offices. A study last year by Interactive Bureau revealed that only half the top 100 companies in the United Kingdom provided their share price online, and some even then buried it so deep in their site that it was difficult to find. Make it easy for the media to find information about you, and they will return for it time and again.

Avoid heavy graphics, splash pages, bad navigation and anything, however pretty and eye-catching, that slows down the seeker from making contact with the information for which they are looking.

Many firms have excellent websites now, but some have too obviously been seduced by their web designers. Trial and test yours in consultation with some valued clients, until you are confident you are providing something that is fast and friendly. For a demonstration example of one set up by the media, have a look at **www.thepressdesk. com/demo/home.php**, which shows a format that works well and efficiently.

Opportunities are provided for interaction, browsing for information, backgrounders and up-to-date real time information, such as relevant news and share prices. This is everything a journalist wants in one place.

Tools now exist that unobtrusively track a user's trail as they browse the Web, and these show that if the information needed by a person is not available at one site, they will go elsewhere.

A whole industry has sprung up to help website builders establish the 'useability' of a website. This discovers how easy it is for a visitor to navigate round a site, and then helps to reconstruct the site to be more user-friendly. In addition, in more sophisticated sites this form of evaluation is used to offer a route to information that is apparently what the visitor will find helpful. When evaluating a website for PR purposes, its useability is a consideration to identify site appeal and the professionalism of the webmaster. A key element is the speed and accuracy with which visitors can find what they want.

The range of audiences

The breadth of reach of the Internet is probably the factor most to be borne in mind when planning and implementing media relations. Ten years ago would Shell have thought that Greenpeace was one of its most important publics? Would McDonalds have envisaged being subjected to expensive litigation and severe reputational damage by two litigants in person who harnessed the Web to spread their concerns?

While law firms rarely speak about their corporate social responsibility programmes, all their corporate clients will be developing their own, and the expansion of legal pro bono work also involves communicating with a much wider circle and building a bigger range of media contacts. Links on the website can reach these new targets.

A campaigning tool

Working from a spare bedroom with a basic home computer and some smart software, global campaigns have been mounted, and lawyers, whether advising litigants or keen to promote their ability to provide legal counsel, should be aware of the techniques used and of the tactics required to parry them.

While it is relatively easy to set up a website and provide a wealth of information, created entirely by its authors, that is available to all who log on to the site, it is a great deal harder to manage the relationship with all those who regularly visit the site, or to counter damaging or incorrect information that finds its way either on to the site itself through chatrooms and discussion groups, or on to other sites, perhaps hyperlinked to your own.

The Sally Clark case provides invaluable tuition. A Cambridge statistician and academic, David MacKay, generously set up, in his own time and at his own expense, a website (**www.sallyclark.org.uk**) so that the team representing Sally and campaigning for her release could communicate easily and cost-effectively with the growing hundreds of supporters from all over the world who were expressing their concern about the safety of Sally's convictions, and writing regularly to her in prison. I also wanted to control a communications channel that could counter the many untruths, misconceptions and inaccuracies about the case that had been pedalled through the popular national and regional media. The website that David created was designed to be quick and easy primarily for those writing to Sally or the campaign team from home computers. If you drilled down you could find the judgments from the original trial and first unsuccessful appeal, all the media coverage that we felt was accurate and fair, a wealth of additional information about the whole topic of sudden infant death syndrome (SIDS) and on the first page were contact details for the team.

Not a day passed during the two years I was working for Sally and Steve Clark without messages appearing, either on my office or home PC, from all over the world, from people wanting to help. Scientists researching SIDS from Canada, Australia, New Zealand and the United States wrote to me. Parents who had suffered multiple unexplained infant deaths wrote from Europe, China and India. Journalists from many different countries, anxious to get the facts straight, wrote inviting me to check their copy. Doctors, statisticians, pathologists, journalists, parents – this huge global community of friends kept in touch with us and with each other through the means of technology and I doubt if we could have managed without this resource. It also provided a time-saving reservoir of research materials for any newcomers who wanted to write about the topic.

It also helped me understand why Internet buffs talk about 'communities'. The day that Sally's second appeal was upheld and she was released, I dealt with the media and their many calls for interviews for hours and then crawled home very late at night. I had already received many hundreds of e-mails from our online friends at my office, but I wearily logged on to my home computer: 330 new messages scrolled up before my eyes, sending messages of congratulations, delight and love from a total of 27 different countries. Disregard this powerful weapon at your peril.

Reach

We are all less good at monitoring and evaluating what we do than we should be. An organisation's website will attract visitors (even the awful ones do) and unless you have some sense of how many visitors your site is getting, you will have no idea how useful this tool is. You can track how regularly your virtual press office pages are visited and immediately get a sense of how far your media strategy is reaching. There are several competing Internet services that can provide you with statistics about visitor numbers. They provide some code that is placed on your webpages to activate their counting computer. Some of the providers include:

- Superstats (**www.superstats.com**): this is a paid or free service. The tracking service can be placed on as many pages as you want, so if you only want to establish how many people are visiting your press release pages, this can be done. If you place its banner advertisement on your page/s, the service is free. Without a banner, it will charge you. If you want to track visitors for a month, there will be a fee.
- Netgenesis (**www.netgen.com**) profiles and segments the visitors to your site, links online and offline metrics.
- Hitbox (**www.hitbox.com**) provides a similar service.

- Stattrax (**www.stattrax.com**) provides a breakdown of the referring pages it monitors, listed by number of referrals. By analysing where people come from prior to visiting your firm's website (and by analysing the content of those pages) you or your marketing professional will be able to identify the place, content and probably the motivation that attracts your site visitors. It can also provide invaluable information about how you are seen in the legal marketplace in relation to what visitors regard as your competitors.

Constituents

Your firm's or chambers' constituents will be diverse and with the additional knowledge acquired by Internet research into who is visiting your website, you can examine in depth your firm's ability to make contact with your targets. Your aim, when researching the content and visibility of your site, is to establish who seems to be interested in its content and whether their interest will mean that they will come back, ideally often and not just occasionally.

Organisations with similar words in their titles can use search engines to research the visibility of competitors' sites and then start researching how to make their own more appealing. If you manufacture widgets, a short Google search on 'widget' will probably throw up most of the companies who do this. With law firms or barristers' chambers it is harder. We use names, if we are solicitors, which are usually connected with founders of the firm, often long deceased, or with the location and address of the set, if we are barristers. But searching on your supposed specialisms can be illuminating. I advised a set that professed to be a leading public law chambers, but when searching on those two words 'public law' a number of other, much less expert, chambers came up. It caused a rethink in how my clients presented themselves online and what links they established. It was also unsurprising that no journalists yet saw them in the way they hoped to be seen.

Discussion and chat

Analysis of the discussion lists available online and the conversations being held on them offers access to very interactive and interested people. The PR industry has tended to avoid involvement in online discussion and it can be very time-consuming, but if you are involved in a campaign, or righting a miscarriage of justice, then this is a very powerful place for building relationships and for effecting change. Campaigning journalists increasingly monitor and participate.

Then there is 'chat'. There are lots of different areas and it can take forever to find relevant chatrooms, but again, once found they can be illuminating and can be monitored in real time.

Empathy

The effect of a website on its visitors and any consequential effect on your firm or online presence is obviously significant to your firm or chambers. It could be a ringing endorsement, a criticism or a call to action.

All relationships with our clients and observers should be dynamic, but this is nowhere more so than in cyberspace where the relationship is transparent and personal, so evident empathy is vital.

Lawyers using the Internet to market and communicate with journalists should just ask if their website changes the relationship. Does it turn surfers into clients, competitors, reporters, employees or other constituents? Is it addressing the issues and social framework of those it is seeking to target and to what extent is it achieving all the firm's objectives for it? Or is it just bragging to other lawyers?

Updating

In 'dog years' I am nearly 400 years old (seven years for every human year), but, as Richard Levick points out, imagine if your age was tallied to Internet years. The Internet changes the way we communicate every three months. How is your firm communicating today compared with how it did it three months ago? How will it communicate in three months' time? Your clients receive information differently. Are you keeping up with them? How are your competitors doing? Are you keeping up with them, or even better, one step ahead? How are you keeping your information up to date and relevant? Do you use direct communications to provide your clients with their own tailored information on legal issues of direct interest to them? Who are your Internet strategic partners? Have you digitised your newsletters yet? When the Internet breaks into channels and surfing is dead, what channel will you own?

If all this makes you feel rather tired, or cross, because of its perceived irrelevance to your small firm or chambers, take courage. There are still the traditional newspapers and their scribes.

Understanding the media from a legal editor's perspective

Frances Gibb is the doyenne of legal correspondents, legal editor of *The Times* and responsible for its weekly Law Supplement.

I asked her to detail her pet hates when dealing with lawyers and their PR people, in the hope that you might learn from them. I list her 'beefs' and then add my comments in parenthesis. In no particular order, they are:

- 'The PRs who ring up and say, "Do you publish a law page and what day is it?"' [If they have not taken the trouble to find out that for some years now *The Times* has published a comprehensive Law Supplement every Tuesday, items for which are finalised four or five days beforehand, they do not deserve to be in legal PR, and their firms do not deserve any profile.]

- 'Those who ring when I am on a news story deadline, just to ask if I have received their e-mail/fax about the latest deal, partner move.' [It is courteous and good practice always to start any conversation with a journalist by asking if they are 'under the cosh', i.e. writing to a deadline, and is this a good time to talk, and if not, getting off the line immediately. The journalist's patience with the caller will be directly related to the newsworthiness of the story. Dull and irrelevant stories can expect, quite properly, to be given short shrift.]

- 'Another failing is to ring with an article idea, wanting to expound it at length (again usually when the journalist is on a news deadline), and clearly not having seen a similar piece we ran two weeks before.' [It is unflattering and just plain dim not to be fully conversant with any publication or programme to whom you are pitching an idea or piece – they are entitled to reject you if you are not.]

- 'Finally, don't ask a journalist, "What stories are you interested in?" The answer is usually, "Any". A story is a story. The trouble is that most PRs don't know what that is . . . unless they have worked as journalists themselves.' [Or, perhaps, unless they have worked in legal PR for some years and have assiduously studied the legal media and the way that legal stories and issues are reported and acquired a sense of what works, and what does not.]

Frances generously offers some advice:

- 'Try not to ring unless it's really necessary. If a journalist is interested in a story, he/she will reply to an e-mail/fax.' [In the case of Frances, she is a busy mother with a surgeon husband and a range of demanding domestic commitments, as well as pressing daily deadlines and a tight weekly deadline for the Supplement. If you think your life is pressured, try a stint as a journalist on a national daily.]

- 'Do always ask if it is a convenient time, the later in the day you ring, the greater the likelihood is that the journalist will be on deadline. And do the research first!' [Try to avoid ringing journalists on nationals after 3 p.m., when they are almost always writing. Most prefer e-mails with punchy, eye-catching subjects, so that they can deal with them when the copy is filed and they have time and energy to do so. Calls can be desperately disruptive to one's train of thought and a brusque response should be expected.]

Frances does not just aim her arrows at public relations professionals. The lawyers themselves come in for their fair share of criticism:

- 'Coming up with a good story or article idea and then pulling their punches, because when it comes to putting something in print, they hedge their bets and/or the client decides against the publicity.' [If you want to be taken seriously, don't waste a journalist's time with a 'punt'. Be sure that if you are putting something to them, you can stand it up, provide a lawyer to give more detail or a quote, and if it involves a client of the lawyer, their permission to publicise the matter has already been obtained. This can give rise to raised expectations that are subsequently dashed, but better that than alienating a potentially invaluable media ally.]

- 'Expecting that newspapers/magazines will want to run a 2,000-word article on the more obscure points of a statute, but being quite unavailable for an instant on-the-spot comment on a news story.' [Don't forget that the legal correspondents on all the nationals not only cover the legal profession, but are always expected to be on the lookout for any news story with a legal dimension on which they are the most appropriate journalist on the paper to write. It is often enormously helpful for them to be able to go to a specialist and authoritative lawyer to check a fact quickly, or get some technical guidance on the content of the piece. One of the surest ways of making a journalist favourably disposed when you want to pitch a story is to have helped them selflessly in the past.]

- 'Imagining that a move, e.g. to a new law firm or chambers, is of world-shattering importance and interest. I was once summoned, in top secret, to see a QC who told me he had something very sensitive to discuss. I raced off to see him somewhere discreet in the hope of the big exclusive – only to find he wanted to tell me about his move to another set.' [What we find of fascination and real importance is rarely seen in the same way by journalists.]

- 'The inability of lawyers (not all are guilty of this) to answer questions concisely – or at all. Lawyers have a tendency to talk *at* you, and to ramble on about a subject, without listening to the question they have been asked, presumably because they usually do the asking.' [At the risk of irritating my readers, can I add that this appears to be a point raised with particular regularity by young, attractive women reporters when the lawyer they are interviewing falls into none of these categories.]

- 'Presuming to know what it is you will want to know and write about, and proceeding to tell you. One barrister suggested I wrote a profile of him, and before I had even replied, submitted his own suggested version of what I might like to say!' [Not only do highly specialist and experienced journalists have a much clearer idea of what they want for their paper, but they have often observed the law in greater depth and for longer than the lawyers with whom they are in contact. Patronise them at your peril.]

- 'Declining to help a journalist, even off the record or for background – even where this could easily be done without compromising the client – and then complaining when journalists get facts wrong. Some lawyers will refuse to give information which is available but will be time-consuming for a journalist to obtain – usually the same people who expect "favours" in terms of their cases being publicised.' [I cannot stress too often the merit of being helpful and responsive to journalists and the dividends this pays.]
- 'Offering a good story – but weeks or even months after the event.' [If you know you are involved in an interesting case or matter, which ultimately you would like to publicise, then alert the journalist, in confidence, well ahead; give them, off the record, the bones of the issue and an indication when you anticipate judgment or being able to give them the full story. They can then timetable your story in among all the others. If you leave it until after the dust has settled it will be old, cold news and of no interest to anyone apart from you, your firm and your client.]

Contacting the journalist

Frances Gibb reports that she gets anything between 50 and 100 e-mails every single day. It is unsurprising when she has to be out and about following stories, attending court and conferences, conducting interviews and filing her copy – as well as striving to balance her life – that she does not manage to reply to those of zero interest. She gets increasingly fewer news releases by fax. She confirms that she finds the most helpful releases are those that say a test legal case is coming up, or a test judgment will be given, and give a short legal commentary, with names/contacts for lawyers who will be able to comment on the day.

She confirms that with big stories, where information is flooding in from several sources, it is much easier for the journalist if the lawyer or PR simply e-mails a reaction over on the day, rather than telephoning and trying to fix an interview. All the big organisations now do this. If the journalists want extra or specific points answered, they will, of course, ring.

It is important to try to send the right news release to the right reporter or department on the paper. For instance, in *The Times'* law section, people changing jobs are covered in a specific section with its own e-mail address. PRs should send the information there, rather than ring the main legal reporter contact, and waste their time by asking where to send it.

Like all professional journalists, Frances is as dependent on good contacts as any. She comments:

The best are those who are skilled in the art of making punchy, relevant points, and are available. Speed and brevity are of the essence when time is short. They are few and far between, which is why the same people tend to be used by journalists over and over again.

Availability outside office hours seems to be a key point. From his earliest days as a regularly used legal commentator, often on topics outside his areas of specialism, Mark Stephens was asked by other, envious lawyers, why the media always seemed to call him. The answer was simple. He had provided them all with his home and mobile phone numbers, took calls cheerfully at any time of the day or night and always meticulously returned messages left for him quickly. This is true of very few.

Never feel that any one level of media is more important or has more status than another. Communicating at any level is tricky and you must become familiar with the audience of the particular medium you are working with at any given time.

4

How to handle the print media

Getting going: dealing with journalists

Media relations are all about people and if you lose sight of this you will flounder. Effective media-handling is dependent on good, trusting relationships forged, over time, between those with information to communicate and those who provide the channel, the journalists. Some say they should never be trusted, others that trust can be safely and mutually established, but takes time. If you deal with them honourably and candidly, on the whole they will do the same with you. There are, of course, exceptions to all sweeping generalisations and, despite many years' experience, I have had uncomfortable run-ins with pushy hacks, but rarely.

Like lawyers, most journalists suffer from public dislike. They work against deadlines, frequently in congested spaces and often are poorly paid. With very few exceptions, they prefer to get things right and produce good stories in an accessible, well-written style, but they are dependent on others for the accuracy of the information they receive and, like most of you, they are employed by businesses that have to be commercially viable.

The risk-aversion trained into lawyers makes us reluctant to venture into unknown territory, but the tendency, which was prevalent a few years ago, to leave all media-handling to the professionals – public relations staff and consultants, practice or chambers managers or underemployed freelance journalists – is waning. Most journalists prefer direct contact rather than a PR filter. Most communications issues are better 'owned' by the firm, the lawyer or the business, rather than someone acting as a spokesperson or interpreter on their behalf. If you are likely to find yourself having to talk to a print journalist, you should first do some thinking to work out what you are trying to achieve and the best route to success, equip yourself with some basic props and struggle through to the end of this guide. Be sure to read through Chapter 3, if you started here, as it explains the media a little more, and Chapter 7, which covers more on the use of the media in the context of marketing, as most lawyers seem most interested in using the media to develop their businesses.

Helpful props

The first edition of this book recommended a number of directories and these still exist, but increasingly the information you need is available online, and simply using a good search engine and searching on the name of a journalist or a publication can throw up a wealth of useful material. For those who prefer the security blanket of books, the following are helpful:

- *Guardian Media Guide 2003*, published annually by *The Guardian*, and available in paperback for £12.59. A comprehensive listing guide and the one that I rely on the most.
- *British Rates and Data (BRAD)*, published annually by EMAP Business Communications, available from **www.brad.co.uk** for £265. To obtain some information online, you must subscribe. Your local library may also have a copy of *BRAD*.
- *Writers' and Artists' Yearbook 2003*, published annually by A & C Black, and available in paperback for £9.09. This lists comprehensively all newspapers and magazines with addresses, phone numbers, e-mail addresses, details of current editors and a brief description of the publication's house style.
- *Blue Book of British Broadcasting*, published annually by Tellex Monitors Ltd. This lists every radio and television company in the United Kingdom (national and regional) with the names and contacts details of all key personnel and schedules.
- *Hollis UK Press and PR Annual*, available for £97.50 from Hollis Directories, Harlequin House, 7 High Street, Teddington, Middlesex TW11 8EL, phone: 020 8977 7711; e-mail: hollis@hollis-pr.co.uk
- *Pims UK Media Directory*, published monthly by Pims UK, Pims House, Mildmay Avenue, London N1 4RS, phone: 020 7354 7000; e-mail: prservices@pims.co.uk
- *Benn's Media Directory*, published annually for a terrifying £325 for three volumes, available from United Business Media.
- *BRAD Monthly*, now produced by Intelligencia/EMAP.
- *PR Planner*: this is a CD-updated quarterly available from Waymarker, which lists events and helps timetable your activities so they avoid conflicts with others, £695 + VAT.
- *Willings Press Guide*: this annual guide to newspapers and journals worldwide is also published by Hollis, as above, and comes in two volumes, UK and international; it is also available via Internet and Windows CD-Rom for £342.50 for the whole package or £170 for just the UK print version.

All professional public relations outfits and nowadays most press offices in larger law firms and chambers have purchased a software programme providing them with a media directory on their screens. The prices and comprehensiveness vary, and none is absolutely 100 per cent up to date as there are so many journalists who move regularly, but the following are favoured:

- *Media Disk*, is provided by Waymaker, phone: 0870 7360010; e-mail: sales@waymaker.co.uk   This not only provides a very detailed list of media contacts, but allows you to organise your data in a sensible manner and offers a slightly more up-to-date service than its rival.
- *Media Manager*, is provided by PR Newswire, phone: 020 7490 8111; e-mail: info@prnewswire.eu.com   This service is better if you want to access European publications, so is the one for firms with international clients or offices.

Online media data include the following:

- *Global Journalism Review*: this is a free online service that has links to papers and Press Councils globally; it is a bit patchy but occasionally useful, particularly if your communications need to be international.
- *Periodical Publishers' Association* has a links page for magazines on the Internet.
- *New Jour* lists electronic journals and newsletters published on the Internet.
- *Media UK*: an independent online media directory, details all magazines, newspapers, radio and TV with an online presence.
- *CSV Action Desks* work within BBC local radio stations, to get charity and community organisation messages across (e-mail: media@csv.org.uk).
- *Campaign for Press and Broadcasting Freedom*: an independent voice for media reform, it can offer advice on the 'right of reply', phone: 020 7630 1966; e-mail: freepress@cpbf.demon.co.uk

Create one or more media lists

From a combination of the above you should create a media list to which your releases, e-briefs, e-alerts and phone calls will go. Larger and more sophisticated firms will need several different databases that segment the media for their different practice areas. These lists get out of date frequently and should be regularly updated.

Alternatively, you could contact PIMS (www.pims.co.uk) at Pims House, Mildmay Avenue, London N1 4RS, phone: 020 7354 7000; fax 020 7354 7053; e-mail: enquiries@pims.co.uk This can provide list management (*Listlogix*) and press release distribution services (*PimsWire*), but as you will discover later I am sceptical about the effectiveness of many releases.

Other essential props are obvious:

- a reliable mobile phone with a long battery life (many PRs have two – one for incoming and one for outgoing calls);
- a genuinely portable laptop with small portable printer if you need to create text or pick up messages on the run, with all the peripherals to connect it easily in hotel rooms, on trains, etc.;
- an easily transportable contact database. Increasingly people are using PDAs: I stick to a time-expired but trusted Psion with over 800 contacts in it, regularly backed up, but there is nothing wrong with hard copy, if you can be confident not to lose it. You will always need numbers when you are away from your desk, as the media tend to operate outside usual or civilised working hours;
- a supply of business cards on which your out-of-hours contact details are printed or written (ideally in advance, to save fumbling during a chance encounter).

News agencies

Many journalists get their information from the main news agencies. Their number has also increased and they operate mainly online, though often ask for faxes as well as e-mails.

It is well worth getting to know them and forging contacts with their key players. At one point Press Association had its own dedicated legal journalist, John Dean, but now the legal brief is shared among the news journalists. All the wires, though, do have dedicated journalists for other topics, and so if you are publicising a banking case or campaigning on a criminal matter you should establish which journalist is covering that brief.

The main agencies are:

- *The Press Association* (**http://pa.press.net**), 292 Vauxhall Bridge Road, London SW1V 1AE, phone: 020 7963 7000; e-mail: information@pa. press.net or for the Northern region, The Bishop's Manor, Market Place, Howden, N Yorks DN14 7BL. PA has separate dedicated numbers/ e-addresses for its individual journalists, but also provides a Television News Release service by phone: 020 7963 7163; e-mail: info@tvnews release.com
- *Reuters* (**www.reuters.com**), 85 Fleet Street, London EC4P 4AJ, phone: 020 7250 1122. Reuters also has different journalists dedicated to different topics and sectors and their details are readily obtained.
- *Associated Press* (AP) (**http://www.ap.org**), International Headquarters, 50 Rockfeller Plaza, New York NY 10020, phone: 001 212 621 1500. AP is the oldest news agency and though based in New York covers some UK news.

- *Bloomberg* (**www.bloomberg.co.uk**). This is the main news resource for City and financial matters; it provides regular updates of the stock markets globally and occasionally covers the law firms involved in major commercial transactions.
- *Newspoint* (**www.newspoint.co.uk**). This is a news agency based in the House of Commons; its Desk Diary has a schedule of the day's activities at Westminster, including Question Time, so if you are tracking the progress of a piece of legislation, lobbying on an issue or protecting the interests of a peer or an MP this can be a useful resource.

There are also innumerable international news agencies, including:

- CNN;
- CBC;
- Africa News Online.

Most countries and some cities have their own and can be found easily, e.g. Athens News Agency (**www.ana.gr**); Czech Happenings covers the Czech Republic and Slovakia (**www.ctknews.com**).

Press cuttings and media monitoring

However assiduous you are it is never possible to be confident you have tracked every single press reference to the issue you are concerned about, and to try to do so is enormously time-consuming. When I was responsible for the Law Society's Press Office its small team would take the first two hours of every day going through all the papers and checking the online media, until we set up a dedicated press cutting service.

Most press cuttings bureaux work by searching for key words (often your organisation's or client's name, but it can be whatever you specify). Some charge for a period, others for a set number of items found, some charge a fee for reading and then an additional charge for each cutting tracked. A press cutting service for a specific client or issue will usually cost between £175 and £500 a week, exclusive of VAT, dependent on the volume of coverage.

The best bureaux are:

- Durrants, Discovery House, 28–42 Banner Street, London EC1Y 8QE, phone: 020 7674 0200; e-mail: sales@durrants.co.uk
- International Press Cutting Bureau, 224 Walworth Road, London SE17, phone: 020 7708 2113.
- Romeike and Curtice, Hale House, 290–296 Green Lanes, London N13 5TP, phone: 0800 289543 or 020 8882 0155; e-mail: info@ romeike.com Romeike and Curtice also provide a service monitoring

Internet publications, news groups and websites (net.cut) and 'Back Research' gives access to the last six months of press cuttings.

- LexisNexis (**www.lexisnexis.com**), phone: 0800 227 9597. This provides legal, news, public records and business information including tax and regulatory publications online and is a subscription service, or pay per use service on which many of us rely.
- Google News: just by searching on Google and then searching its 'News' service you can track many cuttings and references to issues in the news.

It is also worth investigating an early morning cuttings service, like the one provided by Xtreme Information; I am currently using Durrants, which reliably delivers bundles of cuttings to my office before 8 a.m. and delivers them to my home at weekends.

Press Association Library, 85 Fleet Street, London EC4P 4BE, phone: 020 7353 7440, holds over 14 million news cuttings, starting from 1926, and can be enormously helpful if you come to a matter late in the day and need to see how it was originally reported.

Active or reactive media relations

There are just two ways of dealing with journalists:

- you simply wait for them to call and respond to their enquiries (passive or reactive PR), remaining on the back foot, or
- you make contact with them, endeavour to interest them in something you have to say by a phone call, e-mail or release, followed by perhaps a more detailed briefing, an interview, an article, a press conference or a phone call (active or proactive PR), and you are on the front foot.

Most people adopt the first approach. Most smart media relations require the second. Either way it helps to have formed some kind of relationship with the journalist in question before you find yourself in a conversation about an issue.

What is a journalist?

Sadly the caricatures from the old films have gone. There are no visors or trilbies, few trenchcoats, and in 20 years I have only heard one editor talk about 'holding the front page'. As with every profession, journalists are a mixed bunch and there seem to be rather more women than men these days, as is also the case with new entrants to the law.

Most journalists with whom you will come into contact will be graduates, many will have acquired journalism qualifications, some will be qualified but disaffected lawyers (Joshua Rozenberg, legal editor of the *Daily Telegraph*, Marcel Berlins and Clare Dyer on *The Guardian* are solicitors; Robert Verkaik on *The Independent* is a barrister, and many contributors to national and legal publications are legally qualified). The legal editors and correspondents on the national newspapers have mainly been in post for many years and are highly experienced and authoritative. On the legal weeklies (*Lawyer, Legal Week, Solicitors' Journal, New Law Journal, Law Society's Gazette*) and monthlies (*Legal Business, In Brief, Commercial Lawyer, European Lawyer, Independent Lawyer, Legal Director*, etc.), the journalists will often be younger, but nonetheless have gathered a wealth of knowledge about lawyers, firms and the business of law. You patronise them and fail to take them seriously at your peril.

Few will now write shorthand in any form, several will use pocket tape-recorders when conducting interviews. Many may know more about the law business than you do.

Myths exploded

Experienced American lawyer turned legal publicist, Richard Levick, founder of Levick Strategic Communications, promotes law firms internationally. He has assembled 10 myths of law firm PR:

- 'You don't need to return reporters' calls.' Reporters are like stray cats: if you don't feed them they go to someone else's door. Call them back even if it is only to say you can't say anything.
- 'Reporters can't be trusted.' Their job is to write their story, not your story, but that does not mean they cannot be trusted – of the thousand we work with globally, only a few do not play by the rules. Some may not get the story right by your perspective, but most will try to get the story the best they can. The more often you work with them, the more likely they are to get it right.
- 'Moving to new offices and hiring lateral partners is news.' This is as much news as flossing your teeth is news.
- 'A merger is news.' When it is the merger of major firms, it can be news, but usually it is a one-day story. Focusing your press efforts on the merger rather than the firm is like Honda focusing all its press on only the first day of its new model year. To be effective, press efforts have to be ongoing.
- 'The daily newspaper will mention the name of your firm.' The more important the paper, the less likely it is to name your firm. If you are already getting coverage in the legal and trade publications, you may get several name-checks and even a photo. You won't in *The Times* or

New York Times. This does not mean you shouldn't spend time with the major dailies, it just means that you should set your expectations on what is realistic.

- 'Advertising and public relations are the same.' This hoary chestnut keeps coming up. Advertising you pay for and control. PR has far more credibility, but you are in the hands of the journalists and require the help of a third party. You cannot make a reporter write something as you want it, but PR can be managed and journalists influenced. What reporters write, when repeated often enough, has far more credibility than advertising.

- 'Everyone reads the articles as closely as you do.' Lawyers read articles about themselves and their firms like, well, lawyers. But newspaper articles are not legal documents. They are opportunities to get the name of the firm or its lawyers in the press with enough frequency that it develops the benefit of familiarity with clients and prospects – and that is it. Did they include your quote? Spell your name right? Will they call on you again? If the answers are 'yes', then you did well and just need to do it again, and again, and again.

- 'Publicity is local.' In the age of the Internet, there is no local paper. BBC producers read stories produced in Bangkok with the same ease that they read ones from Birmingham. It is called the news stream, and once you get into a newspaper, no matter where, the chances are that clients, prospects and other reporters are going to have access to it. So if your firm is national or international with several offices and there is a bad news story in one city, it should be countered by other stories, so that you don't just leave the one record of that issue.

- 'Publicity begins with a press release.' According to Jim Schachter, Business Editor of the *New York Times,* 'sending a press release to the *New York Times* is like sending a satellite to Pluto'. Press releases written by lawyers have all the appeal, news and timeliness of white rice. Levick's company, which claims to place around 300–400 different legal stories a month, uses a total of two or three press releases a month as a tool to place those stories.

- 'Public relations should be handled on a project-by-project basis.' Law firms conducting their press relations in this way are wasting their money. If Coca-Cola only engaged in publicity when they had a new formula, we would all be drinking Pepsi. Publicity requires reach and repetition. Getting press coverage 'once in a while' when there is a new initiative to report has little value apart from soothing the egos of those who launched that initiative.

Levick stoically maintains that with a little practice (and training and guidance), lawyers can overcome the power of these myths and become good press sources. Many already have.

Segmenting the media

To spend your expensive time effectively, you need to break the media down into distinct sectors, each of which has unique potential for your communications needs, and be clear about the different kinds of interaction you will have with different journalists. One size doesn't fit all.

Avoid media snobbery and be realistic about where most people in this country gain their information. The *Sun* and the *Financial Times* have the same number of editorial staff, but there are more with PhDs on the *Sun*. There are also more A1 readers who read the *Sun*, as its circulation is just so much higher than that of any other paper.

National media

The national newspapers are excellent vehicles for reaching most of your firm's business and higher net worth private clients, and for boosting your firm's image, both internally and externally. As you can see from the circulation figures provided in Chapter 3, for professional service providers the *Financial Times* and the *Daily Telegraph* are the most important, followed by *The Times*. For international commercial law firms, the *Wall Street Journal Europe* is next, and then the other broadsheets. If, however, your practice is a more general, private client one, then your targets may be different.

The national newspapers rarely cover news about developments in the legal market that fall below the scale of a transatlantic merger, unless they have dedicated law pages, like *The Times*. But the journalists on these publications are usually prepared to talk to the lawyers who represent the parties in major pieces of litigation or deals that make the news pages, or able legal commentators who can brief them or comment on these matters. Sometimes if you or your firm feel unable to talk about the case that you have handled, this third party commentary can be a valuable promotional vehicle.

Legal journals

The legal trade press is sometimes derided as 'comics', largely full of gossip of interest only to younger lawyers. It is usually ranked low by senior and managing partners as their preferred media outlet, but as these publications are invaluable tools for those job-hunting, recruiting, seeking to retain staff or to build the number of referrals from outside the firm, they cannot be discounted. They will also be read by your commercial rivals. Most of the senior legal journalists on the national broadsheets will trawl their pages carefully and, if they can find a new angle, and the timing still works, recycle a story with a fresh perspective.

The legal press is also widely read by in-house lawyers who are often the most important clients of many firms.

For lawyers our 'trade' press is also our primary source of professional information and updating. The *Law Society's Gazette* goes weekly to all solicitors with a practising certificate; barristers receive *Counsel*; Members and Fellows of the Institute of Legal Executives receive the *Legal Executive*. Those employed in commerce and industry receive regular newsletters and mailings from the Law Society's C & I Group and have *Legal Director* targeted at them.

The weekly *Lawyer*'s gossipy style is popular with younger lawyers and read online as well as in hard copy. *Legal Week,* its rival weekly magazine established more recently, has its focus more on the commercial and City firms, but these rival publications compete for a wide range of stories, covering specific topics of legal practice in particular ways, covering international as well as UK-based law firms and both carrying many pages of recruitment advertisements. As they come out a couple of days apart, a story featured in the first may be of no interest to the second. There is also *Legal Week Global.*

New Law Journal has been around for years and its weekly summary of developments, mixed with thoughtful articles, is particularly relevant to those in smaller practices around the country, specialising in a mix of private client work, with an emphasis on criminal and justice issues.

Solicitors' Journal is also a reliable weekly read for those not in the larger commercial practices. It has a convenient section for the reader to complete to demonstrate the updating material has been read and understood, which provides continuing professional development (CPD) points. This magazine always features small to medium-sized law firm management topics and is rarely read by those in the larger commercial firms or corporates.

The leading monthly glossy magazine is *Legal Business,* which provides in-depth analysis of law firm management issues, detailed feature articles, carefully researched and sometimes uncomfortably close scrutiny of the biggest and best commercial transactions. It is the primary publication for those involved in the business of law with predominantly commercial clients.

Other legal publications are the monthlies: *Commercial Lawyer, European Legal Business, European Lawyer, In Brief* magazine (which is an easier read than many as it carries car reviews, lifestyle and entertainment articles as well as the traditional legal marketplace and practice issues). The three magazines specifically targeted at in-house lawyers are *Legal Director, In House Lawyer* and *Global Counsel.*

Non-legal trade press

This is a vital and most often overlooked sector. Richard Levick stresses:

> It's crucial that you use the media outlets that talk directly to your customers. The legal press is important for reaching other law firms and partners who are potential lateral hires, but it should not be the only goal of your marketing efforts in the trade press. Research consistently shows that general counsel and other buyers of legal services are influenced by what they read, more so than by almost all other forms of marketing, save personal experience and relationships.

The trade publications in insurance, banking, pharmaceuticals, IT and so on are all read by the managers, executives and lawyers working in companies in these sectors, who all have legal needs but are impressed by seeing reports of law firms that clearly understand their business. The issues covered are of the most direct relevance to the very people who could be hiring or firing your firm. The firms achieving quotes and articles in these publications, however, must emphasise their familiarity with the relevant industry and not just seek to achieve coverage for their firms.

Your selection of publication will, of course, depend on the practice areas that you are seeking to promote. *Corporate Finance,* for example, is the leading UK trade journal for the securities field. *Pink Pages* is read by most in the pharmaceutical world. If you want to build awareness of your employment law expertise, then *Personnel Today* and other HR publications will do the trick. If you are hoping for referrals from accountants, then a piece in *Accountancy Age* might work well. Those running small to medium-sized businesses often read *Director.* Divorce and trust lawyers whose clients come from the top drawer find that *Harpers & Queen* is the place to be named, rather than *Family Law,* and that attending society parties that get reported by Jennifer does no harm either, as referrals in this income bracket tend to come from social encounters. Those whose divorce clients are more likely to be reliant on legal aid might come to your firm if they read about you in *Woman's Own, GQ,* or *Cosmopolitan.*

When advising a group of firms anxious to build awareness of their personal injury expertise, after a little research, I placed a couple of pieces in *Creative Butcher,* having established that butchers suffer an enormous number of work-related injuries! Your firm needs to subscribe to the right publications, which are read by its clients, and the relevant lawyers in the appropriate practice groups need to read them regularly and become familiar with the topics covered by their journalists. Your in-house PR and marketing staff or your consultants will be able to compile a targeted list of journalists to approach, but it is also helpful to ask your major existing clients what is their preferred reading material.

Once you have identified which publications in which fields it would help your firm to appear in, you must decide which journalists on the publications to approach. Lawyers often expect that the entry point is the editor. That is very rarely the case, and a call direct to the top name on the list is likely to confirm the caller's lack of media savvy. Virtually all publications have switchboard operators who can direct you to the right specialist journalist, and online research can show who has covered what topic recently. It is always wise to do this research before calling, and to be clear that you are not offering something on a topic already recently exhausted by that journalist or publication. One financial journalist specialising in the pensions industry told me he received some 50 calls or e-mails from pensions lawyers on the day that Equitable Life's difficulties first became public. Almost all the callers essentially said, 'I'm an expert pensions lawyer. Would you like me to comment authoritatively and at length on the Equitable Life situation?' The journalist had space for just 500 words, and only an hour in which to file his copy, and had already spoken to his preferred pensions contact.

If you cannot identify the appropriate specialist correspondent in the field, start your contact with the news or assistant editor, or the features editor if you are trying to place an article or comment piece.

Regional media

Never forget that a story that originates at local level could quickly arouse national interest. Always devote as much care to a local story as you would to a national one. But for a story to receive coverage in the local papers, it must be genuinely *local* – it must be about people, cases or places that are based in the community served by the publications with which you are in touch. Many people who do not buy or read a national paper are assiduous readers of their local 'rag'. If you are based outside central London you are realistically much more likely to receive coverage in a local rather than a national paper. It is also probably glaringly obvious that the people most likely to instruct you in a regional practice will be resident in the area around your office and may find favourable information about you in their local paper a persuasive reason for contacting you.

The journalists working on local papers are almost always generalists instead of the more specialist writers employed by the nationals. Their legal knowledge may be non-existent or limited, but their local knowledge and their understanding of their readership will be considerable. To succeed locally your story should focus on the locality and on the individual person or people concerned. It should provide details of where they live (the area, but it may be inappropriate to divulge their address), some brief description of their roles in the community and, ideally, a photograph. Avoid any detailed legal background – pare your story to the bones and ensure it has genuine human interest.

The 'Make A Will', 'Accident Line' and 'Save Legal Aid' campaigns mounted by the Law Society received an enormous amount of coverage, over a long period of time, in local newspapers because the lawyers in the regions were at pains to concentrate on the 'people' angles of the three campaigns. Clear examples were given of how vulnerable cohabitees were without a will; how the elderly were sometimes entitled to Green Form assistance in the preparation of a will; how individual clients had been specifically disadvantaged by the changes to legal aid eligibility; how courageous or foolhardy solicitors, attired in the caped crusader costume of Will Power, were offering free advice about wills in the shopping precinct; how local MPs were supporting the campaign to preserve legal aid for their constituents.

The style of local papers varies considerably but is rarely as outspoken, opinionated, detailed or lengthy as any of the national broadsheets. Particularly in the freesheets (which should not be ignored as in many areas they receive widespread circulation) the tone closely resembles a populist tabloid. You will find by regularly reading the various publications in your own region that you will become familiar with the issues, style and interests of each. Some divide their coverage into localities – villages and towns. Many have specific pages or features targeted at women readers, home buyers or the retired.

The *Yorkshire Post* has for many years had the excellent services of its legal reporter, Olwen Dudgeon. Other major regional papers such as the *Manchester Evening News* or the *Birmingham Post* have a regular law page or occasionally devote a special supplement to features on the law firms in their region. Many of these special features are funded by advertisements either co-ordinated by a local law society, or placed by the firms mentioned, and this device has been a useful way of ensuring widespread coverage for various Law Society marketing initiatives to promote specific legal services. The 'Lawyers For Business' campaign was launched with coverage in over 500 regional newspapers, where local solicitors' firms that were members of the scheme purchased advertisements surrounding 'advertorials' (explanatory feature articles) provided to the papers by the Society.

For details of how such schemes can be mounted and contact details for many local newspapers, contact the Newspaper Society on phone: 020 7636 7014, or see **www.newspapersociety.org.uk**.

Andrew Smith, editorial director of NorthEast Press, part of the Johnston Press Group, advises:

Solicitors may be able to build productive working relationships with their local newspapers by offering to advise on general matters raised by readers. Disputes over the garden hedge, noisy neighbours, planning disputes, etc. all lend themselves to stories in these papers. If a solicitor was prepared to provide their local editor with this service, the paper would probably be prepared to print the details of the lawyer's firm in return. Solicitors keen to explore this kind of opportunity should attempt to get an appointment to meet the editor. So many national and local media agencies now offer 'Law Spot' columns, mostly delivered by e-mail, that a letter, even from a local firm, would be unlikely to be persuasive.

Andrew, famed for his canniness and an editor of many years' standing himself, goes on to suggest that when seeking that meeting with the local newspaper editor the solicitor should be evasive about the reason for wanting the meeting, as 'by nature, editors are both curious and nervous of contact with the legal profession and a vague request for an appointment will almost certainly open the diary'.

Contacting journalists

Reasons for contacting a journalist

The main reasons are:

* to offer them information about a piece of news, such as the fact that your firm is changing its name, is merging, or a major new client has just instructed it, or that judgment in an interesting case is expected;
* to offer help with a current news story, by explaining, for example, the practical implications of a new piece of legislation for pan-European companies in their sector;
* to invite them to meet for lunch or coffee or a drink, or visit your firm to meet a few of the partners.

How to make contact with a journalist

Journalists remain a cynical breed, but some still cannot resist a conspiratorial approach that could lead to a story. Although there has traditionally been a degree of comradeship between some lawyers and some writers, and in London the Wig and Pen and Garrick Clubs still stand as testaments to this, it is perhaps harder for lawyers to engage the affections and trust of journalists than other professionals.

Never forget how unpopular the legal profession is as a whole with many members of the public, and remember that some journalists regard lawyers as there only to block them getting to the real meat of the story. Most of them have had, at some time or other, a favourite story spiked or edited at the behest of a lawyer. Some view the laws of defamation and privacy as creations of lawyers to generate extra work. I have yet to encounter a journalist who hasn't suffered personally in some way at the hands of a lawyer and they can tell you tales about the legal profession generally that make your toes curl. Ask them how their last conveyancing transaction went, or how long it took to wind up their late grandmother's estate, or the size of the bill they received when they needed help with a contract – you will wish you hadn't.

At one point just making contact was easy: in London they hung out in El Vino's in Fleet Street or in the Wig and Pen Club opposite the Royal Courts of Justice, or in pubs and wine bars near the regional magistrates' courts or Crown Courts, and seemed always to have some time to spare for a chat. Now the poor creatures have been shipped out to Wapping, to Canary Wharf or to crowded offices dotted round the City. In the regions they seem to spend longer in front of their screens. While there is still sometimes a certain gratitude in the current economic climate for the offer of a square meal or a drink, this is usually coupled with reluctance to travel to enjoy the pleasure of your company unless they can be pretty confident there is a copper-bottomed story at the end of the journey.

Frances Gibb, legal editor of *The Times,* candidly asks, 'Have you a story for me?' before even checking her diary to see if she can squeeze in a lunch with you. If the journalist is too readily available, it probably signals they are rarely filing good copy.

Regional journalists, in my experience, either have fewer pressures or scruples, or are simply hungrier.

Many journalists like invitations to parties, and most of them, certainly in London, seem to accept all they receive. Parties provide an opportunity to meet lawyers and pick up news snippets informally in a congenial atmosphere. But avoid inviting journalists to anything too lavish if you are intending to brief them on the hard times your firm is going through, or they will unhelpfully report the disconnection between your briefing and their experience of your opulent hospitality for a diary column.

Usually, initial contact with a journalist will be by phone or e-mail, whichever feels more comfortable for you, or you have established is their preference. I use e-mail a lot, as I like the fact that the recipient can access it at *their* convenience. Two of my colleagues have a distinct preference for regular phone calls, but are circumspect about getting quickly off the line if it is clear the journalist is writing. 'Horses for courses', but whichever you start off with, try to follow up with the other. Good journalists are busy, pressured and often forgetful, so follow up an e-mail with a call just to check they received and opened your message, and follow up commissions offered or pledges made in the course of a phone call with a short e-mail to tie up any loose ends. But don't become a pest, it is counter-productive – I have worked with people who ring some journalists every single day and sometimes more than once a day, bleating about the story until it is entirely understandable that the journalist loses patience and declines to proceed.

Mary Heaney, founding editor and publisher of *Legal Week,* advises that it is not necessary to call about a specific story, but it must be about something that is of interest, maybe further down the line, and the conversation will help to develop the relationship.

So, how do you get to know them?

When you make your call, or create your message, having done your preparation, always provide the journalist with a context, so they can see why your news item is important, relevant, worth taking notice of. For example, if you are trying to interest them in the fact that your firm has secured a new lateral hired partner, you need to explain why his or her arrival is significant to the firm's strategy, what they will bring, what expertise they offer and what kind of clients will particularly benefit from that expertise. If the news is about a deal, you need to explain that it is the first deal, or the biggest deal, or the most novel approach to a deal, or is using for the first time a new piece of legislation or extending the principle enunciated in a recent precedent. As with everything to do with the media 'first', 'biggest', 'newest' are all good words and if you can truthfully use them, you dramatically increase the likelihood of achieving some coverage.

You may decide, or be advised, to contact a journalist to offer specialist assistance with an issue they are covering. If, for example, there has been a national disaster and you were involved as one of the legal team on the last major crisis of this sort, your input could be really welcome, but you should not assume that the journalist is familiar with the story you would like to comment on. You may need to clarify your credentials briefly for holding an opinion or offering insights on the topic. In your preliminary comments, to save time, you should give an indication of the views you hold or the input you could have. It is always better to say something like, 'I think it was a real error to cancel all train services in the North West in the light of the experience we had on the last major derailment' than, 'I wrote a book recently about the legal aspects of train crashes'.

Julie Lake, the plain-speaking former head of corporate communications at national firm Osborne Clarke, advises:

> You should only talk about things that you know, through your own research or experience, will interest the journalist or their readers, rather than about how wonderful and interesting you and your firm are.

If you are making contact to invite a journalist just to meet you, after a brief introduction, you could simply say something like, 'I've had quite a lot of experience in medical negligence and I'd like to meet you for lunch/coffee/a drink, when it's convenient for you, to talk about a couple of issues that will be coming up in the next few weeks and you might find interesting. I might be able to help you with any articles you will be doing on them.'

Making yourself difficult to dislike

Be understanding if the journalist is pressured when you call. Start by asking if it is a good time for them to talk, and if not, try to find out when would be. Then get off the line – quickly.

We all have different ways of forging friendships, but with journalists, who are more inclined than most to spot charm offensives at a hundred paces, I have found that you can often get under their defences by demonstrating some familiarity with their work. So read some of the latest pieces they have written (often easily obtainable online if your library lets you down and your filing system fails). Think about the attitude they have adopted – do they seem to be favourably disposed to your kind of practice area or firm? Are their pieces prominently positioned in the publication? Are they credited on the details below the leader as just a reporter, or as City Editor? We all soften when it becomes clear someone has taken trouble to think about our work.

If you are a partner, try to make the arrangements and the call yourself, rather than expecting your PA to do it for you. Journalists do not have secretaries and get irritated by a secretary ringing them and keeping them waiting while they put them through to the lawyer.

Be modest: never assume they have heard of you or your firm unless you and it are undeniably recognisable, and even then the names may not ring bells. Tell them briefly about the firm and your own practice and team and then cut to the chase – could they find time to meet? (Never ever let it appear that your time is more precious than theirs.)

Be adaptable about timing and venue. Some like and can make time for nice meals in smart restaurants. Others rarely get out during the day and a drink after work near their office is the easiest. Many now work mainly from home and this may be some way out of town. Some like to be shown round a firm, while some have seen more atriums than they need. If your office is out of town, it is unlikely on first acquaintance that it will be reasonable to expect them to visit you, so a preamble could be, 'I have to be in London for a con with counsel in the Temple on Thursday, is there any chance we could meet for a drink afterwards?'

It is like dating, and just as complicated.

What is your story?

Although lawyers are reluctant to see themselves as salespeople, you must recognise that for effective media relations of this sort you need to have something to sell. The story must always have an angle or 'peg' that gives a reason to run it. The 'peg' could be news of an innovative court decision, the opening of a new law office, a record-breaking award of damages. It must, above all else, be *interesting*.

The story should not try to make more than three points. It should be positive, not negative, but also frank. Journalists are resistant to obvious hype and most have finely tuned 'bullshit' detectors.

You must decide what kind of story you have to sell and precisely to whom you wish to sell it, and this is where professional advice can be invaluable. Your in-house media professional or PR consultant can help you sift through the load of information available to a firm or barristers' chambers, and identify the potential news story.

Fear, greed and sex

These are accepted by case-hardened lawyers and professional journalists as the measure by which all news stories can be judged. A law firm could issue a 'greed' story by pointing out the potential amount of damages that can be recovered by successful litigants pursuing personal injury claims effectively, and add the gloss that their contingency fee service limits the costs exposure. Another firm could invoke 'fear' by setting out the penalties that can now be extracted for failing to observe money-laundering rules, or compliance with EC competition rules or observance of the Clients' Charter. Any firm can use the 'sex' angle by presenting a story or highlighting a case that has a highly controversial or personal basis (the legal position of cohabitees, the highest divorce settlement, a sexual harassment case). It was depressing to observe the unprecedented levels of media interest in a case I was recently involved in where allegations of child abuse were central – avoiding media interest comes later.

The best stories often have facts to support them and research is often the basis for coverage achieved by public relations personnel. The Law Society's first successful 'Make A Will' campaign had its basis in research that showed that only one in three adults has a will, and that most co-habitees assume they will automatically inherit on the death of their partner. We then looked into the reasons why the majority of people are reluctant to put their affairs in order. Armed with the facts, we could focus our campaign.

Selling your story

Having forged some useful relationships with journalists, decided what your story is and the angle you wish to take and targeted the right publication and person working on it, bear in mind the following suggestions to help your story find its way into print:

- Whenever possible, make contact with the right person. On local papers this could be the editor or news editor; on national newspapers it will be the legal or home affairs correspondent, unless your story is in another area, in which case you may need the personal finance, small business or consumer affairs correspondent, as appropriate. Many now list such correspondents on their website.

- *Always* be prompt, reliable and courteous, no matter how complicated your professional or personal life is. If you say you will call back within a certain time, do so; if you think it likely they may want further information, give an out-of-hours number where you can be contacted, and if it is a mobile, make sure it is on. Journalists do not work office hours and invariably are finishing their pieces at 9 p.m. or on Sunday afternoons and do not know which facts they need to check till then.
- Never, ever patronise a journalist, no matter how senior you are or how young or intellectually challenged you may consider them to be. Although you may be a recognised expert on the topic they are covering, they have the power to decide whether or not it should be covered and whether or not you or your firm or set should be mentioned. Treat them as courteously as you would your clients. Be scrupulously honest and avoid attempts to blind them with complex language and legalese. If you do not know the answer to a question, say so, don't bluff, and offer to find out the answer from someone who can provide it. Never forget that some of the longest-standing legal correspondents have probably forgotten more about the law than you will ever know and are usually on cordial terms with all the senior players in the game.
- Remember that one of your aims is to increase the readers' understanding of the law and the issues with which you are concerned. The way you help the journalist could influence how well this is achieved and to some extent the way s/he feels about all lawyers and the tone and style of their piece.
- Try to be as helpful when the story is an adverse one as when it is favourable. The tales are legion about lawyers trying to block and suppress unfavourable reporting about our profession, with occasionally wild talk of injunctions, letters before action and even defamation suits. These never work and simply undermine all future dealings with the journalists. Do your homework, be guarded and careful and you shouldn't say anything that you later have to regret.
- Take the time and trouble to familiarise yourself with the publication concerned, the people working on it, their names, correctly spelled, phone numbers, e-addresses, copy deadlines, and so on. *Read* more than one edition of the publication for which they write. Get to know the audience at whom the story is targeted.
- Offers of practical professional help and assistance are sometimes much appreciated. When your story refers to a report, a publication, a judgment, an article, ensure that you have a clean copy and, if appropriate, that you supply the journalist(s) with copies too.

E-mailing, faxing or biking may be necessary. Journalists can rarely wait long for things to arrive and only have minuscule budgets with which to purchase any materials that cannot be obtained free. Ensure your PA always appreciates the need for speed, if you are delegating the task.

Dealing with an unexpected approach from a journalist

Your first contact with a journalist may come when you are invited to comment on a case or legal issue with which you have been directly involved or on which you are believed to be an expert.

Without appearing overly suspicious, always try to check the credentials of your caller. You will usually receive a phone call that starts with something like, 'Good afternoon, Ms Jones, I'm Keith Small from the *Daily Telegraph*. I wonder if you could let me have your views on the recent announcement by the Lord Chancellor that in future no civil claims can go to the county court without first attempting mediation?'

The rule when handling this kind of call is easy: **Stall but call.** Do *not* be bounced into an instant response. Lawyers are slow and deliberative creatures, but somehow we feel an urge to produce instant quotes to the media when offered the chance. It is an ego thing. Don't do it – and don't get rattled. Remember interviewers are only prosecuting the public's case.

Politely ask Mr Small a few questions:

- Could he kindly give you his name again, publication and office number so that you can call him back shortly? Say when he can expect your call and stick to it – he will have a deadline to meet.
- If you have not seen the announcement to which he referred, ask if he can tell you where it has been reported, or can e-mail or fax a copy to you, or can read it to you slowly enough for you to take down the salient details: Which courts? From when? Where was the announcement made? Is it a suggestion or an imperative?
- Ask him why he has rung you for a comment and if he is asking for comments from others, if so from whom?
- Ask him what kind of piece he is doing, for which section of his paper, roughly how long, and when will it come out?

You should then hang up, collect your thoughts, read or re-read the article or announcement that gave rise to the call, perhaps check with your professional, national or local organisation if they have a collective view – the 'party line' – and then jot down a *brief* comment that you are prepared to have attributed to you. Polish it so it reads well and is memorable. Don't rush it. Brevity does not come naturally to many of us and it is worth taking a little time to get it right. Run it past a colleague, if you can. Once it is in print, it cannot be changed and can be referred to for many years to come.

Then, and only then, are you ready to call Mr Small back. By doing so you will establish whether he is indeed who he says he is, and whether he is indeed employed by the *Daily Telegraph*. If it really is the *Telegraph*, for example, you may want to ask why Joshua Rozenberg, its highly experienced legal editor, is not covering the story as he does not commission others. If the paper given denies all knowledge of Mr Small, try to speak to an appropriate news editor to see if he is a home worker or freelance. If the number he has provided is his own home number, ask who at the paper has commissioned him to write the piece and if possible check with them that this is so.

This may all seem rather paranoid, but many freelance journalists take punts to put stories together without any commission for their publication. This can waste your time and give rise to unreliable coverage in inappropriate publications.

Never forget that all press cuttings, from many decades back, remain in libraries, files and on websites for years and can quickly and easily be retrieved, to trigger a journalist's call or an unexpected question.

Once you know the journalists involved all this becomes unnecessary, but there are still a few whose work ethics leave something to be desired, and lawyers should be more careful than most to ensure they are not conned.

Once you have satisfied yourself about Mr Small, ensure your conversation with him is congenial, that he fully understands the issues raised and your comment. This may require some 'background briefing' and this is where you venture on to dangerous ground.

On and off the record

Some journalists maintain there is no such thing as 'off the record' and advise that if you don't want to see anything you may say in print, you simply shouldn't say it in the course of a conversation with a journalist.

Many law firm marketing professionals tell partners that nothing is ever off the record and that they must never ever say anything to a journalist that they would not be happy to see in print. The more sophisticated recognise that 'off the record' is a necessary tool of their job as well as of the reporter's. Chris Hinze, former worldwide director of communications for Andersen Legal and now an independent PR adviser, had to handle much of the adverse press interest resulting from the Enron scandal. As he puts it:

> If I cannot have sensible background conversations with journalists as part of rumour control, conversations in which I do not fear that what I say will be attributed to me or to my firm, then I cannot operate.

For novices, the safest route is obvious – *if in doubt, leave it out*. But there are some unwritten guidelines that dictate the conventions of professional journalism. These are understood by all who work seriously in the profession, are supported by the National Union of Journalists, taught on journalism courses and for media study degrees and are, in my experience, very rarely breached.

'On the record' conversations are those that can be attributed to the person talking or to their firm: 'speaking today, Jonathan Hill of the Quill Law Partnership said, "Our firm is thrilled . . . ".'

'Background', 'not attributable' or 'not for attribution' conversations are those that can be used in print as part of the journalist's own analysis and conclusions, as long as the source is not named: 'It seems the Quill Law Partnership is pleased to find itself . . . '.

'Off the record' conversations are those that cannot be reported in any form, although it is possible that the information contained in them may become public through other channels.

'It all comes down to trust', says Chris Pullen, head of marketing in the London office of American firm, Weil Gotshall & Manges:

> If you can develop a good relationship with a journalist, the better the chance you'll have of getting quoted and quoted in context. Of course there's a risk involved, but the worst that can happen is that other people won't agree with you, or like your views on an issue. Does that matter? No. What matters is that next time that journalist wants a quote, they come to you. That's what matters.

When the topic is technical and complex, all good journalists are at pains to ensure they get it right and are grateful for assistance to help them understand it fully. It will be particularly necessary with regional journalists who are most unlikely to specialise only in legal stories.

So, the safeguards go like this: at the start of the conversation with the journalist, before you say a single word you are not prepared to see in print, say clearly and distinctly, out loud, 'This is off the record, do you understand?' or 'This is for your background, you can use it as long as it is not attributed to me or my firm. Understood?' Once they confirm that it is, you can almost always safely provide the background information they need to understand the issue better, confident that your comments will not be reported. It would clearly be stupid to make defamatory or intemperate remarks, which you could subsequently find embarrassing, even when speaking off the record, but it is very rare that this convention is broken (and has only happened twice in my fairly long career).

Robert Verkaik, former barrister and legal correspondent, now with *The Independent* after a stint on the *Law Society's Gazette,* comments, 'When you are faced with a journalist, you have to decide how well you know them, and how likely they are to breach your trust. That has got to be a call that you make every time.'

The 'off the record' quote is used widely. Whenever you read that 'a friend of the Prince of Wales and Mrs Parker Bowles said . . .' or 'an eminent barrister said . . .' or 'a well-known criminal law solicitor told me . . .', you can be sure that a journalist has persuaded someone to divulge some sensitive information on the basis that it remains non-attributable, or the person who features in the story has arranged for someone to brief the media on his behalf.

Watch out if your memory is unreliable

Imagine a conversation with one of your clients. During an hour's conversation, the client mentions two points that are not to go any further. Can you honestly say you would remember precisely what you are able to repeat, should you wish to do so, and what you were expressly asked not to, unless you made a note at the time? Have you ever blurted out something a friend has asked you to keep to yourself? You should carefully stipulate where an off the record or background comment ends, and where the conversation goes back on the record. Good journalists will ask you this themselves, but don't rely on their doing so.

Journalists are only human (with a few exceptions) and it can be difficult for them to remember exactly what you said they can and cannot print, unless they took a meticulous verbatim note. When briefing be sure to allow sufficient time for them to get it down properly – so few write shorthand these days.

But, once again, for the avoidance of doubt: if you can't risk seeing it in print, *don't say it.*

Granting exclusive interviews

It is sometimes the case that a publication asks you to confirm that you will only talk to them and to no other publication. The issue might be fairly confidential or major to your firm, e.g. a high-level lateral hire, a merger. The publication gets to publish the news first and gets a clear run at it. Journalists take the promise of an exclusive interview on a newsy topic very seriously.

Sometimes large sums of money are offered for the exclusive rights to a story and clients are now more knowing about the value of their stories and the sums they can achieve. Sometimes they expect their lawyers to negotiate for the highest price. The bidding war can be fierce if the story is a big one and the tabloids are interested. Think hard and long before you attempt to get into this arena unless you have had appropriate experience. A small number of skilled media lawyers will be happy to handle the negotiation on your client's behalf.

'If you're holding off publishing a story at a firm's request, and it then it gets broken elsewhere, you'll be very reluctant in future to do that firm a favour by holding off a story for them', says Matt Swallow, associate editor of the *Lawyer*. It is also necessary to be aware, if you agree to an exclusive for a print publication, whether that exclusivity also relates to the Internet and is for a day, a week or a month.

These exclusivity agreements are invariably verbal, unless money is changing hands, so be very clear exactly what the journalist wants and what you are required to do, so that you can honour this agreement scrupulously. If for any reason you have to change the terms of the agreement, or are forced to or accidentally break the exclusivity deal, always ring the journalist with whom you made the original agreement and explain. Many firms like to give exclusive interviews to publications that have been kind to them, and to shun those that have reported them negatively. It is an understandable, but flawed, strategy as it simply recycles the negativity and builds no bridges for the future.

How you are described when being quoted

This often exercises lawyers a lot. Decide how you prefer to be described in print. Informality is the norm, so it is more likely to be 'Petrina Bacon' rather than 'Mrs/Miss/Ms Bacon' and thereafter the convention is just to use surnames, regardless of status or gender. So you will probably find, 'George Bridges, managing partner of Smartfirm of Chelsea said today, "it's outrageous that . . ."' and then further on in the body copy, 'When asked if he thought this was the thin of the wedge, Bridges commented that . . .'.

All marketers want to make sure that their lawyers, firm, chambers or organisation get mentioned, and preferably with some reference to their specialism and locality. So 'Smartfirm of Chelsea, the personal injury specialists' would make them happiest. This is hard to control, particularly as all copy filed by journalists can be tampered with by sub-editors, but ask how the journalist intends to refer to you and your firm, and try to indicate your preference.

If you are speaking on behalf of an organisation such as the Association of Personal Injury Lawyers (APIL) and your comment does not match exactly APIL's line on an issue, you may want to make sure that you are not referred to as 'speaking on behalf of APIL' or 'an APIL spokesperson said today', but are just quoted by name with or without your firm.

Just decide which role you are playing and ask that your attribution reflects this. Check the spelling too, as people will increasingly work out e-mail addresses from the scant information provided and try to e-mail you, but if your name is incorrectly spelled, this will be hard.

Richard Levick, who gets more name-checks for his law firm clients and himself than most, reminds us that 'no journalist is under an obligation to cite you as a source of some insight, much less mention the name of your firm when doing so'. To maximise your chances of being quoted, he advises that you should give colourful examples of your work and your firm's activities and, if you feel you can, express strong opinions. At the end of the interview, reiterate the spelling of your name and that of your firm, and your exact job title, if it is relevant. Clarify how your firm should be described: as 'international', 'national', 'local', 'award-winning', 'a boutique' and so forth. Good journalists ask for these details, but don't wait for them to do so. Follow up the conversation or interview with an e-mail providing background details of your firm and practice to ensure the journalist has them all to hand when writing.

Paul Jaffa of Grandfield Public Relations, and stalwart of the Professional Services Marketing Group, makes the point that:

> All the journalists know is what you tell them. Unless you know that you are speaking to a specialist in the field under discussion, treat the journalist as an intelligent lay person. There's no earthly reason why a general legal journalist should understand some obscure financing mechanism. Make clear why the mechanism is important and interesting, and also clarify to whom you're selling your legal services.

Can I ask to check the piece before it goes to print?

Usually no. It is most unlikely that the journalist concerned will be prepared to let you see the final copy before it goes to print. In any event, sub-editors can tinker with it, to edit it down to length, give it a heading, re-order paragraphs, or update it if another news story affects its relevance. If there are complex technical legal points you want to check have been correctly used, you can always ask the journalist concerned to fax or e-mail you the relevant extract for copy checking, but do not be surprised if this is refused.

When, however, the story is on a ground-breaking area of law, or one that only you control, as with the Sally Clark case, it is easier to strike a bargain that you will provide the journalist with information to enable them to write a compelling piece, but this will be conditional upon you retaining editorial control and checking the final copy before it goes to print. If they want the story enough, most journalists will agree to these constraints, particularly if they know you understand their business.

But the whole issue of not being able to check the journalist's copy is one that burns up an inordinate amount of wasted time and is often the most troublesome aspects for lawyers. We are all trained to check and double-check all written materials. We read things literally, demand clarity of meaning and are rarely able to read without a pen in our hands as we believe that we can always improve on the original text. Not having control over press articles makes us anxious and tetchy, and overly ready to criticise those who produce them. Of the two professions, in my experience, the journalists win hands down in the writing stakes.

The press interview

Careful preparation is essential for all effective media relations – the single biggest failure by lawyers is to assume they can 'wing' it. Training and thinking pay off. Research the papers and journals where you feel you may have a contribution to make. Look at the style of reporting and writing. If the publications issue style guides, obtain them. Look at the length of articles. Check circulation figures and readership demographics. Determine the type of reader you will be addressing. Consider which topics the individual writers seem to cover most and which have been their most recent issues. The more carefully you can match your comments to the style that is most commonly used, the more likely the journalist is to be interested.

Assess how much background information a journalist is likely to have on the topic. If s/he is a legal correspondent on a national daily, it will probably be considerable. If s/he is a news reporter on a regional business magazine, more explanation and a different angle will be essential.

Think through all the possible questions the journalist may have and prepare your answers to those questions. Decide if there is any area that you are not prepared to cover and be ready to handle the situation positively and guide the journalist back to the topics you are prepared to discuss.

Be clear what you want to get out of the interview, or you will be responding to the journalist's agenda. Before the interview, prepare a list of key points you wish to make, regardless which questions you are asked. Have ready any key facts and figures that can be used to support your case, and have them in a format that can be e-mailed or faxed easily to the journalist, together, perhaps, with the briefest profile of your firm and a few lines of biography about yourself (not the exhaustive version detailing your O levels and golf handicap).

In many ways, it is like preparing a case for trial.

Coping with the press interview

Most of these are now done over the phone. It's always better face-to-face, so try if at all possible to invite the journalist to meet you, if time permits, rather than deal with a faceless voice.

During the interview the reporter will use a notebook, a tape-recorder or both. If it is a phone interview, as few use headsets, you may have to allow time for them to juggle holding a phone and pen. If you are sitting together, you will find that they may ask you questions without appearing to make a note of your answers. This is unnerving for those of us anxious to be reported accurately. If there is something you particularly would like to see in print, attributed to you, you can try saying, 'I'm happy for you to quote me on this' and then slowly and distinctly utter your compelling comment, in the hope that they will capture it. But it is always their decision, and their editors, what they think is interesting and should be printed, not yours.

They should always ask before using a tape-recorder, but it is very easy after a few minutes to forget if a small recorder is running. Take care. There was an embarrassing case recently when a chief executive of a major company claimed she had been misreported. She wished she had never raised the matter when the tape of her interview was transcribed and the journalist was found to have reported her verbatim.

At some point in the interview, the journalist may ostentatiously close their notebook and put it away. Be alert. This is an old hack's trick. You could be walking to the lift, chatting informally and then find you are standing finishing the conversation for a few minutes. The notebook may have gone but the interview continues. Because they know that taking notes in front of people can inhibit them, reporters, like policemen, often train themselves to make a mental note of what is said and then transcribe it quickly afterwards, in the car, the loo, on the train or in the pub. They may not recall, word for word, what you said, but they will usually get the gist of it. But remember that you are talking 'on the record' from the moment the reporter identifies themself to you, face-to-face or on the phone, until you bid them goodbye, unless you make it very clear to the contrary.

Very often the reporter who approaches you already has the story 'in the bag' from other sources. They may be approaching you as part of a 'fishing expedition' to try to substantiate what they have heard elsewhere, or just to get a quote from you. Your quote will be just some comment or reaction to what has been said, announced, happened elsewhere. This kind of story will probably not disappear if you decide not to cooperate. It will still appear, but without your contribution, or you may even be reported as declining to comment (which is never ideal as it sounds as if you have something to hide or nothing to say).

If your firm, profession or client are in trouble, an invitation to comment may be an opportunity for damage limitation and a chance to say something in mitigation. It may sometimes be a good ploy to ask, 'Have you talked to anyone else about this?' Beware, though, of falling for the fishing hook and confirming someone else's rumour or speculation by dignifying them with a quote and thereby providing the journalist with a story where they previously did not have one.

'No comment' is a very unsophisticated way of dealing with a reporter's questions and leaves the impression of evasiveness. Try to say something, however bland and even unusable, unless the matter is genuinely *sub judice* (in which case, see Chapter 2).

When dealing with the tabloid and more popular papers remember that they specialise in 'human interest' stories. You can exploit this by remembering that no matter how arcane or complex your particular area of law, at some point it will inevitably involve people, and try to position your comments from their perspective. Generally speaking, the popular papers rarely make things up, but they do tend to simplify, exaggerate or dramatise the stories they cover to make them more appealing to their readers. And they love big photographs to break up their copy.

These tendencies are often shared by those whose stories they are telling. The function of the popular press is primarily to entertain – it is no more sinister than that. When they publish an untruth it is usually because someone has lied to them. Max Clifford, the scourge of real public relations professionals, readily admits he invented both the story that Freddie Starr ate small furry rodents and that David Mellor performed sexual athletics while wearing his favoured football club's strip. Both stories emerged, but the paper was not lying, the publicist was.

In a family law matter that I recently handled, the other side's management, while publicly proclaiming their dislike of the media scrutiny their client was receiving, regularly briefed the tabloids with factually incorrect material, which was published. Countering a steady stream of misinformation proved difficult.

If you are not in London, it is often useful to insure yourself against the possible attentions of the national tabloid press by cultivating a relationship of trust with your main local weekly or evening paper, which is less likely to behave mischievously. When handling a major hiccup in an MP's private life recently, I was very grateful he had a solid, trusting relationship over many years with a reporter on his main local newspaper, who was prepared to run a more positive version of the story ahead of the national red tops. As the MP's primary concern was to maintain the confidence of his constituents and keep his seat, it was imperative that they saw and read the real version of the situation, portrayed in the most sympathetic way achievable. We managed to contrive this before the story broke nationally – inevitably in a rather more hysterical way.

The serious national broadsheet press is more concerned to inform, or even educate, but they still need angles to their stories to ensure their papers sell. It would be a mistake to shun contact with the press because you believe that they are attempting to damage, defame or destroy you, your client or your firm. The press can be used by you, to get your messages to a wide audience – you just need to say the right things to the right people in the right way at the right time.

A precaution

Sometimes you may be dealing with such a sensitive issue, you remain nervous about it being accurately reported. Taking your own tape-recorder to an interview and insisting that you be allowed to use it works well, even if it inevitably creates a rather tense atmosphere with journalists and could not signal more clearly a lack of trust on your part. Tony Benn, the former campaigning MP, has used this technique all his life and has many hours of fascinating tape as a result, which have provided invaluable records for his books and diary.

Veteran media trainer and television presenter Peter Wheeler lists four essential points for his media trainees to remember when approached by the press:

- Don't get 'caught on the hop', ask to ring the journalist back to give yourself time to think.
- Know who it is you are talking to – check the journalist's credentials.
- Keep the interview short and only make statements you have thought about.
- Listen carefully to the questions and the question behind the questions.

When they get it wrong

Most weeks I get irate calls from a client, or legal contact, fuming about the inaccuracy of a press report and demanding that I help get a retraction or a printed apology or correction. These calls most often relate to an item in a legal journal about the firm, its management or profitability and the caller wants a follow-up piece, 'setting the record straight'. It simply is not going to happen and it usually is not worth expending energy on. You must learn to accept that for most journalists it is as irritating to have a lawyer trying to double-check their prose, as it would be for us to have a journalist asking us to redraft our contracts or leases.

Ninety times out of a hundred, it is better to let the matter go. Although the piece may be available online for longer than you would wish, it will also, in hard copy, be wrapping the chips by the end of the week. You are very unlikely to get a printed apology, unless the matter has given rise to a Press Complaints Commission (PCC) grievance or even reached the courts. You may feel personally better if you blast off a letter to the editor for publication, but in the majority of cases by doing so you will be drawing further attention to the matter a day or two later, when many will have forgotten it. If, to protect your own, your client's or your firm's reputation it is clear that something must be done to correct an inaccurate report, then it must be done *at once*.

Law firms are a nightmare to advise in this kind of situation, as they want to consult all the partners, or the management board, or the senior partner at his holiday retreat, or all affected clients, or all the above, before reaching a decision. Ideally, if the paper is out before breakfast, the riposte for publication should be on the Letters Editor's desk by e-mail or fax within an hour or two. If he has not got it by 2 p.m., he will not use it the following day and the moment has passed.

Richard Levick points out, 'Most mistakes are genuine errors caused by extreme time pressures under which journalists work. While the primary goal may be to obtain a correction in print, the secondary and important goal is to maintain the relationship with the journalist in question.' It is very stressful, particularly for a junior journalist, to be told they have made a mistake, and if it has to be corrected in print they will be reprimanded by their editor and may even risk losing their job. If you are kind and understanding when you point out the error, and calmly request that it be put right, you can win a journalist's loyalty and trust.

Neil Rose, features and news editor on the *Law Society's Gazette*, recalls when they got the date of an Act of Parliament inadvertently wrong:

> The lawyer involved got remarkably worked up and asked the law firm's PR department to write us a very aggressive letter. But the firm's press officer rang me and said, 'this lawyer's a bit mad'. That took the sting out of it. We published the correction and everything was fine, because he had dealt with it in a friendly way.

But whatever action you decide to take, or not take, let it go. Don't stew bitterly on it, blaming yourself for letting it get away from you, or the journalist for wrecking things. Don't boycott the journal and sulk in your tent. Retain a sense of perspective and move forward.

Encouraging the journalist to contact you again

If, after all this preparation and careful thought, the piece emerges and is satisfactory or better, let the journalist know that you are pleased with it. It is flattering to them, and just good manners if they have helped you. Jessica Smerin, formerly a journalist on the *Gazette* and *Legal Business* and now in Levick's London office adds, 'When you contact the reporter to praise the story, let them know that you are happy to be contacted again.'

Make it clear that you do not mind their ringing just to check facts on a story with which you are not involved, read their work regularly and comment positively on it occasionally. Such encouragement can pay invaluable dividends and in any event, it is fascinating to watch good journalists develop their skills and understanding of the profession over time.

Journalistic rivalry

I found it fascinating when I used to organise events at which all the legal journalists were present to see them vying with each other for the best angle on a story, and peering over each other's shoulders at the screens of their laptops to see what their rivals were running with, while helping each other decipher unclear shorthand outlines in the most companionable manner. The legal correspondents in particular on the whole know each other well and get on very cordially. Many have been in post for a very long time and have a very astute understanding of each other. They do, however, have directly competing imperatives. So it is not a good idea to flaunt your closeness with one journalist to another, or make reference to a deal for sponsorship you have brokered with one paper, while trying to sell a story to another. Try to be even-handed, while having the interests of the client or firm you are seeking to promote as your driver. When dealing with the national newspapers, you are entirely at liberty to refer to things in the legal periodicals. They are not in competition with them and regularly pilfer them for story ideas.

News releases

It surprises me that in this day of instant e-mails, so many firms and other organisations still churn out press releases and send them to literally hundreds of outlets most weeks.

I have been by Frances Gibb's desk in *The Times*, where she has been legal editor for many years, and seen the huge pile of faxed releases, entirely ignored, accumulating by the fax machine, until someone throws them out. I recall Jean Eaglesham, when legal correspondent on the *Financial Times*, mentioning with surprise the hundreds of releases she received each day, promoting very minor deals and transactions of absolutely no interest to the average *FT* reader.

'Only send press releases about your most important transactions and deals', pleads Martha Sellers Klein, immediate past editor of *Legal Business* and now editor of the *Legal 500* and editorial director of the publisher, Legalease.

I have advised firms that put out on average 10 releases a week, who wonder why only one or two ever get picked up and used. My role has often been to work out their strategy for promoting their business and then to identify the real targets and go just for them.

However, with over 400 journalists reporting legal matters, it is not easy to keep a contact database clean and up-to-date, and there is often the wish on the part of the lawyers who employ and pay the marketers that news of their matters should be sent to the widest possible pool of potential users. Those marketers do not always feel able to resist the pressure imposed on them by their paymasters, even though they know the results will not work. PRs often find it hard to beat the lawyers in arguments.

Despite attempts in the first edition of this book to encourage firms to rechristen press releases as *news* releases in the hope of concentrating minds on the fact that their contents should be *news*worthy, to reduce the volume and target more carefully, I fear that little has changed. One still sees news releases that should never have been written, let alone sent – desperate attempts to fascinate busy journalists in issues of only scant interest to just a few of those in the firms responsible for the release. And one rarely hears from editors or journalists complaining that they have space to fill and insufficient material to use, but rather that they are deluged with rubbish from firms and often wonder whether the senders ever read their particular publications.

There are lots of basic rules about good and effective news releases, but never forget that even today about 90 per cent of those produced find their way automatically into wastepaper baskets throughout the land, before their second paragraphs have even been scanned. The 'delete' button makes it easy to consign an electronic release to oblivion just on the basis of its subject and the identity of its sender.

When I had to judge *Solicitors' Journal*'s Golden Shredder Award a few years ago, to find the worst press release issued by or on behalf of a law firm, I found it hard to believe some of the entries. One public relations company devoted two and a half pages to a fulsome description of a solicitor's office, which had revamped its reception area. Three releases announced the new accounting systems that the firms had installed. Literally hundreds were full of turgid prose telling us that various worthy individuals had joined law firms or chambers, with desperate 'mug shots' (often taken by colleagues, judging from the quality). The prose involved was often unreadable, typos and grammatical and punctuation errors abounded, but most importantly, they were all deeply, deeply dull – and their contents certainly were not news.

It is depressing that a similar competition run today would reveal much the same story, despite the increased level of sophistication and the number of media studies graduates there must now be in marketing roles in firms.

Fiona Bawdon, highly experienced legal journalist, now editor of *Independent Lawyer* and co-author of the definitive text on conditional fees, advises:

> First rule, have a point to your press release. There is one very good firm doing very good work, which puts out far too many releases relating to the same cases. When it's about to come to court, when the verdict is given, when the application for leave to appeal is filed, when leave to appeal is granted, when the date for appeal is fixed, just before the appeal is heard, during the appeal, when the verdict is given, when they pledge to take the case to the European court, etc. Less is generally more. This overload of information means my eyes glaze over and the firm will find it much harder to get anyone's attention when there really is something to report.
>
> What would I like them to do? Phone me up or e-mail me when something comes up which might be of interest to my publication. I'd like the relevant lawyer to make contact, not their PR person, and a little goes a long way. Just a call to say, 'I know you're always interested in key legal aid cases, wondered if you might want to know more about this . . .' or 'Have you heard what the LSC is up to . . .?' This is quicker and often much more effective than a press release – it also helps to build a really good personal relationship between lawyer and journalist.

I certainly use e-mail a lot, when communicating with journalists. Possibly too much, as a phone call builds a relationship much better, but I am mindful of the pressures under which most journalists work, and that my matter is just one in a long list vying for their attention. An e-mail can be opened by them when they have time to do so. A phone call can catch them on the hop, but if you choose to phone at least just ask if they are 'under the cosh' (i.e. writing to a deadline) and free to talk before launching into your spiel.

Either way, e-mail or phone call, having established they are free to talk, just offer a sentence or two about the case, matter, client or issue you think they might find interesting and then only burden them with detail if they ask for more. Every single legal publication complains about unfocused press releases thudding on to their screens and fax machines, on matters in which the recipient publication and its readership have little, if any, interest.

Making your news releases work

Richard Levick of Levick Strategic Communications, working all over the world on law firm publicity, agrees that sending a press release to a wide range of publications is not the most effective way to generate media coverage. But as many firms and organisations still use this system, I should provide some guidance, though you will by now have discerned that I am personally sceptical about whether this is a useful way of either getting your stories into print or spending your firm's time and money.

As a starting point, as noted above, always call them *'news releases'* not press releases, just to concentrate the mind and remind all those sending them that they are intended to contain *news*. This title is also more appropriate for the broadcast and online media, which do not regard themselves as 'press'.

Objectives

If your release is to work, it should have these objectives:

- to present the facts about something you consider newsworthy (note, *you* the media handler, consider newsworthy, not Mr Eisenhammer, a junior partner);
- to supply these facts in good time for publication;
- to supply them in a form that is ready for publication;
- to supply them only to those you genuinely believe will be interested.

Think of your story as a product that you are selling. This is an alien concept for lawyers, but it helps you understand the approach you need for this work.

An alternative approach

If some information has to go out but really is not newsworthy, think of heading it Fact Sheet, or Information or Briefing Note, rather than News Release. At least you are signalling honestly the content.

The reality, however, as confided by many PR professionals, is that lawyers often insist that many releases are sent that the communications professionals know are without merit. They do as they are told, but simply limit the distribution and make no efforts to sell the story in, for fear of irritating and alienating their media contacts. Unfortunately, this regularly gives rise to complaints on the part of the lawyers about the efficiency of their PR people when the doomed release fails to be reported.

On more than one occasion I have been asked to help a law firm get a more visible profile and told that its in-house personnel just are not up to the job. It often becomes very clear that they are perfectly fine, but that the lawyers simply do not understand how the media operate and what is and is not of interest.

When to send out a news release

There are four reasons for producing and distributing a release:

- when you want to get the information to more people than it is practicable to communicate with at once by any other means;
- when your release is planned, relating to an event that has been known about for some time and diarised (a seminar, office move, promotion, court judgment, change in legislation, provision of a new legal service); or when the release is timely (offering advice on consumer finance at Christmas when people are spending heavily): good marketing teams have a 12-month calendar prepared, timetabling a steady flow of such releases, but take care each is genuinely worth issuing;
- when your release is reactionary, reacting to an unanticipated event (the economic situation and its impact on the conveyancing market, an unexpected change in the law or regulations, a query raised by a case or a press comment, to counter some negative matter);
- when you know the recipient publications prefer to receive their information in this way.

Getting your news release read

Bearing in mind the volume of news releases, it is often hard to get yours read beyond the first line.

A few tips:

Top of page

Use a special e-mail template or News Release fax header paper and make sure the originating organisation is clearly identified and that the release is clearly identified as a release and prominently dated. If there is an embargo (see below) this should be very clear in big bold type giving the time up to which the embargo is in force.

Heading

Provide a clear indication of what the release contains, don't try to be clever and write a witty headline, that's for others to do, e.g.:

Exeter law firm Devenish offers Speedymove – a new affordable conveyancing service

First lines/first paragraph

Put the most important piece of news in the very first sentence, e.g.:

> From 1 December 2003, Devenish & Partners, Exeter solicitors, will be offering all those moving house a new, online conveyancing service at the fixed price of £500 + VAT per transaction.

Second and third paragraphs

Provide some background detail and more information about the news item or activity itself, e.g.:

> Devenish & Partners is launching Speedymove, the first wholly online domestic conveyancing service offered at a transparent fixed fee by a solicitor's firm. This follows market research throughout Devon in collaboration with six major local estate agents. This initiative responds to home owners' concerns about the rising cost and uncertainty of the legal fees charged when moving house. It recognises that most home owners nowadays have access to a computer at work, but are unable to visit their solicitors or telephone them during the working day. All the documentation . . . [*more information and detail*].

Fourth paragraph

This could contain a quote from the firm's senior or managing partner, the head of the conveyancing team or the firm's IT Director if the focus is on the user-friendliness of the technology. Quotes are used less often in the national media, but almost always taken up by the regionals, e.g.:

> Speedymove will revolutionise the home moving process for many people. 'We've trialed it with about a hundred clients over the past three months and know that it works', said Laura Montgomery, head of the residential conveyancing team at Devenish . . .

Further paragraphs

These should follow only if there is genuinely more information that needs to be got over. This could include reference to third party endorsement (always the most valuable PR tool), commending the firm on its new service. It could include a comment from a local estate agent or a satisfied client.

Never worry about a release being too short. Only worry about it being too long.

Notes for editors (very last paragraph)

This (another media convention) is the place to put all the factual information about the firm, the lawyer or the service.

This can be as skeletal or comprehensive as feels appropriate in relation to the length and topic of the release, but at the least should contain the following:

- name of firm (if recently created by merger, say so, and when and with whom);
- number of partners and staff;
- offices, if there is more than one;
- brief list of legal services provided;
- any accreditation or other distinguishing features of the firm or its lead lawyers.

Give the contact details for the new service clearly and in larger print size.

Contact details

This is the most important part of the release – be sure to give clearly and prominently the name (or preferably two names) of people who can be contacted at any time, day or night, weekday or weekend, to provide further information. These people should be sufficiently familiar with the detail of the topic to be able confidently to provide more information than is contained in this release to an enquiring journalist. Although it is commonplace to give details of a press officer or PR person, unless they are wholly up to speed with further and better particulars, they in turn may need to contact a conveyancer or legal specialist to answer some of the journalist's questions, and so it is preferable to provide their number too.

Give the titles of the individuals whose contact details appear and all necessary co-ordinates, including e-mail address, home or mobile phone numbers. And do ensure that, when you have done this, these people are prepared to take the calls, have their mobile phones on with batteries charged, will check e-mails and pick up messages regularly. It is very easy to get a reputation for being hard to reach and very quickly the journalists will stop reading your releases, ringing for further information or bothering with your firm at all.

Checks before you send your release

- Is this really worth sending out?
- Is there any better way of doing this?

- Does it answers the questions –

  - Who?
  - What?
  - Where?
  - When?
  - Why?

- Are you clear whom this is intended to reach?
- Is the headline catchy enough to get noticed?
- Is the release correctly dated and embargoed?
- Is all the technical detail included properly in the Notes for Editors and in the body of the release?
- Are the right people identified as contacts with all their contact details clearly given?
- If you received this, would it interest you?

Embargoes

An embargo is a request (or instruction) to an editor or publisher not to print a story before a certain specified date or time. It has no legal binding force, but all professional journalists and publications understand the convention and try hard to observe embargoes, unless there is no justifiable reason for the embargo to be imposed. It can give rise to a complaint to the PCC if an embargo, imposed reasonably and properly, is broken by a journalist or publication.

The main purpose of putting an embargo on a release is to enable the receiving journalists or editors to have sight of a news story in advance, so that they can undertake research and obtain additional information to prepare a substantive piece, hold space to run it and generally investigate the issue in further depth.

It is also an essential device when sending something to periodicals with long lead times before print. It ensures that the topic receives coverage in a fortnightly or monthly publication without making the information available yet to those that go to print sooner.

It is a good idea to put an embargo date on a press release if an event you are publicising is a few days in the future, e.g. the release announcing Devenish's conveyancing initiative, which is to go live on 1 December 2003, could go out, under embargo, in mid-November as it would be of interest to weekly and even monthly publications as well as dailies.

It would then have at the top, before the content of the release:

November 20 2003 Devenish & Partners, Exeter

News Release

EMBARGOED UNTIL 01.00 DECEMBER 1 2003

This means that articles on the topic can appear in print from very first thing on 1 December, but not before.

I released, under embargo, the skeleton argument prepared by Sally Clark's QC for Sally's appeal, as I was anxious that the many journalists and broadcasters following the case should be fully aware of the detailed points Clare Montgomery would be making to the Court of Appeal. The document was embargoed until the time that the court hearing was due to start, whereupon the arguments would be made in open court in front of journalists and members of the public. This was a high-risk strategy as court start times can change at the last minute, but a risk worth taking to get the information out there. No one breached the embargo, though several journalists held genuinely newsworthy information in their hands ahead of the appeal. That way, they all had access to the detail of a complex and vehemently disputed case and my client's interests were as thoroughly protected as possible in the circumstances.

Presenting your release

The styles and look vary enormously, but now we all have access to modern technology there is no excuse for not presenting your release in as eye-catching and appealing a format as possible. The accepted and preferred layout and style is different from the way you present your business documents. If your release looks like a lawyer's letter, it deserves the treatment it will get.

Never forget if you are faxing a release, or might be asked to do so, having sent the document first by e-mail, that by fax the quality can degrade and some colours do not fax well or clearly.

Ensure, if you are e-mailing your releases – as recommended – that you have a proper and stylish template on your system identifying your firm or organisation clearly at the top.

Try to keep to a minimum all those hundreds of words of disclaimer that all law firms now seem to have at the end of their e-mails and some faxes. They may not be needed at all for a news release, and they clog up the memory and slow down transmission appallingly. Increasingly bright firms are putting all this stuff in an attachment, which the recipient can choose to ignore or open just once and in no subsequent exchanges.

The stylistic conventions to observe when writing your release

The following stylistic approach is the one recommended by media studies courses and the Institute of Public Relations, but some publications elect to have their own house style so always check with the style guide, if one exists, when writing for a new publication, and conform to its preferences.

- Always include the words 'News' or 'Information' right at the top of the sheet or first page, with your organisation's name and logo. Some firms are becoming more informal with headers such as 'News from the Rightlaw Partnership', which is entirely appropriate for the modern world.

- If a time embargo is involved (see above), show this as prominently as possible at the top.

- Ensure your layout is as clear and straightforward as possible. Your aim is to make your release easy and quick to read. Regional press will often reproduce a good release virtually unaltered if they like it, which should be your ultimate objective.

- Pick a punchy headline. Your own is unlikely to be reproduced, but it tells the copy taster or editor receiving the release what the story is about. Don't try to be clever, just ensure it saves the reader wading through the text to find out what it is about. Use capitals or bold to make it stand out.

- Avoid sub-headings, unless your release is about several different topics. If you must use them for clarity, put them in bold and use them as mini-headlines.

- Double-space your release, always use only one side of paper. Use the clearest font you can – Times New Roman is always preferred rather than a trendier one. Justify your margins, with ideally one and a half inches each side. This allows the recipient to add comment and notes.

- Use 'book style' for paragraphs, i.e. don't indent the first paragraph, but indent all succeeding ones.

- The use of capital letters is a vexed issue over which arguments rage. It is a major style change over the last few years. Editors nowadays usually restrict capital letters to proper nouns, initials and geographical places. Business positions are no longer given capital letters, while official ranks and titles are, e.g. 'The Lord Chancellor said' but 'the chief executive of the Law Society' and 'prime minister, Tony Blair MP'. I struggle with this and you may too.

- Full stops are dying out. They are no longer used when giving initials and are only usually included when indicating an abbreviation, e.g. or i.e. but 'PJK Smith'.

- Quotation marks should be used only for quoted speech or to differentiate an object from an organisation, 'There is a train named after the Law Society, it is "The Law Society", and is quite separate from the Law Society, the professional body for solicitors'.

- Underlining is used in the printing and publishing world only to instruct that the underlined section should be set in *italics*. Do not underline in a release as the editor will decide what, if anything, needs to be emphasised by italics. Use capitals or bold instead for emphasis.

- Signs and symbols are used in printing and publishing sparingly. The percentage sign (%) is rarely used, and 'per cent' is more common. 'Etc.' should never be used. Aim for consistency: if you use 'one and a half', don't later use 'one-and-a-half' or figures.
- Figures can be problematic. A sentence should never start with a figure and if there is any question of it being misread, spell it out in words. A story is told of a supermarket being reported to have made a presentation to its 1,000th customer, since its opening five years previously. This should have read one millionth, which would have been rather more impressive, but the figure in the release had been misread or typeset incorrectly. The general rule is to spell out one to nine and write 10 upwards in numbers, but with the larger numbers best spelled out.
- Continuing a news release to a second or even third page is a sign that you may be in trouble. Always aim for just one side of A4 if at all possible, but if it must run on then put 'more' or 'more follows' or 'continued' at the centre or bottom right-hand corner of the first page. On the second (and if you must, the third) sheet, in the top left-hand corner there should be a brief indication of the subject and issuing organisation or individual. Pages can easily get detached and all pages must be numbered and identified clearly.
- Author's name or another's name and contact details together with any other source for additional information should always be given at the end of the release, even if this appears at the top as well.
- The date of issue should be given clearly on all releases, either at the very top or at the end. It should be written month first, e.g. January 1, not 1 January and omit the 'st', 'th' and 'nd' – again, be consistent.
- Try to avoid words such as 'recently', 'yesterday' and 'today' within the release and give the actual date instead. This avoids confusion if the release is not used immediately or is used in a different time zone.

Evaluating your release

This is obviously only possible if you are clear what you were seeking to achieve, so are able to assess whether you have been successful. To evaluate properly you also need to be confident that you can track the take-up and reach of your release.

There are a number of media evaluation agencies which with clever technology can assess whether agreed objectives for a release are met. You can identify the key messages you are hoping to get over, the negative points you hope will not arise, the audiences you are most keen to address, the prominence you would like the story to attract. You can even assess which journalists consistently file positive or negative stories about your firm or your practice area.

The best of these research agencies is Echo Research, which provides the most useful service I have found to date.

Echo's chief executive, Sandra Macleod, has more than 20 years' experience in communications and reputation analysis. She and her team can be contacted at Echo Research Ltd (**www.echoresearch.com**), Friary House, Station Road, Godalming, Surrey GU7 1EX, phone: 01483 413600; fax: 01483 413601; e-mail: info@echoresearch.com

It is not too difficult to get a sense of whether your release has worked at least at a superficial level. You need to consider:

- length of article;
- wording of the heading;
- prominence in the publication and on the page;
- use of additional information provided in interview or briefing;
- successful correction, or retraction if required;
- names of individual lawyer, firm or client correctly used;
- quote used, all or in part;
- balance in favour of positive rather than negative angle.

Targeting

Most press offices, PR consultancies, savvier firms and chambers know the wisdom of targeting their material carefully, but too many still tend to deluge every publication or programme with a copy of everything they issue. Some consultancies and all distribution agencies charge by the number of copies they distribute, so it is clearly not in their interests to be more restrictive. But the scattergun approach is not only wasteful of time, paper, energy and electricity, it is seriously counter-productive in establishing rapport with the media. Most organisations and individuals, having received a welter of useless releases, will habitually bin everything they receive from that source, allowing the one possibly usable gem to go unread with the dross. If the recipients come to expect something worthwhile from you or your colleagues, they will read it with care and consider its merit properly.

Things not to do with your release

- Don't send it to the wrong journalists or publications.
- Don't send it too late to be read, researched or used.
- Don't take more than the first paragraph to tell the nub of the story.
- Don't take more than the first sentence to attract attention.
- Don't puff yourself, your firm, your chambers, your organisation or your client.
- Don't cover stale or non-news.
- Don't forget to check and recheck all your facts.
- Don't send more than one page if you can possibly avoid it (the rest can follow if the publication expresses interest).
- Don't send incomplete information.

- Don't use clichés, goobledegook, legalese, jargon or language designed to impress.
- Don't forget to spell check.
- Don't leave off relevant contact names and numbers.
- Don't send it without having checked that someone will be available at your end to field any enquiries it may trigger.
- Don't send out too many releases.
- Don't fail to prepare for its impact.

News on the wires

I recall sending by e-mail to the Press Association newswire recently an announcement about a high-profile family law case on which I was advising. We timed the delay between my hitting the 'send' button on my PC and the story appearing on the *BBC Online* and *Sky News* websites. It was less than 10 minutes. The phone calls started immediately and as the Internet is, of course, global, an entirely domestic matter can reach the widest corners of the world and generate interest in the most unlikely places. As this particular case had an American dimension, with the time differences, I fielded calls about it for some 12 continuous hours, since the American media started ringing as soon as the UK journalists filed their copy and headed home. The learning point – be prepared.

Profile pieces

All the legal publications like to profile interesting lawyers. *Legal Business* will devote several pages and a couple of huge photographs to one individual if they are thought to be of sufficient interest to readers. *The Times'* Law Supplement, the *Gazette* and *Lawyer* run 'Lawyer of the Week' columns, and most of the others feature individuals from time to time.

While it can be very valuable for a firm or set to have one of its members featured in this way, these pieces often give rise to personal angst on the part of the person profiled. We each have our view of how we are perceived and it rarely accords with how another sees us or writes about us.

Many lawyers seem to feel that being interviewed for a profile piece, apart from being recognition of their worth, will be safe. After all, talking about ourselves is easy. We know all there is to know. But profile pieces, like all media activity, require careful preparation, and if you grant an interview without doing such preparation, you deserve to be unhappy with the piece that eventually appears.

The preparation should cover the following:

- Why am I giving this interview or arranging it for a colleague?
- What am I, and my colleagues, hoping it will achieve?

- How do I want to be seen?
- How will my clients feel about this piece, if they see it?
- What is the best that can come out of it? (Satisfied clients and colleagues and potential new clients?)
- What is the worst that could come out of it? (Irritated peers and clients, no new work and delighted competitors?)
- What are the aspects of my own professional career and personality I would most like to see covered?
- What are the ones I would prefer not to have reported?
- What, if any, aspects of my firm or chambers or company are likely to give rise to interest on the part of a journalist at this time?
- What is the line on these?
- What is the readership of this publication?
- What is the background and particular interest areas of this journalist?
- Are they bringing a photographer or are we expected to provide a photo?
- Will there be any chance of my checking the copy before it goes to print?
- Will my personal life be mentioned? Am I (and my family) comfortable with that?
- If a client matter has caused the interest in me in the first place, have I checked with the client that they are entirely comfortable with my mentioning their matter to this journalist? (If not, you may not be able to give the journalist the interview for which they were hoping and it would be better to level with them about this before you start, to avoid wasting anyone's time.)
- How long will the interview take? It is rarely advisable to grant an interview that lasts more than 45 minutes. Any professional journalist should be able to obtain enough for a worthwhile piece in that time. A longer interview will probably run the risk of your straying beyond the appropriate parameters. Indicate when you make the appointment how long you are prepared to give and set up a system to have the interview terminated by a phone call reminding you of another meeting, or some such, if it is in danger of over-running.

Fiona Bawdon, editor of *Independent Lawyer,* has done many such profiles of lawyers, particularly when a reporter on the *Lawyer.* She contrasts two experiences:

Many moons ago I happened to do two profiles of senior women lawyers. Both of these women were unhappy with certain aspects of what I had written. One of them went into a massive sulk and refused to speak to me again about anything, even though she was a leading player in the field of law in which I specialised. One time when I tried to call her about something, she got her secretary to tell me she wouldn't talk to me 'because she didn't recognise herself' in the profile I had written.

Woman lawyer No. 2 took a rather different approach. She got on the phone and said, 'Hey, Fiona, I don't think some of your profile of me is fair' (relating to some derogatory comments about her by some male lawyers I had quoted). We had a good chat. I was able to explain why I had included this stuff (to allow those making the comments to be seen in their true light). We ended the conversation amicably. She remained a good contact of mine, and for other reporters on the publication, whereas the first woman lawyer became notorious on the newsdesk of this publication as One to Avoid. Woman Lawyer No. 2 has gone on to much, much bigger and better things, which she acknowledges are due at least in part to her regular exposure in magazines like mine. She and I have now become real friends, and she is someone I like and admire, and who inspires me in equal measure.

Leader columns, opinion columnists and 'op ed' pieces

In truth, not many readers will have issues and matters that are the appropriate subject matter of leader columns in the national papers (though they may for the regionals), or of interest to the small group of well-known opinion columnists (Polly Toynbee, Melanie Phillips, Libby Purves, Simon Jenkins, etc.) who file topical opinion pieces most days. The articles opposite the editorial or leader columns ('op ed') are also some of the most prominent and most read in all the nationals. These outlets are well worth considering, but it is probably more effective to ensure that the approach is made through a professional consultant or in-house adviser who has a relationship with the leader writer or columnist in question and can ensure that the material or idea is of potential interest.

Use of photographs

In the years since the first edition of this book, we have become an even more visual world. Then (in 1994) I said that we must remember the tired cliché that one picture is worth a thousand words. I pointed out that this is particularly true when dealing with the regional and tabloid press, who like to break up their text with as many pictures as possible. Increasingly, pictures and graphics are skimmed across the Internet, and with digital cameras, phones containing cameras, and most offices having scanners, coupled with dwindling attention spans, I forecast greater rather than less use of photography in legal media relations.

Fiona Bawdon, editor of *Independent Lawyer*, begs for less of:

those dreadful 'wacky' (painful) photos of Lawyers Having Fun in a Good Cause, or whatever. They're only used as a send-up in the diary columns of the *Lawyer* or the *Gazette*, and perhaps on internal office noticeboards. I cannot imagine what they think these things achieve, other than to make them look like sad human beings. Let the quality of your work speak for you to show how interesting you really are.

There are a few guidelines to remember when seeking to enhance a story or feature article with a photograph:

- Use only professional quality photos.
- Have them available in hard copy, neg and jpeg or pdf (e-mailable) formats.
- Have colour as well as black and white and be sure which the publication requires.
- Be prepared to bike them over, never post, as picture desk editors often come in at the last minute just as the publication goes to print and time is always short.
- Try to be a little imaginative in the style, but be familiar with the format used by the publication in question.
- If you are announcing that someone has joined your partnership or chambers, try to get away from the standard group shot of people in identical suits, all in a line, with fixed grins, posed in front of a row of law reports, or outside the firm's front door. Single studio shots of individuals also often lack life, and shots with some animation and informality can work better. A group in discussion, with some seated, some standing, can look more interesting. A lawyer at work at their desk, or on site at the client's place of work, can give a better sense of what they do than a sterile studio portrait.
- Be mindful of the background. If you want to portray your firm as cutting edge, avoid rows of legal tomes behind your people. If you want to show your expertise in property and construction, consider being photographed on a site, rather than in an office.
- Be clear about the culture and brand of your firm you want to communicate and be aware that this is done more compellingly by photography than by words. Now that many firms still dress down, despite a reversal in the trend in some City offices, it would be discordant, if your ethos was one of informality and youth, to have all your people pictured formally be-suited and be-tied.
- Be careful about the power of images and their ability to linger in the memory. When Mark Stephens was representing the families of young men killed by American 'friendly fire' in the Gulf War, he used a long continuous computer print-out to demonstrate how many unanswered questions he had put to the US government. That long roll of paper showed vividly just how much information was required. While representing Sally Clark we carefully rationed the use of pictures of her two baby sons who had tragically died, as we knew their little faces were likely to remain in the memories longer than the detailed medical evidence and legal issues we were trying to get across.

Sending photographs with releases

It is always worth actually making it clear on the release itself if a photograph accompanies or is available on request. The release and photographs can get separated in a busy newsroom, or on a picture editor's cluttered desk, so it is imperative that all the details are clearly shown on the back of the photograph, and the people, places or objects photographed are referred to on the release.

When the release goes out electronically, as the majority now do, the photo can be scanned in and also dispatched this way, and you should make it clear on the release that a photo or high-resolution scan is available. Scanners are one of the cheapest and easiest-to-operate pieces of equipment; if your firm has not yet done so, consider investing in one.

Photographs for the wires and news sites

I keep mentioning the immediacy of modern media, but it bears repetition as it runs so counter to the thoughtful, risk averse, delaying tactics usually employed by lawyers.

If you do not provide a photo to the newswires they may simply dig one up from the archives, and it could be an out-of-date shot you would prefer not to see back in circulation. As with the print media, there is a enhanced chance of your story being taken if you can back it up with a usable photograph, and so when preparing any story or matter that might deserve media attention in due course, be sure to think of the visual potential. If it will feature a particular lawyer or team, have to hand, in the right formats, some up-to-date shots. If it features a client or business, get something from them or arrange a photo shoot. If you have a particular publication or news service in mind, talk to the picture editor and establish their preferences.

All this will not only increase the chance of your material appearing, but will make you appear professional and astute.

The photo caption story

This is a device for achieving coverage that works particularly well with regional newspapers and some journals and tabloids. The photo must be interesting, professionally taken and, with the caption, must tell the story.

Never be surprised, however, if the most carefully arranged picture never appears. I still recall with irritation the photocall I laboriously organised a few years ago with all the solicitors involved in major miscarriages of justice. It was to be an historic shot and its timing was carefully planned to attract awareness to the amount of work in this field, often pro bono, that was undertaken by solicitors, and the inadequacy of legal aid remuneration. Many busy lawyers gave up their time, an excellent photo was taken and despatched to the picture editors. The following morning it appeared in only one paper. An hour after our picture reached the newspapers, Paddy Ashdown held a news conference to confess to adultery and pictures of 'Paddy Pantsdown' took precedence everywhere.

Conversely, the decisions on what is the priority of news can be your salvation. A potentially worrying leaked photo of a senior member of the Law Society's staff in an advanced state of undress at a private staff pantomime never, fortunately, saw the light of day, as it landed on a picture editor's desk on the same day as a major rail crash.

What to do with research findings and other supporting documents

Sometimes news releases make reference to publications, surveys, reports, cases and other documents. It is frankly unlikely that many journalists will plough through these unless they are professional legal correspondents, but they should always be given the chance. Ideally, the news release should contain a straightforward summary of the document in question, with its recommendations or findings, if any, highlighted at the start and/or end of the release. A copy of the document should then be dispatched with each release, as an e-mail attachment, unless this would be prohibitively difficult to download. If it is not possible to provide the full text of the document, consider attaching just the summary, or introduction or conclusion, as appropriate, or at least making it clear how a copy of the full text can be obtained, if required.

It is unrealistic to expect journalists to cover a publication if they are required to go to any lengths to acquire it or are required to pay for it.

How to distribute your news release

If you are responsible for distributing your news release yourself, there are six ways available to most lawyers:

- e-mail;
- fax;
- bike or courier;
- phone;
- post;
- Document Exchange.

It entirely depends on the urgency of the release and the resources of its distributor as to which combination of these you use, but increasingly the preference of both senders and recipients is e-mail.

If you are sending it out to a large number of recipients you may wish to consider using a distribution agency like PIMS (see above) or one of the others. They will set up, if given enough advance warning, a customised electronic distribution list for you, tailored to your requirements (they can fax you lists of journalists and then you can mark those you wish to receive your news). You provide them with the release and a template or sheet of your firm's news release paper and any other materials that are to be distributed. They will then despatch electronically at an agreed time your release and any other information, confirm to you that it has gone and charge an agreed fee. For large circulation releases I recommend this route. It can save hours of staff or consultancy time.

If you are handling the distribution yourself, and your story is of potential interest to national and regional newspapers and broadcast outlets, always e-mail it and then fax it to the Press Association and the other newswires (see earlier for details), and then e-mail or fax it to all your other targeted recipients. This can tie up a PC and a fax machine for quite some time, so ensure that your press office or firm has available machines to handle incoming messages while the distribution is going on. If the wires find it interesting it will then go out straight into the newsrooms of all major papers and radio and television stations within minutes.

E-mail

Virtually every journalist now has a readily available e-mail address and many who work from home have access from their homes to their office e-mails. That said, always check with your key journalists that you have their latest e-address and that they are likely to be near a screen when you anticipate the release will reach them. I often ring the most important journalists to check that they will look out for it. Their screens are often clogged with messages of limited importance, and if they are writing they may be deep in their Word program and not checking for e-mails very often.

Fax

Most national journalists (both print and broadcast) like to receive releases as early in the working day as possible and if not by e-mail then they must have them by fax. Some like to have the belt and braces of getting them by both means or sent to office and home.

Because they very rarely have their own personal fax machine, unless they are working from home, they also often appreciate a quick phone call in advance, warning them that a fax is on its way. This is a wise precaution to avoid your fax being consigned to the bin unread, particularly if you have been deluging the publication with unusable material for some time, as your release may be doomed as soon as your organisation's letterhead or logo has been identified.

Before faxing the release, check you have the correct fax number of the journalist or editor to whom you are transmitting and whether they are working in their office or their home that day. This may be obvious, but it is so often overlooked. Do also check that your fax has indeed been sent – most newsrooms' fax machines are busy 24 hours a day, and often run out of paper. It is only too easy to forget to check that your transmitting machine kept trying until it got the message through.

Bike or courier

This is still occasionally used, if you want to be sure that your news release reaches its destination and is particularly favoured when sending information to some of the major regional and national papers. It is expensive. Phone in advance to let the journalist or editor know something is on its way or it may sit at reception for hours.

Phone

In extreme cases you can still telephone through your release to the appropriate publication or individual and simply dictate it over the line. Though few newspapers still have copytakers as e-mail is so widely used, they can usually find someone to take down a short piece at dictation, provided it is sufficiently newsy. Phoning is probably only an appropriate option when you are sending last-minute information to the news agencies or national papers from somewhere without a modem or when quickly announcing the outcome of a case from court.

If you are obliged to dictate a story to a copytaker you should appreciate that this could try their patience and jeopardise a valuable working relationship with a publication, unless the item is really worthwhile. You must make sure that the person receiving the copy appreciates that you are effectively dictating a news release that the publication is free to edit/rewrite or jettison as it sees fit. Most publications and organisations will simply ask you to e-mail or fax stories to them, however late in the day you are making the call. If you have no alternative to dictating a story, ask for the 'copytakers' and ensure you dictate punctuation and spell proper names and complex phrases carefully.

Post

Unless the information you are communicating is of really low news value and without any time element, I would advise against using the post for any news releases at all, though some firms still do. Not only is it impossible to be sure that it will be delivered the following day, it also indicates to its recipients that the contents of the release are non-urgent and can, therefore, be disregarded.

Document Exchange

If the news you are communicating is not urgent and is designed for other lawyers, then you can use the Document Exchange, but be aware that few publications or broadcast outlets have this facility.

Addressing your release

If you are sending the release to a known journalist, correspondent or editor be sure that his/her name is prominently shown on the fax frontsheet. If you are sending it 'on spec', without having established any working relationship with the publication in question, telephone their switchboard or check one of the directories mentioned above to establish the name of the appropriate editor – Home Affairs, Features, Consumer Matters. Sending out a release without a target name dramatically reduces the likelihood of it ever being used. If necessary, use the information in the directories referred to above to put the right name to the right job, but don't rely on any of them to be 100 per cent up to date – none of them can be.

If, for whatever reason, you are forced to send out a release to the publication in question without identifying the individual you hope will read it, it will probably be filtered by 'copy tasters' who wade through the welter of unsolicited and 'junk' releases that they receive each hour. You will now appreciate the importance of an eye-catching headline and an attention-grabbing first line or two, as they rarely get much further.

You can sometimes 'talk the story up' by a preparatory phone call, but again this only really works if you are in a position to telephone someone with whom you have already had some contact.

Be prepared

Although the whole topic of crisis management is discussed later, if your client, organisation or firm is under attack or involved in some high-profile activity that is likely to attract media interest, and you are sending out a release on the topic, don't wait till the first phone call comes. Try to anticipate what you are likely to be asked and mentally (and ideally on paper) prepare your response and identify the individual(s) to whom such enquiries should be channelled.

Jot down all the tricky questions you think you might be asked and draft some safe answers you could convincingly use. This is a task for which PR and issues management professionals are ideally suited, as their objectivity can often identify the real bear-traps, which the lawyers familiar with the matter may have overlooked.

Press conferences

These used to be much loved by public relations consultants, particularly when 'launching' something. Most professional journalists, however, share Marcel Berlins' view that rarely is anything added by attendance at a press conference that cannot be gleaned from a well-presented news release.

Though press briefings one-to-one or in small groups are still commonplace, the full-blown press conference is going. Apart from the prime minister, who holds press briefings regularly at No. 10, and car manufacturers, who still launch new cars with a great deal of razzamatazz and dry ice, this is a dying event.

The main purpose of some of the few press conferences held today seems to be to enable its organisers to say: 'At a press conference today . . . '. There is, of course, real value in a press conference if a key spokesperson is going to be available to flesh out the information contained in the news release and thereby provide additional material for attending journalists and his or her time is too precious for them to be able to brief journalists individually. The last I organised, at least six months ago, was for my clients, a City Council which had just emerged from protracted litigation that had gone against it, with the highest award of defamation damages. The chief executive, in the interests of openness, was advised by me to make himself available to answer any questions the journalists might want to put to him, which was only practicable in a press conference format or the rest of his week would have been taken up with this. Some 40 journalists and three camera crews attended – both national and regional – and then further interviews were granted on a carefully selected basis with individual national journalists afterwards.

The optimum time for a London or regional press conference, bearing in mind the travelling many journalists have to undertake since the demise of Fleet Street, seems to be around 11.30 a.m. with coffee available on arrival. The session should be chaired by someone suitably authoritative and (ideally) familiar with the journalists likely to attend. There should be a *brief* introduction setting out the purpose of the conference and clearly identifying the people involved. The key spokesperson should then make whatever *brief* statement is appropriate (not just a recitation or reading of the information contained in the news release that has already been distributed, but a more expansive and informative version) and then should be prepared to field questions.

The journalists should be invited to identify themselves before putting their questions, unless the chair can give their name and paper or programme, and a note should be taken of all who attend.

It is often felt appropriate to have more than one person present to assist with questions if the main spokesperson's expertise does not cover the full remit of the story. If others are there to deal with questions, allow them to do so. A Royal Commission launched one report at a major press conference with all 10 Commissioners present in a line on the platform. The chairman declined to allow any of the Commissioners to deal with any of the questions asked by the many journalists in attendance and fielded them all himself, even though it was known and reported that several Commissioners had dissented from the majority view on various points. It simply looked like stonewalling and encouraged the press to seek out the dissidents for individual interviews afterwards.

If resources allow, and it is appropriate if the event is a launch or a positive story, it may be civilised to offer a quick buffet lunch to all attending the conference once the formal business is over. Do not, however, be surprised if many journalists prefer to sneak away to file their copy without delay. Such an occasion can, however, offer them a further chance to gain additional information informally and provide a small reward for those who have been responsible for the initiative that is the subject of the conference. It also allows more important relationship building to go on. But however sociable the event, remain on guard and aware of the journalists' deadlines. If the story is very hot, it may be necessary to provide points for the journalists' laptops or even phone lines for them to use, so they can file their stories immediately. At the Royal Courts of Justice in the Strand there is a fully equipped press room near the entrance to the cells. When high-profile trials take place elsewhere the Lord Chancellor's Department sometimes makes arrangements for press facilities to be available and sometimes sends one of the press team to act as a liaison point.

It is always impossible to know precisely how many journalists will attend a press conference as they are notoriously bad at formally accepting or declining invitations, usually because they are unclear until the last moment whether there will be a more demanding call on their time. Numbers at press conferences can range from 10 to over 100 without much warning and this can cause caterers apoplexy. It is always wise to phone round beforehand (ideally on the morning of the conference) to try to establish numbers, if this information is needed. Do not feel your event is a failure if very few journalists turn up.

Press briefings

These are more popular. They are more informal gatherings with a few journalists, usually over coffee, a light meal or drinks (breakfasts, while fashionable in some quarters for businessmen, rarely appeal to journalists). While the format is social and relaxed, don't lower your guard too much or you will find that your indiscretions have been recorded and reported.

The ideal briefing probably would involve a small number of journalists from different publications, who perhaps do not yet know each other (they always seem to enjoy each other's company) – perhaps someone from a national paper, someone from a monthly magazine, someone from a trade journal and someone from a local newspaper. Their hosts should be represented in equal numbers and should include people who are really familiar with the minutiae of the story, not just the senior partner or head of chambers.

Media lunches

The larger firms and chambers have always been good at holding annual press parties, and entertaining and feeding journalists in some style regularly, but media lunches are becoming more popular with smaller law firms and with barristers' chambers. Many journalists seem to find them enjoyable, choosing to accept such invitations in preference to others. Such events are designed to provide an informal opportunity for a journalist to meet several members of a firm or chambers, off the record, to see their premises, perhaps meet some of their staff, and learn a little about the ethos of the organisation. Essentially they are opportunities to gossip and bond.

Large law firms often include influential clients in the lunch mix and this can add to the congenial atmosphere; clients are often refreshingly impressed by meeting journalists, though the converse is not always true. Never expect to receive favourable, or indeed any media coverage as a result of inviting a journalist to attend such a lunch. Journalists, on the whole, feel no sense of obligation, they are objective observers.

One-to-one lunches regularly with journalists remain useful to maintain the relationship, learn about developments on their publication and generally keep a grip on issues of interest to them. I am often asked to play the informal 'marriage broker' and introduce a legal client to a journalist they want to meet. I will arrange the lunch for the three or more of us and then endeavour to withdraw at a suitable time so that the lawyer(s) can get to know the journalist on their own.

Regular legal columns

Regional, professional or consumer publications have for years run these, which provide a valuable opportunity for lawyers, firms or set to publicise their work and specialisms. Many of these columns are already written by legal journalists, some are provided to local papers by news agencies on a syndicated basis, but increasingly magazines that have traditionally run agony columns advising on the complexities of personal relationships are extending these to include more detailed legal advice in response to readers' enquiries.

Most local newspapers already have a legal column, either produced by local law society members or by a proactive local solicitor who has volunteered their services. Be warned, however – they take up a considerable amount of time, if the information provided is to be accurate and up to date (which is clearly essential, but sadly not always the case) and it is recommended that the task should be shared on a co-operative basis between three or four lawyers, each specialising in different topics. The most common enquiries relate to neighbour disputes, wills, family breakdowns and faulty consumer goods, in that order.

It is also frankly doubtful whether this activity generates the kind of quality of work that most of you will want. It may build your profile and that of your firm in your locality, which has some merit, but it can also give rise to some of the oddest and saddest letters you have ever received.

Ensure that you include some kind of disclaimer about accuracy; a suggestion that in any doubt further advice should be sought from a solicitor and, even if you are using the column to promote your practice, don't agree to respond to readers' letters privately, or you will have no time of your own ever again.

And, to answer the perennial question – yes, you sometimes do have to make up the letters in order to provide the answers you feel the readers need!

Book reviews

These are not perhaps immediately thought of as part of media relations. It is often, however, worth considering obtaining a review copy of a book that has been published in the area of law (or more general life) in which you can reasonably be regarded as an expert. A review, particularly if written in a humorous and non-academic style, could well be printed if submitted unsolicited to the appropriate publication and could be the start of your receiving invitations to contribute to that journal on a regular basis.

Diary and gossip columns

Snippets of legal gossip are always pounced on with enthusiasm by journalists. If you have a little story – amusing and non-defamatory – pages like 'Tulkinghorn' in the *Lawyer*, 'Obiter' in the *Law Society's Gazette*, 'City Diary' or Edward Fenell's section in *The Times*, *Private Eye* or Marcel Berlins of *The Guardian* would be glad to hear from you. The funnier and more scurrilous the story, the better.

Articles

Many lawyers contribute on an occasional or a regular basis to a wide range of publications. Unless you wish to risk the wounded pride of rejections, it is worth trying to establish in advance whether an article on your chosen topic would be of interest and securing a commission before you spend valuable time writing. Many major newspapers with legal pages, such as *The Times'* Law Supplement on Tuesday, are always on the lookout for contributions and welcome unsolicited approaches to the law pages editor. Others tend to have their own stock of tried and tested contributors to whom they will always go in preference to untried ones. Ideally you should e-mail a brief summary of what you are proposing to write to the relevant journalist or publication and then phone a day or two later to see if they have had a chance to consider it. If, however, you feel you have something new and interesting to say, by all means submit an article (ideally between 750 and 1,250 words, double-spaced on just one side of paper) to the editor or appropriate journalist on the publication of your choice. Don't submit it to more than one journal at a time, although you are free to send it to another journal once it has been rejected by the first.

Attach or enclose a short note explaining why you are the right person to be submitting this article and why you believe it is of importance, relevance and interest to the readers of the particular publication to which you are writing. Provide an e-mail address (your own, not your PA's), and a daytime telephone number where you can be contacted, should it be necessary to obtain your agreement to changes to the text.

If the article is accepted, you should reasonably expect to receive payment at the NUJ (National Union of Journalists) rates of pay that currently prevail, unless you agree to waive or reduce a fee because you feel the article is potentially useful to you or your firm.

Research-based stories

Research materials are the tried and tested basis for much news coverage achieved by public relations personnel on behalf of their clients. Research can be commissioned from a wide range of organisations and can be complex, expensive and of real academic relevance, or 'cheap and dirty', of more populist interest and available within a few days. It is true that one or two 'amazing facts' will turn an otherwise fairly pedestrian story into a newsworthy item of national interest and much legal work lends itself readily to statistical analysis.

Journalists are always asking the Law Society's Press Office if this is the largest damages claim, or the longest case, or the harshest sentence or the highest fee paid to a barrister. Though they would often love to have this information, it is not collated, to my knowledge, in one place, but research could provide the answers. Readers, however, are more interested in research information about people and the fact that more than one in three marriages fails, or only one in three adults has a will, is immediately comprehensible.

The Law Society has its own Research and Policy Planning Unit, which commissions, produces and publishes a raft of research materials each year, analysing trends within the legal profession, the public's attitude to lawyers, the areas of work undertaken by a changing profession and its profitability. These materials can always be referred to (with proper attribution) as the basis for some news story of your own. The information about the public's perceptions of lawyers is helpful when preparing for any media exposure.

Alternatively, research can be commissioned from Gallup, NOP (National Opinion Polls), RSGB or many other organisations into the specific area in which you have an interest. You can pay MORI or others to ask a representative group of 100 MPs a question or two when they conduct their regular omnibus surveys.

Whenever undertaking research for profile-raising purposes, you should never ask questions to which you do not at least suspect the answers and should ensure that the questions asked will provide the best news platforms possible, rather than just findings of interest to you and your colleagues.

Once you have obtained the research findings and distilled them into manageable form (and the raft of figures that are sometimes initially produced are not necessarily in a format that the public and the media can readily digest), draft your news release. It should clearly detail who undertook the research (e.g. 'Gallup for the Solicitors' Family Law Association, revealed today that . . . '), how it was handled ('methodology'), what the sample was and which are the most newsworthy findings. The full report should ideally be available to those interested in receiving it (with the consent and full knowledge of the research company involved) but often a summary will suffice. A welter of statistics is often counter-productive, and it is better to extract two or three really interesting findings that you wish to stress.

Keeping the story running

Some stories 'grow legs' or 'spin' in a different direction. This means the original topic extends and coverage of the same issue can continue, from a slightly different angle, for several days. An example some years ago, which is still remembered, involved a defamation case brought against a newspaper that had alleged that a television soap opera actress had performed oral sex on her fiancé in a Range Rover parked alongside a major road. By the third day of the trial, a breakfast television programme was demonstrating to its viewers 10 things they could do in a Range Rover and a video of the lady in question performing other feats at a party was doing the rounds! Thinking up ways to give a story 'legs' or 'spin' is a very specialised knack and one that several lawyers have mastered with distinction. The more often the key message is repeated, the more memorable it will be.

Bear-traps to avoid to achieve results

When dealing with the print media, strive to avoid the following:

- sending out news releases by scattergun technique to all and sundry without targeting properly;
- arranging to see a journalist without having something they can use for a story – they have to justify their time too;
- not providing short, pithy quotes – lengthy explanations and caveats are useless to journalists;
- not responding quickly to requests for information from journalists; their deadlines are very tight and they do not have time for you to undertake lengthy research and contemplation;
- criticising your competitors or opponents;
- dropping your guard for quotes: be wary when a journalist puts words in your mouth; if he says, 'Would you say that . . .?' ensure you use your own words or his quote could be attributed as said by you;
- asking a journalist to see an article before it is printed; printed corrections are rare and can often bring the original error to the attention of readers who missed it the first time;
- being pompous, elitist, patronising, verbose or inaccessible.

And if the piece never appears?

Don't be disappointed or surprised if a newspaper story in which you have invested time and effort never appears in print, and don't blame the journalist who was writing the story. Often last-minute news developments and space constraints mean perfectly good pieces are harshly edited or spiked by the sub-editors responsible. Don't give up. Try again.

Litigation PR

The appetite for readers of and listeners to the popular media to pore over the details of court cases increases. The claim made by Mr and Mrs Michael Douglas that their privacy had been infringed when one of the two main celebrity glossies took pirate shots of their wedding, after the couple sold the rights to the rival publication, filled many pages not just of the tabloid press in February 2003. A trivial case involving celebrities will attract global media scrutiny. A major matter involving people no one has ever heard of may go unremarked.

Lawyers are becoming more sophisticated about using successful cases to market the legal expertise that resides in their firm or set, and also to ensure that their clients' reputations are enhanced by the issues in their cases being effectively communicated beyond the courtroom.

All of us involved in helping solicitor Sally Clark remain clear that mobilising public concern about the safety of her convictions by a carefully planned media campaign, was vital in achieving the second, and successful, appeal, which saw her released from prison on 2 January 2003.

Joshua Rozenberg, former solicitor and veteran legal journalist, who spent 25 years as the BBC's legal correspondent and for the past couple of years has been legal editor at the *Daily Telegraph*, is clear that we have much to learn if we are to impress legal journalists and get news of our clients' cases published:

> Law firms often send me press releases announcing cases they have won for their clients. At best, these reach me on the late afternoon of the judgment; at worst, they arrive several days or even weeks later. This is hopeless.
>
> If the case is important enough to merit a press release, I need to know about it *before* judgment is delivered. I do not expect to be given advance notice of the result, when known; that is confidential to lawyers and later, their clients. All I need to know is when and where a reserved judgment is coming out.
>
> Some lawyers tell me they are unwilling to alert me in case they lose. That, too, is deeply unimpressive. Competent litigators should have a pretty good idea of how the case has gone by the end of the hearing. And if the result is a defeat, it is even more important to explain the client's position to the media.

Most of the time law firms, particularly the lawyers within them rather than their professional marketing staff, are unnecessarily nervous about tipping off journalists about a potentially interesting case, for fear, as Joshua says, of attention being drawn to the firm if the case does not succeed, or through inherent anxiety about client confidentiality, which regularly scuppers much timely legal communication.

Not once in some 20 years of legal communications have I been wrong-footed by a professional legal journalist breaking an embargo I imposed, and only a couple of times has someone failed to honour the understanding that a comment was 'unattributable', or a briefing was 'off the record'. All the journalists on the national and legal publications can confirm that I regularly alert them to potentially newsworthy cases coming up, often provide them with briefing materials embargoed until the date of judgment or talk them through the detail of the case, and indicate its likely outcome.

To brief properly on detailed cases obviously requires the full collaboration of the lawyers who have the conduct of the cases, and often at the very time they are at their busiest preparing for trial. But often marketers report with irritation that the dilemma they face is the professed wish of the lawyers to have their expertise better recognised, but without the same lawyers making time, at the right time, to provide the necessary information – so this simply cannot happen.

Key rules when handling high profile cases

This topic deserves a book on its own, and given time I would love to try to produce it, but I am aware that many of my readers will not be undertaking the kind of legal practice that involves statements on the steps of the court and television cameras outside their clients' homes. Much that has gone before in this book on the professional rules and legal constraints, and some that comes after on the use of the broadcast media will, I hope, be helpful, but these are the guidelines that should, I believe, influence everything:

- Ensure that at all times the client whom you are advising or representing is fully aware of, comfortable with and gives proper, informed consent to anything you propose to do that involves the media having access to their case. It is *their* case, not yours.
- If in any doubt about your client's instructions in this respect, to clarify their thinking and protect yourself, draw up a simple agreement setting out what you propose to do for them in terms of media contact and ask them to sign this to signify their consent.
- At no point use the media's interest in your client as just an excuse to promote yourself or your practice.

- If the client is able and willing to do so, they should speak about their own case to the media themselves. You should help and support them throughout but only speak on their behalf if they expressly ask you to do so or it is apparent that they are simply not able to do so themselves. In terms of public sympathy and media interest, it is always better to hear from the parties to the action than from their legal ciphers.
- Do not make jibes or score cheap points off the other side or comment or behave in any way, however helpful to the course of the litigation, that could bring you, your firm or profession into disrepute.
- Do not take personal advantage of any media offers involving cash, unless you have cleared it with both your client and your professional body and squared it with your conscience. Sometimes lawyers are now offered money for details of a case or to tell the whole story from their perspective. I have been on several occasions, but have always declined.
- Don't embark lightly on courting the media or drawing attention to a case. It can take over your life, invade your private life and make it challenging to fulfil your responsibilities to your other clients. Once the tap is turned on, it is often hard to turn it off.
- Don't ever forget that you are, if a solicitor, an Officer of the Supreme Court and owe a duty to the court as well as to your client. It is possible to get carried away in the heady world of the media, particularly if you are new to it.
- Try to ensure that everything you do and say in the media context supports and assists the legal work being done on your client's behalf.
- Be meticulous in adhering to all the constraints that apply to media coverage of court matters.

See Chapter 8 for much more guidance.

5

How to handle radio

There is something dangerous, scary and addictive about broadcasting. It should be approached with caution and care, but at the same time it can be the greatest fun.

Many lawyers first find themselves in contact with a microphone or a camera when a case in which they are involved hits the national or local headlines. Ideally, if there is any risk, however remote, of your having to perform on radio or television you should undergo some training first. If your job requires you to act as a spokesperson, insist on receiving some training; the skills you will acquire will be valuable in all your communications.

It will also be helpful to wade through the previous chapters before embarking on a radio broadcast. While contact with the radio station may come from a producer or researcher, most have a background in journalism, many have been print journalists, and the knowledge you gain from understanding how the print media operates will hold you in good stead when you embark on a radio interview.

Preparing for radio communications

The best radio broadcasts are eavesdropped conversations, with an easy, informal style. The key to competent broadcasting is preparation. Take time to prepare before all interviews, no matter how many you have given. This may seem dull, but it is essential if you are to survive and it is the least you owe your client or your employer if you are putting their case across. Just as you would never go into court without having done some homework, the same is true of a studio. Although a down-the-line interview or over the phone interview may feel informal and quite natural, it still requires thorough preparation if you are to be satisfied with your results.

Let us assume that the first contact you will have with a radio programme will be when you are invited to participate in an interview or discussion on a legal topic or case with which you are involved. When you become more confident and experienced you will feel able to approach programme-makers yourself with stories you feel may interest them.

Questions to ask when approached by a radio programme

- Why have you contacted me?
- What kind of programme is it? (Ask this carefully in order to avoid offence – you will probably not be familiar with many daytime programmes, even though they may attract high audiences. Try to do some research first, but the programme-makers' description will be illuminating.)
- Will my contribution be live or pre-recorded?
- Who else will be interviewed or contributing to the programme?
- If the package is to be edited, in which order will the contributors speak?
- Who will be conducting the interview?
- Who are you? (the researcher, series editor, producer, interviewer?)
- How long will the interview last?
- How long will the item or programme last?
- What angle are you taking?
- How much, if any, background information on the case or topic have you got?
- Will there be any follow-up programme, publication, phone-in?
- How will I be introduced?

and most importantly, ask yourself:

- Am I the right person for this?

From many broadcasts by lawyers, it is clear that this last vital question has never entered the minds of many of them. It is deeply flattering and exciting to be asked to broadcast to thousands or even millions of people and our every instinct is to accept the invitation and worry about it later. There are, however, occasions when it is appropriate to decline. Never forget you have the right to say 'Thank you for asking, but I don't think I'm the right person for this – let me suggest someone who is . . .'.

Without clear and convincing answers to most of those early questions it would be frankly irresponsible to agree to go on air, but many people do every day. Many must live to regret their temerity.

Preparing for the interview

The extent of the preparation that is possible for you to undertake is very much influenced by the kind of programme to which you are contributing and the timescale involved. The same methods of preparation are needed whether your interview is for radio or television. The intellectual process is also very similar to that required to conduct effective interviews with print journalists.

Interviews often fall into two categories:

The informative interview

This is where clarity is essential. You are there to provide and perhaps explain information. There must be certainty about your material and authority comes with your familiarity with it. Decide in advance which main point you wish to put over and make subordinate points in descending order. This means that if the interview is cut short for any reason, only the less important points will be lost.

Not only should the most important point be made first, it should be re-made if possible midway and, if time permits, at the end as well. A final restatement is often useful, but ensure you only use a few simple words as the ending comments can be cut short if time runs out. If you are stopped mid-sentence, you can look and sound ridiculous, despite the preparation you have done; and the last impression is the one the audience is left with.

Since the whole point of this kind of interview is to pass on information, the interviewer should have little objection to discussing the questions with you in advance, if circumstances allow. Do not expect too much airtime, however important you feel the subject to be. It will part of a busy programme schedule and two to three minutes is the usual maximum length. Sometimes a comment can be edited down to just 30 seconds, and that allows for only two or three pungent sentences.

An information interview should be comparatively painless, unless nerves cause you problems, as you will be there specifically because you are perceived as knowledgeable and will be encouraged to share that knowledge. It is unlikely the interviewer will seek to trip you up or in any way discomfit you. Careful preparation is the best way to avoid any anxiety and never forget to base your approach to your performance on the listener's point of view. Provide what they need or want to know, in the manner they find most comfortable, rather than delivering what you may most enjoy telling them.

The critical interview

This kind of interview is obviously trickier. You may be defending your organisation, client, profession or opinions. Once again, preparation is paramount, coupled with an absolute mastery of your subject. Again, consider your topic from the listener's point of view. This should give you some indication of the areas of questioning you are likely to meet and of the style, tone and language you should strive to adopt.

In all probability, your interviewer knew nothing about your subject yesterday and is unlikely to remember much about it tomorrow, but for the purposes of today's interview they are as expert as you. The research team will have dug up the key facts, perhaps they have cuttings or comments made by you or others in the past, and they will have a clear idea of the line that questioning will take. Despite requests, you are unlikely to be told in advance what those questions will be, but the areas for discussion will be established before an interview of this kind. Always bear in mind that some interviewers have spent weeks researching for your interview, and beware of any skeletons in your cupboard.

It is quite within your rights to make clear in advance any areas that you are simply not prepared to discuss. There have been many cases where a lack of liaison between researcher, producer and interviewer has resulted in questions being asked that the interviewee did not expect and is either unable or unwilling to answer. The resulting embarrassment can lead to accusations of dishonesty, or even worse, a half-baked attempt to answer the question, usually very unconvincingly. This is not in anybody's best interests and makes for edgy and uncomfortable listening.

If, despite everything, you are asked such a question live on air, say straight out that it is in an area on which you are not qualified to speak. Don't be afraid to point out that you had received an assurance that that particular subject would not be covered. Do this politely and firmly, not aggressively. Then sit back, wrapped in righteousness. Leave your interviewer to get out of the mess without your aid.

Should such an interview descend into a contest, short answers do much to discomfit an interviewer, although like all advice, it would be dangerous to carry this to extremes. Here, preparation assumes an even greater importance. You are likely to have a good idea of the direction of any criticism, but if in doubt, a little role reversal will serve as a good guide.

Having decided where the attack might come from, and the form it could take, work out the shortest satisfactory answer. This will prove the most manageable line to defend. Having established your line, stick to it. Don't fall for 'interviewer's nerve', a well-known ploy; this is when your interviewer listens apparently sympathetically, maybe even nods kindly and says nothing when you stop talking. He or she will look you steadily in the eye, giving you the impression that they are riveted by what you are saying. Their expression will imply 'Surely you've not finished? It's absolutely fascinating. Do go on.' If you do, you could find yourself in trouble.

Resist the temptation to break the silence. The pause may last a second or two – although the first time you try this ploy it may feel like a lifetime. Don't let it embarrass you. Return the interviewer's kindly gaze and keep your mouth shut. The ball is in their court and they will have to return it to keep the interview alive. Whoever ends the silence, claims it.

Do not try the politician's game of not really answering the question at all. It irritates the audience, who can spot this one a mile off and may make the interviewer even less favourably disposed towards you. You run the risk of their commenting, 'Very interesting, but I wonder if you would now answer the question I put to you.' Now that so many more people granting broadcast interviews have undergone media training, both the sophistication of audiences and the rigour of interrogation have increased markedly.

It can be a pretty undignified position to find yourself in apparent conflict with the interviewer, and often sets the viewer or listener immediately on the side of the interviewer and against you. Even the most terrier-like interviewers (the names Paxman and Humphrys spring to mind) have devoted fans who cheer them on silently as they press for answers to their questions. From then on, everything you say will have less impact and is unlikely to be persuasive to the audience, unless you maintain a calm and principled stance.

If the interviewer has got you on the spot, admit it; not all of it, but as much as suits you. 'I've got to admit there's a lot in what you say. We made mistakes. But we've learnt from them and they won't happen again.' It is a good and attractive approach, distinguished by truth and human fallibility. It quite often throws the interviewer off the trail – satisfied that he has shown he was right, he moves on to another subject, and you still have not revealed the real skeleton in your cupboard.

But don't rely on this to bail you out. The really sharp interviewer will spot that you have told only half of the story and will still press for the whole tale. Once again, you may appear to the listeners to be evading the point, with a resultant loss of credibility. If at all possible, don't forget the oldest trick in the book is honesty. It is invincible, easy to remember and it is usually possible to select a safe strand of argument within your case and stick to it. It just requires forethought.

The requirements to withstand a critical interview on radio are similar to those of any reasonably tough legal negotiation or courtroom contest. The skill is to be able to remember and apply them in the totally different world of the radio studio, a world where your interviewer is completely at home and you may be feeling like a fish out of water. The interviewer therefore starts with an in-built advantage. But don't forget, at the end of the day you, not they, are the expert in your own subject and ensure that it appears that way.

If you have real anxieties about issues that rigorous research could reveal and on which you might be questioned, then you should perhaps reconsider whether it is wise to agree to be interviewed at all.

The news and current affairs programme interview

A typical information interview is probably the most common for lawyers and the one you are most likely to encounter in connection with your work. Like press newsrooms, radio newsrooms have reporters working to news editors who select stories. Current affairs programmes are run by editors or producers who decide on their content and set up interviews, with the assistance of researchers. Many programmes, particularly on the less well-resourced stations, now rely heavily on their presenters (who all have journalistic backgrounds) who not only conduct the interviews but may do some of the research as well.

Your first contact will probably be with a researcher or producer who is responsible for lining up the interviewees and providing the person conducting the interview with appropriate background information and questions to ask.

Don't be miffed to be called by a rather ill-informed and youthful person who appears to be floundering their way through a complex topic on which you are an acknowledged expert. Remember the budgetary constraints under which all broadcast outlets labour and be patient if you want to get it right. It is in your interests to ensure that accurate information is provided and understood or you will find yourself fielding unintelligible questions and participating in a half-cocked interview.

Having established the kind of programme, the angle of the item, its length and all the other essentials outlined, start working out *what you want to get out of the interview*.

Most people being interviewed on radio or television seem to have as their objectives simply answering the questions they are asked and getting out of the studio alive. This is not good enough. If you have been entrusted with £300,000 worth of airtime, you should aim to make it work for you in a rather more positive way.

If you are commenting on a case in which you are involved, be clear about how much you or your client are prepared to have said. As advised earlier, *never* comment on a client's case without first obtaining their consent to do so and ideally agreeing the line you propose to take. If appropriate, get them to sign a disclaimer to this effect.

Jot down the key points you want to make and, if uncertain, ensure that the programme-maker who has contacted you is clear what the boundaries are. Remember, they will expect you, as the lawyer, to give guidance on the rules of *sub judice* and to be clear what you can and cannot say, so don't rely on them to guide you. If in doubt, seek help from your professional organisation.

If there are areas into which you legally cannot be drawn, say so clearly. If there are topics you are simply not prepared to discuss, take care. Don't just say, 'Please don't ask me about . . .' because this will indicate that the real meat of the story is being concealed and any researcher worth his or her fee will try to ensure that the interviewer probes this area. If there are genuinely no-go areas, explain carefully, as a lawyer, why these cannot be discussed and make it clear that the programme-makers could be in trouble if they ignore your professional advice.

There are many stories of lapses by novice broadcasters, but one of my favourite is told by Peter Wheeler, the veteran Manchester broadcaster, who has been providing media training classes for decades. He was once interviewing an official in connection with the potential dangers associated with a nuclear reactor for which he was responsible. During the interview live on air, Peter was slipped a piece of paper with the one word 'Scunthorpe' printed on it. Not knowing what this meant, but trusting the intelligence of his researcher, he simply said, leaning forward earnestly and fixing his interviewee with a gimlet gaze, 'Now tell me about Scunthorpe.' The man from the nuclear industry went ashen, gulped, floundered and dried up completely. Apparently, just as he was being shown to his seat in the studio, he had confided to the researcher, 'I do hope he doesn't ask me about our plant in Scunthorpe – it's a bloody time bomb, that place.' The researcher had just done her job.

Learn from this story. Never let your guard down, however charming and hospitable the programme-makers are to you beforehand. It is their job to try to find chinks in your armour that could enliven the piece and make a more newsworthy and entertaining programme.

So, having jotted down what you are prepared to say and having made mental, but not written, notes of what you are not prepared to say, work on getting your messages into short, digestible, plain English phrases. Two or three main points are the most you can wisely include in a radio interview, which will probably run for a maximum of two minutes and may be edited down to just 20 seconds.

Even if you have been advised that your interview, once edited, will run for longer than two minutes, don't be tempted to stuff in more facts, figures and information. The attention span of your audience is limited and it is always preferable to emphasise the key points, rather than introduce supplementary ones and risk distilling the impact of the messages you want your audience to retain.

Know your audience

As with the print media familiarise yourself with your audience. Listen to (if necessary by arranging for someone to tape) a couple of editions of any programme to which you will be contributing, so that the style and language is not a surprise.

Think carefully about the tone and style of the programme and the other sources from which its audience probably gets its information. Seek to communicate in an appropriate style. Particularly guard against pomposity and complex language on the more informal programmes.

When granting interviews on a complex legal issue, I often found that if I could explain it in advance to my younger son in a way that he could understand, then I was probably going to be able to explain it to a radio audience satisfactorily. Now he too is a qualified solicitor, I am having to find other helpers.

Don't forget that there will be very few lawyers among your audience and never underestimate the intellectual challenge of finding a way to explain a complex issue simply. On radio, more than on television, the person being interviewed is expected to explain the story.

Remember the reason that *you* have been asked to appear on the pro-gramme is probably because you are believed to be an expert who can explain the topic to the audience. It is, therefore, your duty to be comprehensible.

Learn to know your voice

Most of us used dictaphones on a regular basis until e-mail took over, and so are familiar with how we sound by this method, but the radio micro-phone paints a much truer picture of the real you. I recommend practis-ing using your voice with the best quality audio-recorder you can find. It is an embarrassing experience, but reading extracts of novels into a recorder to gauge your inflections and speech patterns is very valuable, and if set speeches have to be made, it is always worth rehearsing them on tape. Your family or colleagues will think you are mad, but when you compare the results of those who made this effort and those who did not, the difference is pronounced.

Get used to how long two minutes lasts – it is time for about 360 words only. If you are finding it an unhappy experience, two minutes can feel like a lifetime. If you have a lot of information to impart and have not focused your thoughts, you can find that the time is up before you have even covered the preliminary ground. Verbosity is the primary enemy of broadcasting lawyers. Advocates, particularly, find it hard to be succinct.

Experiment with your vocal instrument. Most of us use only a very small amount of our vocal range. We all tend to forget that using our facial expressions influences how our voices sound. Something said with a smile sounds totally different on radio from something said deadpan, and anything that brings warmth and animation to your voice is essential in making your message easy to absorb.

Think about what makes you turn up the volume on your car radio when you are driving. It is probably not so much the topic being dis-cussed as the inflexions used by the people talking – not the content but the tone. The variety and animation in their speech patterns is what makes you really listen, otherwise it is often just background noise. Much radio broadcasting is received by people engaged in other activities at the same time. To catch and hold their attention requires more than just careful diction and well-thought-out phrases. It requires animation: energy, enthusiasm and enjoyment.

Practise getting some light and shade into your voice. Listen to how different you sound when you say a simple phrase with and without an accompanying smile. Even if the topic is a serious one, you can greet your interviewer or open the interview with a pleasant smile and this will welcome your listeners too.

Use your personal volume control. Many people get louder when trying to emphasise a point. On radio it is often more effective to slow down a little and get a bit quieter. Be aware of the speed – many people tend to talk too fast particularly when they are nervous, and have to make a conscious effort to slow down when broadcasting.

We have all been taught that nature abhors a vacuum and when in a studio novice broadcasters often rush to fill any silences, as they find them awkward. But allow a moment or two of silence to elapse after you have made your most compelling points. It permits your point to sink in and allows your audience to digest it.

Invite people whose judgement you trust to be honest with you about your diction, your breathing, your phraseology. Colleagues are always flattered to be asked to help and one might even be prepared to role play an interview with you to give you practice. Most lawyers that I know seem secretly envious of Jeremy Paxman or David/Jonathan Dimbleby and would love a chance to swap places.

Regional accents

Never, ever worry about or try to correct a regional accent. Provided they are comprehensible, they bring life and colour to radio and are welcomed by programme-makers. I will often actively seek out a lawyer with a slight accent in preference to a 'plum-in-mouth' City lawyer to suggest to programme-makers if I am trying to get across a complex point to the consumers of legal services in the regions.

There is an inherent compatability with a regional audience if the broadcaster clearly comes from their patch, but it works on the national stage too. A recent tricky issue was made easier by the fact that one of the two senior managers in the firing line had a delightful soft Geordie accent. This made him seem much less 'stuck-up' than his colleague with public school received English. As the alleged autocractic stance of the management was in issue, it was helpful to have a 'man of the people' as a spokesperson.

The radio studio

Many believe, naively, that radio is an easier medium on which to appear because you do not have to worry about how you look. In fact, it is often far more difficult to perform ably on radio when you only have your voice to work with and no other help or distraction. Some say your real personality is easier to discern on radio, as you can play fewer games to disguise it.

If you are being interviewed in a radio studio, the environment is normally dark, small and rather cosy. There is something comforting and womb-like about many radio studios and many of us prefer them instinctively to the more clinical television studio.

Often the presenter/interviewer and you will be seated in close proximity, each with a microphone on a stand in front of you, suspended from the ceiling or sticking up from the centre of the table. You may also be asked to wear earphones ('cans'), particularly if there are to be questions from listeners telephoning the programme. These are not the small portable ones you use for your Walkman or mobile phone, but large earmuffs that entirely cover your ear, with padding and an adjustable headband. Old hands always work with just one of them in position, and the other tucked behind the ear so that they can hear sounds other than the talkback or programme – don't emulate them. The technicians are usually in a small adjoining control room nearby behind a glass screen with their control panel. The two are linked and everything that is said in the studio will be audible to them.

You, however, will be protected from the remarks of the technicians unless they throw a switch to speak to you. Your interviewer may, in these miniaturised and hard-up times, be operating the console him/herself, particularly if the interviews are interspersed with calls or music (as on BBC Radio 2's *Jeremy Vine Programme*, which has replaced the redoubtable Jimmy Young). Try not to be distracted by the technology.

Depending on the type of programme, you may be asked to wait outside the studio, listening to the programme as it airs, and then be ushered into the studio only a few minutes before you go on air. It is often wise to arrange to be at the studios in sufficient time to sit outside the studio, or in the control room, for a while beforehand to absorb the style and atmosphere of that day's programme and to familiarise yourself with the other items.

An awareness of the variety of items that make up magazine programmes is particularly important with regional programmes when there can be music, perhaps lively contributions from listeners, traffic and weather reports and a melange of items as well as the one you are on. It is imperative to hit the right tone, if you are to succeed in communicating effectively with each particular programme's audience. When I was interviewed by Jenni Murray for *Woman's Hour* on Sally Clark's case,

I followed immediately after her chat with Goldi Hawn and Susan Sarandon who were promoting their latest movie, *The Banger Sisters* – a fairly major step-change was required.

The start of the interview

What to say at the start of the interview often worries novice broadcasters. Do I use the interviewer's name? Their first or their second name? Do I say 'Good morning' or 'Hello'? It is best to gauge by the style of the programme, but aim for friendly but professional informality. You do not need me to tell you that while 'Hi' probably works for Radio 1, it will be quite wrong for Radio 4.

Check with the researcher or the interviewer beforehand how it is proposed you will be introduced – if your name is tricky, make sure they can pronounce it correctly – and ask what the first question will be. Another media convention, which is vital to remember but often forgotten in the heat of the moment, is that virtually every interviewer is prepared to let his/her interviewee know what they are proposing to ask as their first question. They may not use the exact words they outlined, once on air, but it is really useful for you to know how the interview is going to begin and to have an opportunity to align a few of your mental ducks before the start.

If you are introduced as 'Ms Jones from the Shropshire Law Society', it may well be appropriate just to say 'Hello', or 'Good evening' and await the first question. If a chatty style is employed and you are introduced with 'And now we have Jane Jones, a local solicitor' or 'This morning I'm pleased to welcome Mark Forbes, who has just won a ground-breaking award in a personal injuries case' then it would feel right to say, 'Hello, Michael' to your interviewer. Avoid over-use of the interviewer's name – it sounds cloying and insincere and jars. And do avoid that politicians' trick of often wasting valuable airtime with something like, 'Good morning, Jim, and thank you for inviting me to take part'.

Always guard against getting the time of day wrong on pre-recorded interviews. It sounds very silly to hear someone saying 'Good morning' when the interview they recorded at 9.30 a.m. is being transmitted at 7 p.m. and it is the sort of thing that can slip past a hard-pressed editor. Alastair Cooke always records a 'Good morning' and a 'Good evening' to cover the two transmissions of his weekly *Letter From America*. 'Hello' and 'Thank you, goodbye' are safe. Similarly, take care with phrases like 'a few hours ago' or 'today' if the programme will be transmitted some time later.

A common introduction on a local radio news item will be something like: 'Lawyers in Greater Manchester today have met to discuss withdrawing from the local duty rotas in the light of the government's proposed changes to legal aid. Joseph Bloggs is the regional co-ordinator and he is here to explain the position.' You may then have to try to boil down the history of the issue, the reasons for what has happened and your view representing local solicitors into a couple of sentences.

You may try to protect yourself by saying, 'This is a complex situation that can't be explained in a couple of sentences, but basically the position has arisen because. . .'.

When it comes to editing the tape, most producers and reporters will not be keen to start an interview in this vein. They think listeners get bored if people start talking about 'complex situations'. In any case, journalists pride themselves on being able to explain *anything* in a couple of sentences. So the tape will be edited and, in answer to the question implied by the introduction ('the reason for the situation') you will appear to begin by saying, 'Because. . .' and your first phrase about complexity will be lost.

So it is better to start off sharply, with a single wrap-up sentence: 'The position is bureaucracy gone mad. The government is . . .'. This way you get the background in, but as a support for a sharp opening and it is unlikely to be edited.

The interview

Don't turn away from the microphone at any point when speaking, or lean into it or increase the volume of your voice, but do look throughout at your interviewer, or if taking part in a discussion with others, at whichever person to whom you are addressing your remarks. Just maintain your distance from the mike. The sound technician will ask you to say a few words for 'level' and will then adjust the recording equipment appropriately. Use your ordinary conversational voice and try to avoid adopting a special 'telephone' or 'broadcasting' voice – you will hate it when you hear it later. I have often noticed that when broadcasting many novices also often crank up the volume a notch or two. Don't – quiet works well and the sound technician can make necessary adjustments.

Sit still, don't swivel in your chair or rustle any papers on the table. Try not to let your knees knock, your feet tap and keep your hands away from the mike. Don't bang or tap the table to emphasise a point or play with a pen or pencil. Don't light a match, blow your nose, sniff or click a ballpoint pen. Don't wear jewellery that could clunk on the table (even though it usually has a felt or baize covering) or mike stand, or fidget with your cuffs. All these sounds, which we are quite used to ignoring in normal conversation, are mannerisms most of us, quite unconsciously, acquire when nervous, and all will be picked up by the mike as quite dreadful thumps and clicks.

Rustling paper particularly sounds like a waterfall or worse. If you absolutely must blow your nose or cough, wait for a suitable moment, turn away from the microphone, taking extreme care not to kick the table or scrape the chair, then return to the mike once the deed is accomplished. Have a sip or two of water, if nerves are making your mouth dry, while the interviewer is talking.

Wear something comfortable. It may seem strange to mention clothes when you are on radio and could be naked, but how we feel very much influences how we sound. If you are doing a serious, legal piece on a difficult topic you may feel better in office clothes. If you are participating in a chatty phone-in programme where your contributions are sandwiched with pop records, you may feel more at ease in jeans. Now that so many lawyers are able to dress down at work, it is easier to be comfortable and it genuinely does affect your conversational style.

Points to remember for good radio

Keep your answers short. This makes unfriendly editing more difficult. It also allows the momentum of the interview to gather pace, which gives it and what you are saying more impact.

Identify your purpose in granting the interview. This is not as obvious as it seems. Depending on your judgement of other media coverage and of the current situation, your objectives in a radio interview can vary considerably. For example, you may want to get your side (or your client's side) of the story across in the face of slanted press coverage; you may want to inspire sympathy for your cause or your client; you may want to enhance the image of your firm, chambers or profession.

You must also *decide what audience you are chiefly aiming at*. Are you speaking to members of your profession not involved in the issue? Are you speaking to the public at large? You can tailor your replies to your specific audience with phrases such as 'This issue is much wider than one for the legal profession'; 'I'm not sure the public realises what's going on here'. Never ever make a threat on a radio programme or aim to frighten or upset your listeners, but if you can alert them to how the issue you are addressing can affect them personally, they will be hooked.

For local radio, subject to comments above about pre-recorded interviews, *keep it local and immediate*. A test of immediacy is to see whether or not you can work the word 'today' into it. Not 'Lawyers in Kent are concerned about delays in the county's magistrates' courts', but 'Lawyers in Kent have today sent a message of protest to the Lord Chancellor about delays in the Maidenhead Magistrates' Court'. In fact, this is one of the simplest ways of making news immediate: send a letter (to almost anyone – Prime Minister, Lord Chancellor, MP, Chairman of the Bar) about the issue you want to publicise and then tell the radio station and other media about it. Better still, send them a copy of the letter with an embargo saying 'not for use until 10 a.m. Monday', i.e. the time the letter is expected to reach its destination.

If you do this, *always make clear in the letter itself that you are releasing it*, with a phrase like, 'Because of the great concern about this issue, I am making this letter immediately available to my colleagues and the public'. Remember, immediacy can only stretch to yesterday, or what will happen tomorrow – beyond that, we are in the realms of ancient history or the uncharted future.

Be friendly and as helpful as possible. Don't begin by being hostile to an interviewer before the recording starts. Ninety-nine interviewers out of a hundred are not interested in doing you down. Their interest is in making the most of the story, in producing 'good radio' with lots of impact.

Take time to explain the background. A lot of radio reporting is straight voice-pieces, or reports with odd bits of interview cut into it. If you have any written material you are providing for newspaper reporters, or leaflets for the public, send these or deliver them to the radio reporter before the interview takes place. Never assume that the reporter knows enough about the issue but don't overwhelm them with too much information for a short item in a tight timescale. Yours will be only one item of many.

If you are mentioning on air *a publication* of public interest, give clear information about its availability and ensure sufficient stocks exist to satisfy demand.

If providing *an address or a telephone number*, dictate it slowly and ensure that it is repeated later in the programme for those who were without pen and paper the first time.

However complicated the story, the reporter in nearly all cases will usually need to do the interview with you in a *maximum of three minutes or less* and he or she will be lucky to get all of that on air. Don't blame the reporter for lack of time; accept it and structure your replies accordingly.

Try to be positive. Don't say, 'I don't know' unless it is a question on an issue of law genuinely outside your remit. Say, 'We haven't considered that yet', or 'It's a very difficult situation and any comment I make at this stage might be misleading'. But be ready to speculate: 'Lawyers are angry and there is very strong pressure to withdraw from the duty solicitor schemes', or 'It will be for the local committee to decide, but there's a fair chance they will vote for some kind of action'. If speaking about a client's case, you would obviously be more guarded if a decision, for example, about an appeal, has yet to be made. Local radio often comes back for more.

If you do an effective interview and if you get on with the reporter or presenter, you will be remembered as someone to come back to if the issue continues or develops, or even on topics beyond the immediate issue. Some reporters use the initials 'GT' after names in their PDAs or Filofaxes. This means 'Good Talker' – someone who can be relied upon to talk in a friendly, accessible and informative manner on a range of issues.

Be careful with figures. Never be tempted to fudge the exact amounts involved in a money dispute. If cash is at issue, whether it is the hourly rate charged by solicitors, a barrister's brief fee, the amount of a contract, the quantum of damages, always give the exact amount, unless you are legally prohibited from doing so. Any rounding up or down and you are vulnerable to criticism for putting out inaccurate information. The same is true of numbers generally. It is safer to say 'all 483 women will be involved', rather than 'about 500 women will be involved'. It is quite likely that the radio journalist in writing a news item or an introduction will say 'about 500 women' but you should still try to get the precise number in at the beginning, even if you use the generalisation later. Lawyers, more than most, are expected to be factually accurate and taken to task if they are not.

Don't be rude. It never pays to be rude or argumentative. Most listeners will side with the person who is attacked, not with the aggressor. If an interviewer is being unfair to you, the listeners' sympathy will be with you; but if you go rudely on the offensive, their sympathy will switch. You cannot win if you are argumentative in a recorded interview. If you lose the point, the interviewer may leave it in, because anger makes good radio and your losing the point makes the interviewer look good. If you win the argument, the interviewer may cut it out, because although it makes for good radio, it also makes him or her look foolish.

By all means be scathing about the government, the opposition, the court structure, your opponent in a case, and anything else you like within the bounds of defamation, provided you *ensure your criticisms have their basis in fact not prejudice.* Use colourful language too if you must, but remember that the strongest swear-word likely to be broadcast is 'bloody' and even that as little as possible. In any case, once in an interview is the maximum. Too common use of any expletive lessens its dramatic impact and simply indicates the poverty of its user's vocabulary. Swearing by lawyers on air would probably give rise to public and professional complaints as well.

Avoid jargon. Legalese can be meaningless to anyone other than fellow lawyers. If your language makes your listeners feel excluded they will not feel inclined to support your viewpoint or absorb the information you are imparting. See the Plain English Campaign's website for the most exhaustive list of alternatives to legal words and phrases.

Don't be embarrassed by your mistakes. Even with lots of preparation, and a good amount of experience, you will still make mistakes. Sometimes words come out jumbled up. Perhaps you will get a figure wrong or stumble over a difficult name or phrase. Quite often it is the phenomenon of the tongue being slightly in advance of the brain – you don't say the words you intended to say. If anything like this happens, don't worry if the interview is pre-recorded, go back and begin all over again. Say to the interviewer, 'Sorry, I've got that wrong' and go straight on to say the sentence you meant to say without pause. The reporter can edit out your fluff easily.

Drying up is also quite common. You would be surprised at the number of professional broadcasters who do it. If your mind goes blank during a recorded interview, just let the tape run on while you wait to get going again. If you want to stop altogether and have a moment to think and get yourself into gear again, say 'I'm sorry, can we do that bit again?' Many people are surprised, however, at how unexpectedly fluent they become when the interview is live – adrenalin may be responsible.

Go somewhere quiet to pre-record an interview if you are not in a studio. Extraneous sounds on tape will spoil the impact of what you are saying and will be distracting. The reporter or sound recordist will be aware of this, but it is as well to show you have thought of it too. At a news conference, for example, it is wise to have a side room available for interviews. Out of doors, it may be necessary to go and sit in a car. If it is your office, ensure that no phones will ring nearby or doors unexpectedly open or close.

In a radio discussion with others

In all broadcast panel discussions, you have to be ready to talk directly to the other participants, if necessary across the presenter. In a radio discussion, if you want to cut into someone else's chatter, do so decisively and seize control of the discussion, as two people talking simultaneously across each other sounds completely unintelligible on radio. On television the audience can tell where the different voices are coming from as they see the faces. Radio forces the listeners to rely on the evidence of their ears, which is much more difficult. If you must intervene, do so with a strong point that forces the others to give way. Conversely, you can refuse to be put down or interrupted yourself by carrying on speaking in a determined fashion. The professional interviewer or presenter will realise that it sounds like garbled nonsense on air, and so will give way to allow you to finish your point. You may need to allow time for the presenter to identify you before your contribution, 'James, I believe you have a view on this'.

Whatever happens and however much you feel you are not getting your fair share of the airtime, don't lose your temper, become loud or aggressive. You will immediately lose the sympathy of your audience. Try to retain a sense of humour. When I first did *Any Questions?* many years ago, it was really hard to get a word in edgeways between the opposing politicians. I determinedly gently made the point that their rather arid sniping was one of the many things wrong with the current political system. It won me a round of applause and a chance to make the rather different point I had been wanting to make for some time. Intervening successfully gave me confidence, reassured Jonathan Dimbleby that I could hold my own and that he could safely come to me for comment more often.

Never lose sight of the fact that many programmes have cult personalities presenting them. These people may well articulate views with which you personally disagree, but never underestimate them or forget that they have their followers and many see it as their role to advocate the case of their listeners.

Toe-curling tales are told of a certain presenter on local radio in Birmingham who has clearly made a personal vow to embarrass as many solicitors on air as he can manage. I can only assume he had an unhappy divorce experience, or an abortive conveyancing transaction, or a woman lawyer did not succumb to his advances, but to enter his studio without being aware of his personal agenda would be unwise.

Try to appreciate that when an interviewer is raising what seem to you to be naïve, irrelevant or just plain stupid points, they may well be doing so on behalf of listeners who share these very views.

Remote studios

The way that radio programmes are made today has become more minimalist, streamlined and changed beyond recognition. There are now many more satellite stations dotted round the country. Hundreds of digital stations have sprung up and with the expansion of broadband and ISDN lines many organisations and some of the largest law firms have their own in-house studios from which they can conduct broadcast-quality transmissions. Even small local radio stations now have fully equipped radio cars they can send to your home for quick interviews.

One has to travel less and less to take part in a radio programme, but if in London, it is still usual when working with the BBC to go into Broadcasting House, or to one of their studios in Millbank or at White City.

In one of the new wings of Broadcasting House there are now a number of tiny studios, with just one technician controlling the output from them all. You may be asked to pop into one, say your few words and then go, without ever seeing or meeting your interviewer.

If you are based out of London and a national BBC Radio programme wants to use you, it is quite likely that you will have to go to one of the BBC's local radio stations or to a regional radio centre and be interviewed 'down the line'. The BBC also has an increasing number of remotely controlled studios, which have to be activated by the person being interviewed. Some of these are in bizarre places such as underneath a football stand, opposite the gentleman's lavatory at the Royal Courts of Justice or in Coventry Cathedral crypt. If you have to go to a remote studio, you will be given precise instructions how to get there and what to do when you arrive.

My favourite was always the remote studio in Broadcasting House, before it was replaced by the new Five Live suites. There was a handwritten message stuck by the door, saying 'To turn this studio on switch the red switch' and another saying, 'Don't forget to turn the studio off when you leave'.

If you are using a remote studio and do not have a technician for guidance, give yourself a little time to read all the printed instructions on the door or table that tell you how to work the equipment. Don't worry if you get mixed up. It is very straightforward and there is always a telephone that connects you directly with the control room in London or the regional centre. If you have not made contact after the allotted time, the producer or engineer will come through on the phone and explain what to do, or they will arrange for someone on site with you to ensure that you are all set up.

It is normally quite simple. You usually just have to put on the earphones, throw a switch and speak into a strategically placed microphone. You will then be given guidance by the engineer from the main centre and in due course will hear your interviewer's voice coming down the line into your 'cans'. (You see, even the jargon's quite easy after a while.)

It is undeniably hard, though, to generate energy and enthusiasm for your topic without any feedback at all in a solitary room with no audience. When it is a one-to-one conversation, you will find you treat it very much like a telephone conversation, but should guard against losing focus on the brevity and punchiness of your comments. It is particularly hard when you are participating remotely in a discussion going on elsewhere. Be ready to come in with your point without being asked. The chairman cannot see you and once the first question and answer (which may act as a voice-over introduction for the participants) is over, it is very much up to you to intervene as you think best.

Being a guest on a phone-in programme

Every programme is becoming more interactive. At regular intervals on almost all, even traditional ones such as the *Today* programme, phone numbers, website details and e-mail addresses are given out and listeners are invited to contribute.

Lawyers are regularly asked in as guests on topical phone-in programmes, and legal advice sessions are featured on almost every radio station. Many general current affairs programmes such as Five Live's *Weekend News* invite the audience to e-mail their questions or comments, as well as telephoning in while the programme is going out. Participating in these is often a good way of getting additional publicity for a legal issue and, if the programme went well, you can suggest that a phone-in be set up off-air to follow an interview, if you feel it has further potential interest for the public. You may also be asked to provide information for the website and, perhaps, for the team in Glasgow operating the BBC's

AdviceLine, which provides fact-sheets and other information triggered by all the BBC's programmes.

The technique for phone-ins is a little different from participating in other radio interviews or discussions. When I used to contribute to the *Jimmy Young Programme* I had the luxury of being advised in advance of the calls and topics that would be taken the following week and had a little time, with the help of researchers, to prepare my answers and check them for accuracy. Many programmes, though, provide cheap and cheerful radio with only a few seconds' time delay, so callers' questions are put through and you may be expected to give immediate answers live on air.

As with other interviews, you will usually be invited into the studio and given a pair of earphones through which you will hear the questions. You may be able to see the computer screen now used by most presenters on which the callers' names and brief details may be displayed by the producer or researcher in the control room, who has fielded the call in the first place. The very short time delay is often so that any really unacceptable calls can be screened out.

Here are a few pointers:

Always have a pad of paper and quietly take brief details as the questioner is speaking.

However trivial the question or abrasive the caller's manner, the matter will be important to them. So always try to be informative, sympathetic and conciliatory. Remember that although thousands of people are listening, most of them are doing so in the privacy of their homes or cars and probably on their own. A loud or over-authoritative guest makes a poor impression and confirms the suspicions of many that we lawyers are an arrogant, bombastic lot.

Don't worry too much about giving a legal lecture or producing short, snappy answers – treat it as a gentle conversation, but do try to ensure that you always give sound advice as there are bound to be others in your audience with similar problems, who may be listening carefully in the hope of finding their own solutions. A phone-in programme is one occasion when the general broadcasting rule about projecting yourself is not essential (although, of course, you should keep alert).

If you are invited to be a phone-in guest, and there are some very particular points you would like to put across, you might even consider asking some friends or colleagues to phone in with a friendly question to ensure that topic gets covered.

Be warned: most phone-ins with a legal dimension major on neighbour disputes, ruined holidays and the refusal of some retailers to replace unsatisfactory goods. They can also feature lawyers' fees and complaints about solicitors. Most experienced practitioners in general High Street practices will find the information requested easy to provide, but those in more specialist practices may find them a struggle.

Flatter your questioners. Start off by saying 'That's a good question' or 'That's an interesting point' – it will give you a little thinking time, but then provide the requested information succinctly, or gently rebut any hostile arguments and make your own points.

If you are fielding legal questions, do not feel the need to present yourself as a walking encyclopaedia. You cannot be expected to know the answers to all questions fired at you and if you try to bluff, you will be found out. It is much better to say something like, 'I'm sorry, it's a long time since I did any conveyancing, but if you let our switchboard have your number, I'll look that up and get back to you', rather than fumble your way through an inaccurate answer. Learn from phone-in doctors who always adopt this tactic rather than make dangerous diagnoses on air.

Some lawyers seem incapable of saying 'I don't know' and some of the black letter law being relayed to listeners by lawyers who are not consulting others before they broadcast is dangerously out of date. If you don't know, say so, but always offer a way of providing the listener with an answer soon. Try to avoid anything that could be construed as touting for their business by suggesting they come and see you at your office. The backing of the AdviceLine or the website means you can usually offer to ensure that up-to-date information will be accessible after the programme. Say so, but don't make promises you cannot fulfil, and if you have promised to provide additional information to the production team, be sure you do so. Sometimes a topic is inappropriate for discussion on air, but the caller clearly needs help. You can always arrange to speak to them off-air, but should guard against getting drawn into spending overmuch time on one person.

Be generous to your callers. If they raise an interesting question or provide you with an opportunity to get over some useful information, thank them with something like, 'I'm glad you raised that, Sara, I know lots of people worry about travel insurance'.

'Fluffs' and 'dries'

This includes stumbling, making mistakes or grinding to a silent halt. If the interview is being *pre-recorded* for insertion into the programme later, always try to get it right first time, but do not be too shy to ask to do it again if you know that you have not made a point well, or are really unhappy with how you expressed yourself. Now that it is often the case that the presenter/interviewer is 'self-op' they will be operating the recording machine as well and it will be easy for the glitch to be re-done and improved. The production team or presenter will also want to get a good interview and will be prepared to allow you to improve your performance.

If there are time constraints or the presenter is not receptive to re-takes, on a pre-recorded interview the only certain way of getting a re-take is to stop dead and remain silent for a while.

If the interview is *live*, simply gather your thoughts and start again. The interviewer will often bail you out and eye contact is an important trick here. If you are looking at your interviewer, not only will your speech be more conversational and intimate but your eyes will signal to him or her that you are in trouble and they will usually throw you a verbal lifeline. Although you may be mortified at your stumble and may blush every time you recall it, very few of your audience will even have noticed and those that did will feel instinctive sympathy.

One memorable interview on the *Today* programme is still played to trainee presenters. It involved a man who was so paralysed with fear that he only managed to emit strangled grunts and gulps throughout a whole three-minute interview. Brian Redhead, one of the most experienced pros in the business, managed to keep a flow of conversation going for the entire three minutes and by interpreting the facial expressions of his guest, even managed to convey to the listeners the essence of the points that the man would have made if his larynx had allowed him.

Using notes

Although some people rely on notes, try to avoid this. It always gives rise either to rustling or to a stilted, hesitant style, unless the broadcaster is very experienced. If you have to quote statistics (and if you must, prune them to the minimum and make them really clear and simple), then by all means have a note in case your mind goes blank but *never* try to write out verbatim what you intend to say. Jot down the main points you want to make; reduce them down to key phrases; then distil them down to key words on a small index card.

Radio interviews conducted over the telephone

All radio stations now make extensive use of interviews over the telephone or 'down the line'. (The same phrase is also used when the interview is conducted from a remote studio.) Quite often the request to do a telephone interview will be made early in the morning or later in the evening, when you are at home. Sometimes, they are arranged for a time when you are in your office, or chambers or at court. You may not be as fully prepared as if the reporter had given you more advance warning, so remember, if the interview is to be recorded, you can always ask the journalist to phone back in a few minutes so that you can prepare yourself for the interview, jot down a few points and gear yourself up to put them over effectively. Quite often, however, you may be telephoned and asked to take part in a live programme and have limited time in which to marshal your thoughts.

It is strangely comforting to be in familiar surroundings when you are broadcasting and this can lead to its own traps. It is easy not to engage the brain fully and it is hard to get quite the same adrenalin rush to power you through the interview.

If you do nothing else before a telephone interview, clear your desk and remove any distracting pieces of paper that could be in your eyeline. Those of us who have found ourselves idly reading items on our desk while broadcasting should be prevented from ever gracing the airwaves again.

Once it has been agreed at what time the interview will take place, you can expect to be telephoned by the programme-makers about five minutes before you are to take part in the programme. If the interview is going live into a programme, after they have checked your sound level, you will have a few minutes during which you will hear, over the phone, the programme going out on air. This will help you get a sense of its style. The interviewer will then probably wrap up the previous item, introduce the piece in which you are involved and then will speak to you, just as though you are having an ordinary telephone conversation. Never forget, however intimate and informal it may feel, your conversation is being transmitted simultaneously into possibly millions of homes. When the interview has ended, you will stay on the line for a few more moments until one of the production team gives you the clearance to hang up.

If the phone interview is being recorded then there is, of course, scope to repeat one or two of the questions and answers if you are unhappy with your first responses.

The end of the interview

No matter how well your interview has gone, a killer interviewer can completely distort the essence of what you have been saying by a curt final line or two. An interview that ends with, 'Well, I'm afraid we have no more time, but I must admit I'm unpersuaded that the Office for the Supervision of Solicitors is dealing with the public's complaints efficiently' can destroy all the hard work you have put in during the previous three minutes attempting to reassure the listening public.

The interviewer has control of the timing of the interview and will know precisely how long they have left to get out of the interview. If you find that this cheap trick is being pulled on you, don't smile weakly, or worse, say 'Thank you' or 'Goodnight'. Instead say something like, 'Well, you perhaps misunderstood what I was saying', or 'Maybe I can come back on another occasion to go into this with you in more detail' to salvage something from the potential wreckage.

If all has gone well, very briefly thank the interviewer and say goodbye.

Follow-up calls or correspondence

Be warned that participating in many radio interviews on topics of popular interest can give rise to e-mails, telephone calls and letters from listeners in surprising numbers. These may not just find their way to the radio station or your office, but may also invade your private life if your address and phone number are listed. It is also surprisingly easy to work out many e-mail addresses. Lawyers are easier to trace than many professionals and you may find you are invited to enter into lengthy correspondence with people with legal problems, some of whom exhibit obsessive tendencies and appear to be vexatious litigants. They will have liked your friendly manner on air and will have found it a refreshing contrast to the solicitor(s) to whom they have previously gone. You may be asked to take on their case or requested for further material on the issue on which you spoke, or they may simply want to avail themselves of the therapy of pouring out their sorry tale to an apparently sympathetic listener. They often just want free legal advice.

Adopt a policy of friendly non-co-operation and stick to it, unless you are prepared to surrender a considerable amount of time. A fact-sheet that can be mailed by the programme-makers or radio station to all who express an interest in the issues is a valuable option, if the station or programme has the resources to handle this. It was cautionary to know that the *Jimmy Young Programme* received nearly 100,000 requests for leaflets on will-making after I represented the Law Society in one programme promoting the need to make a will and to use a solicitor to do so.

You may also find to your surprise that you receive wounding and acerbic letters from other lawyers taking issue with the advice or information you gave or challenging your approach as too populist or 'broad brush'. Such communications may be helpfully intended or may be symptomatic of a little professional jealousy. If you are like me, you will remember the one critical letter from a fellow solicitor, not the 50 supportive ones from the public.

Some tips from a broadcaster

Scott Chisholm, veteran CNN journalist, now media trainer with Electric Airwaves, is clear about the importance of remembering the following:

- 'Radio is very personal – it's in your kitchen, your bedroom, your car. Get rid of all corporate speak; use "I", "we", "you", not "they" or "one".

- Be firm when dealing with interruptions, don't be deflected, just keep going. Try "Let me finish", "You asked me a question, please give me a chance to reply".
- Never, ever let an interviewer or producer know that you have undergone media training.
- Before any interview, you have certain rights:
    - to know what the story is;
    - to know what angle the programme/interviewer will take;
    - to know what the programme is;
    - to know who else will appear/be interviewed;
    - to know what the programme-makers want from you;
    - to know what the first question will be.

- Most of us speak at about three words a second. Most radio interviews last a maximum of two minutes = 360 words only. Choose them with care.
- Pitch your messages as if to an intelligent, enquiring 13-year-old child and you will reach the average listener exactly.'

Jim Naughtie, veteran interviewer on the BBC Radio Four *Today* programme told me recently, 'If the person I'm interviewing comes across as second rate I have a duty to let the audience know this. If they're just not properly prepared – it's obvious.'

How to handle television

Television is a deceptive and seductive medium. Unlike on radio, it is possible to produce a convincing and authoritative performance with only skeletal material. Conversely, even the best prepared material can be destroyed by an inept performance. You can talk authoritatively and knowledgeably, but if you do not *look* authoritative or knowledgeable the audience will not believe in you.

The types of interview you are likely to encounter and the types of programme you may be invited to participate in are similar to those discussed in Chapter 5 on radio. The biggest difference – glaringly obvious though this may seem to you – is that you will be visible as well as audible to the audience and how you look will influence how you are perceived and how what you say is heard. Your appearance can even cancel the impact of your words.

That first contact

The first approach from a television programme or company will probably be a call from a researcher or, if it is a programme on a small regional channel or made by an independent production company, from the producer or editor. It is virtually unheard of for the presenter or interviewer to make contact with contributors to the programme and you often do not even get to meet them until a few minutes before the interview is recorded or goes on air.

Do not feel slighted to be approached by someone who may quite evidently be young, inexperienced and entirely unfamiliar with your area of law, if not with all law. Young people seeking to learn the craft have traditionally started as researchers on news, consumer and current affairs programmes. Initially they are tasked with finding out more about a chosen topic and/or person and providing the interviewer with background notes and possible questions to form the basis of the interview. As they become more experienced, and particularly on regional programmes and those made by 'indyprods' (independent production companies) where the staffing is even tighter, the researchers are often expected to come up with ideas of potential interest for the programme's viewers, and work up an entire item, including in some cases conducting the interview on film or tape for insertion as a complete 'package' into the programme.

As more and more programmes are put together by small indyprods, you may find that you are approached by one that is just at the preliminary stage of putting together a programme idea and has not yet pitched it at a channel, let alone secured a commission. Such approaches can be very time-consuming and you should be careful to manage their expectations of the time you are prepared to commit to helping them put together an interesting proposal.

Questions to ask before you appear

- Why have you invited *me* to participate? (The reasons may vary and sometimes it may be on a flawed recommendation about your particular expertise.)
- Precisely what kind of programme are you making? (Even if you have viewed the show before, check what this particular programme is all about.)
- Am I required for a one-to-one interview or to take part in a discussion with others?
- Who will be interviewing me? Will I have a chance to have a chat with them beforehand?
- Will my contribution be pre-recorded or live?
- If others will be involved, who will they be?
- Will the interview or discussion be preceded by any film or other interviews? If so, with whom, on what and will I have an opportunity to see it/them first?
- How long is my contribution likely to be? How long will the finished programme be?
- Where will the recording or programme take place? Will cameras come to my office to pre-record a piece or will I be required to go to the studio?
- What time will it be transmitted? Will it be repeated, if so when?
- Will I have any opportunity to view the programme or my contribution to it prior to transmission, if it is to be pre-recorded?

When you are satisfied with such answers as you can obtain to the above questions and perhaps have taken advice from a media professional, you must then make the crunch decision: should you agree to appear?

You can always say no

It seems to be forgotten by some that they always have the option of saying 'no' when asked to appear on television. There is something inside each of us that is so flattered at being asked to broadcast to millions that, no matter how frightened we are at the prospect and how unprepared we may feel, we still accept and only repent our decision when we reach the studio or are watching the transmission of our performance later.

Although a competent appearance on television can be professionally and commercially very advantageous, an incompetent one can do damage that you may never be able to remedy and may cause permanent injury to your self-esteem.

There are some programmes that seem to have a clear agenda to discomfit as many lawyers as possible, and others where the informal approach and format are such that most who have undergone a legal training will feel totally out of place. It is unwise to agree to appear on such a show unless you are genuinely confident you can deal ably with anything that comes your way and can adjust your personal style to fit the format.

There is a huge difference between appearing on something like *Watchdog* explaining the sale of goods legislation to a sympathetic Nicky Campbell or Kate Sanderson, and appearing on *Kilroy* when the producers have filled the studio with over 100 people who are dissatisfied with the service they received from their divorce lawyers. The former is an opportunity to inform the public and promote the profession, the latter is more likely to be a bloodbath.

Familiarise yourself with the programme

As with radio programmes, it is essential to have at least a working understanding of the programme on which you will be appearing and the audience to whom you will be speaking. Daytime programmes are inevitably largely a mystery to lawyers but they have a style and a devoted audience all their own and often represent valuable opportunities to correct misconceptions about the law and the legal profession, if used wisely.

The proliferation of low-audience but consumer-oriented programmes that are now available via cable and satellite are also probably viewed by few lawyers, but are often the easiest to get on. Again, it is vital to establish the style and culture of the programme before agreeing to appear.

Essential preparation

Skimp this at your peril! Much as with any form of presentation, and as advised in previous chapters, the quality of your television performance will be directly affected by the time and effort you put into preparing for it.

It is often assumed by bright people like lawyers that they can 'busk' their way through interviews simply by answering the questions put to them. But this is simply not an ambitious-enough objective. If you are a novice broadcaster, there will be sufficient unfamiliar things going on, so you cannot afford to be unrehearsed on your messages.

Once you have decided to take part in the programme, work out precisely what you, your firm, your organisation or your client would most like you to get out of this broadcasting opportunity. It used to be commonplace to work out how much, say, five minutes of prime television airtime would cost if it was an advertisement and advise the participant not to squander that value. In a volatile marketplace it is hard to say with accuracy, but you might well find that if you are taking part in a prime time programme on BBC 1 or ITV that you are being given the advertising airtime equivalent of £500,000 or more for every minute you are on screen. This should concentrate your mind on using this opportunity wisely.

Having worked out just what you want to achieve by participating in the programme, jot down the key points you want to get across – never more than three. Come up with a few punchy phrases that convey the meat of these messages. Say them aloud. Are there any words that trip you up? Are there any simpler words you can substitute?

If you are to be one of a group or panel, try to research who your companions will be and what lines they are likely to take on the issue. How can you counter their arguments? What evidence can you summon up to support your viewpoint? Is there any recent research you can quote or authority you can cite? But best of all, is there a case history or human interest story you can refer to, to bring the issue to life for your audience?

Invite colleagues or family or friends to engage you in a debate on the issue playing 'devil's advocates', so you are pressed on the points you intend to make and forced to see if your opinions withstand scrutiny.

Think long and hard and as you get closer to the recording or broadcast date, cut down your material, until it can be got over in a minute or two, no more, as that may be the maximum amount of time you have in which to make your point.

Pre-recorded or live?

Views differ. Some experienced broadcasters always say they prefer prerecorded interviews as they know they will have the opportunity of remedying defects. But I am a staunch advocate of the merits of live television because, unless you are an experienced television performer, you are likely to give your best, most spontaneous and most interesting performance the first time; even if the interview is pre-recorded your first 'take' will almost certainly be your best. The main advantage of pre-recorded items is that real howlers, 'fluffs' (stumbles or mistakes) and 'dries' (grindings to a halt) can, if necessary, be corrected. But with each take you are likely to become more mechanical and 'rehearsed'.

The most common situation is for there to be a fairly lengthy interview from which a few select snippets are edited for inclusion in the final programme. If it is a news programme, the snippet may just be a 'sound bite' of 20 or 30 seconds and it is always worth trying to compress your key message into this length and formulate a punchy sentence or two in readiness.

Increasingly current affairs and news programme-makers put together 'packages' on particular topics. These can include some location filming, some library footage, some graphics showing statistics and several inter-cut interviews. The entire package may run for up to 10 minutes but your contribution may, after editing, be only one or two minutes or even less. It is often difficult to gauge precisely what others will say and how the whole item will be treated once the footage is completed, edited and inserted into the programme. The producer responsible for the item may not be entirely sure what they will use in the final edit until they get to that stage. You can only ask for guidance from the programme-makers and try to ensure that any footage preceding your interview is at least explained to you, if you are not to have the opportunity of viewing it.

Many interviews are now conducted 'as for live', which means that the recording will not be stopped unless something goes disastrously awry and the interview will be timed by the interviewer to run for the required final length. Programmes like *Question Time* are done this way, in the interests of spontaneity.

Handling the pre-recorded interview

For pre-recorded packages there is always the danger that you will allow your guard to slip and will begin to relax as the interview wears on. Experienced interviewers will often spend up to 40 minutes interviewing a subject, knowing that the finished interview will be edited stringently, in the hope that the careful phrases at the start of the interview will become less veiled as the interviewer establishes rapport with the interviewee.

You may find that the same questions that have been asked at the start of the interview, and to which you believe you have provided satisfactory and perhaps guarded answers, are being asked again. If you are genuinely content with the original answers you provided and have nothing further to add, do not be drawn into expanding but politely indicate that you believe you have already dealt with that point and perhaps the interviewer would care to move on. As, however, the style and angle of the interview become clearer to you, you may wish to take the opportunity of replying rather differently to the question and, if at all possible, should indicate that your second answer is, you believe, the more accurate. In general, the shorter the answer to a question, the more likely it is to be used.

If the interview is filmed at your office or somewhere on location, there will only be one camera and once the interview has taken place, with the camera looking at you, you will have to suffer 'the noddies' and reverses. This is when the camera is re-set looking over your shoulder at the interviewer or presenter, who may ask some of the questions again, and will be required to look interested and give encouraging nods and smiles, as if listening, so that appropriate shots can be intercut with your replies. You will also be asked to provide a few yards of footage sitting silently yourself, so that there is scope to edit between questions and answers.

If the interview takes place in an ordinary television studio there will be two, three or four cameras on moveable rostrums, the pictures from which will be relayed to a bank of monitors in the control room or gallery above the studio. The director will be able to select from the range of shots of those taking part in the programme and the vision mixer will cut between them. In the smaller news studios there are usually just two cameras operated remotely by a vision mixer in a control booth. Invariably there are wide angle establishing shots of the couple or the group to set the scene at the start of the programme, sometimes under the titles and introductory music, and then it may well be that there is an opening shot of the presenter, introducing the topic, and the participants. There will then probably be two-shots and single shots of the interviewer and interviewee as appropriate.

Although a red light will appear on the camera whose picture is currently being used, you should make no attempt to watch these lights or 'work' to the respective cameras. Do, however, remember that you may be on screen even though you are not talking, and so avoid grimacing, or reacting in any inappropriate way to what anyone else is saying. Unexpected reactions can entirely alter the way that a participant is perceived by the audience. A standard trick on *Question Time* is to cut to the panel member representing the opposition as they display derision at the utterances of the Cabinet spokesperson, or the audience member who asked the question to signal their dissatisfaction with the response he or she is receiving.

What if I grind to a complete halt on live television?

This is the stuff of which nightmares are made. It is probably second only to drying on the West End stage, but surprisingly rarely happens. Many normally quite reticent people find that under the scrutiny of a television camera they become surprisingly fluent, sometimes even overly loquacious. Provided you are in eye contact with your interviewer, if you are in danger of petering out they will probably throw you a verbal lifeline. It is their job to ensure that the interview continues smoothly, not yours. If you stumble over your words, or do not express yourself as clearly as you wish, simply plough on or correct yourself. The same rules apply as in ordinary conversational speech. If we make a mistake, we correct it and carry on.

Your audience may well not even notice and, working on the premise that like radio, good television is a conversation observed by cameras, it is appropriate for speech patterns to contain the same flaws that ordinary conversational speech contains. Most people, particularly if they are delivering an unappealing message, assume that the audience will be delighted to see them trip. Research has shown that on the whole the audience reaction is one of sympathy and a willingness to forgive.

What shall I wear?

As we all invariably unconsciously, form 80 per cent of our opinions about other people within the first 10 seconds of seeing them, it is unwise to ignore the effect that your personal appearance will have and how this can affect the way your message is received.

You should appreciate that most of the public still believes all lawyers are white, male, middle-aged, middle-class and dress in dark (often striped) suits, with white shirts and club or old school ties. You may conform to this image exactly and may be entirely comfortable with it, and it may be appropriate for the type of programme to which you will be contributing.

Alternatively, if you do not personally fit this stereotype for reasons of race, gender, age, class or style, you may wish to send out a different message by your appearance. It is perfectly possible to be interestingly and fashionably dressed while still retaining the necessary authority and gravitas to reassure your clients. Hundreds of lawyers demonstrate this most ably every day. Although the 'dress down' craze that swept City law firms for a few years seems to be reducing, there is a greater informality in how younger lawyers present themselves and there is usually no need to disguise this when participating in television programmes.

As soon as cameras were allowed into the Palace of Westminster, many MPs and a few peers sought the help of image consultants about their wardrobes, hair and faces. They appreciated that their constituents would be more likely to see them on television than in the constituency and would form opinions about their abilities by what they saw. Emma Nicholson MP ruefully reported that when she returned to her constituency at weekends, her electors often commented favourably on 'that lovely blue suit you wore last week', but when challenged about the content of her speech in the House had no recollection of it whatsoever. Tony Baldry's penchant for striped cricketing blazers attracts more interest than his views. Theresa May's kitten heels will be remembered from her first Tory Conference as Chairman, but I doubt if you can recall what she said.

I was much comforted after my first rather amateur outing on *Question Time* many years ago to receive kind letters from strangers who had found what I said sensible. I know that I talked unfocused rubbish much of the time as terror had turned my brain to blancmange, but I talked my rubbish convincingly in a smart jacket and in a well-presented way.

Advice about men's clothes

Although television technology has advanced extraordinarily in recent years, there are still a few items of clothing that can cause problems for the machinery: houndstooth-type checks, broadly striped suits, shirts and ties can all 'strobe' and distort the picture.

Under some studio lights bright white shirts can cause 'flare' and be distracting. They can also cause the skin tone to look anaemic. For safety, wear plain fabric clothing or suits and jackets with a very small and subtle check, stripe or print with plain pastel-coloured shirts – pale blue, pink or cream work particularly well and are flattering to most skin tones. Whatever you choose to wear, ensure it is spotlessly clean, well pressed and fits properly. Many men find a crisp new shirt gives them confidence in unfamiliar situations.

Pull a chair up in front of a mirror and see that your jacket and shirt do not gape when you are seated as you will be on television. Our body shapes alter dramatically when we sit, and clothes that appear to fit well when we stand (particularly as we instinctively suck in our tummies when we look at ourselves in mirrors) can let us down once we are seated and allow ourselves to relax. Television is always said to add pounds and makes even the very slim look potentially a little overweight. Avoid anything that is too tight or restricting and, if in doubt, err on the side of generous, overlarge clothing, which can give the illusion of slimness.

Personally, I have a penchant for men who wear imaginative, colourful ties and an abhorrence of club ties, which are dull and, to me, seem to signal some exclusive grouping to which the viewer – and most women – can never belong. You should choose whatever you feel best reflects the personality you would like to project, but try to avoid stereotypes.

Men might also consider using bright handkerchiefs in their breast pockets, as so little can be done to make the traditional male suit and shirt interesting to look at when shot from the waist up. They help to break up those expanses of dark suiting which is all that will be on show once the early shots have shown the group in which you are seated. The received wisdom is that a matching tie and handkerchief indicate that the wearer has no imagination or received them as a present from an offspring or spouse. A different but co-ordinating tie and hankie, however, apparently indicate a free-ranging and creative individual!

Always ensure that your socks are long enough and appropriate. A distracting glimpse of pale whiskery flesh between sock and trouser bottom can deflect a viewer's attention and although red socks with dark suits seem currently almost the norm for some iconoclasts, consider whether this is really the image you want to project.

Be aware that flashy watches, cufflinks, bracelets and rings glint under the studio lights and often attract more attention than under natural light. If you are talking about welfare benefit law or the plight of prisoners on remand, you may feel that some restraint in your accessories is called for.

The essence of dressing for television, however, is to ensure that you wear something *appropriate* for the programme, which does not distract from what you are saying or send out a contrary message. If you have been invited to appear on one of the breakfast television programmes and the format of the show is sofa-based with presenters in informal sweaters, then you will probably feel more comfortable (and certainly look it) if you turn up to the studios in a jacket or blazer, with casual trousers and perhaps an open-necked shirt, or even a jumper, rather than a suit. If, however, you are appearing as a legal expert on an investigative programme being transmitted later at night, the presenter will almost certainly be suited and you will choose to be too. When talking to cameras outside court, you will obviously be in court attire, but if an advocate should ensure you have removed both wig and gown.

I recommend that you always ask the researcher, or whoever contacts you from the programme, for guidance on the dress code and, if in any doubt, take an alternative change of clothes with you to the studio. There are few things that get in the way of marshalling your thoughts more than worrying about whether you are going to look out of place.

A valuable tip is to contrive to sit on the tail of your jacket once you are seated, whether in the studio or at your desk. This prevents the collar of your jacket rising up behind your ears, something that seems to plague politicians and trade unionists particularly. If the viewer is worrying about your tailoring, s/he is not listening to what you are saying.

Always ensure your shoes, collar and cuffs are clean and in good condition and polish your shoes beforehand if possible. Although the majority of the interview will be shot from the waist up or closer, establishing shots often show the whole body and some lawyers' footwear leaves a lot to be desired! There are subtler ways to signal that the profession is not as affluent as the public seems to think than displaying scuffed or holey shoes.

Increasingly, television crews come to the contributor and you could easily find that you are to be interviewed in your office, chambers or outside the court. When the coverage relates to a court case it is rarely possible to spend time or energy worrying about your appearance and your responsibility to your client would make this inappropriate in any event. If the crew is coming to your workplace, it is possible to have more control and ensure that a change of jacket and a fresh shirt and tie are always available.

Advice to women

In many ways women have more choice, so it should be easier for us to find something that fits in with the format of the programme on which we are to appear. But there is often a dilemma for the woman lawyer who will want to look every bit as authoritative and knowledgeable as her male colleagues, while presenting herself as interestingly and as attractively as possible.

This can be a problem particularly for the young woman lawyer who is anxious to be taken seriously without adopting a dowdy style. Most women lawyers tend to dress as female versions of the men. Dark suits, light shirts, discreet or no jewellery are the norm and often all this is entirely suitable. But again it is wise to establish the style of the programme and adapt to it. Since the first edition of this book, the ubiquitous trouser suit has become acceptable uniform for all professional women at almost all times. Worn by Cabinet Ministers and Prime Minister's wives – and even once in public by the Queen – it is a comfortable option for which many of us are grateful. But you may want to differentiate your style between something that is right for an informal interview on an afternoon women's programme and something that works for an insert into *News At Ten*. Appropriate garb is also influenced by the area in which you practise; media lawyers tend to be the funkiest, particularly in the shoe and jewellery departments, and those handling commercial property transactions seem to be the most conservative.

The guidelines for women are flexible but it is always worth checking what any female interviewer is likely to be wearing so that you can ensure a similar style yet avoid colour duplications or clashes. I once turned up to do a show in an almost identical pink jacket to the one being worn by Sue Lawley and was grateful I had thought to bring a change of clothes with me. I suspect that pink jackets are also very 'daytime presenter' now and not right for a serious lawyer.

Obvious dangers are too short skirts or skirts that ride up when you sit down (tugging distractedly is almost as irritating to the viewer as unexpected glimpses of thigh); clothes that crease too much; anything that is too tight or constricting or gapes when you move; and, again, patterns that strobe and upset the cameras. Cleavage should be concealed at all times. Strong, clear colours seem to work best as do simple, unfussy styles. Don't rush out and buy a new outfit unless this is a necessary confidence-builder for you. Wear something you are familiar with and comfortable in. Ask your colleagues what they like you in best.

That initial establishing shot of the studio or the group will reveal your legs and shoes. While comfy shoes are great for radio and can warm the voice and relax the mind, *all* of you will be on view, if only momentarily, on television. The colour of your tights, the length of your trousers and the style and condition of your shoes should all be taken into account. Ensure your tights or stockings are intact, unpatterned, non-shiny and of an appropriately neutral colour (a spare pair in the bag is comforting) and again, that your shoes will withstand scrutiny. Very high heels are said to send out a particular signal, but as Margaret Thatcher wore ever higher heels as her term in office drew to an end I am unable to fathom this.

Jewellery should be understated and undistracting. Earrings should not dangle or catch the light and bracelets and necklaces should not chink or jingle. As with the men, be aware that jewellery, whether real or costume, catches the light and looks more obvious on camera. It is impossible to distinguish between costume and valuable jewellery. Otherwise, wear what you feel comfortable in and perhaps you will help change the public's view of lawyers.

There are many books now available offering guidance on one's appearance. Mary Spillane's *Branding Yourself* (2000) provides many answers. I would tend to avoid Trinny and Susannah's offering, as it seems to be more focused on presenting yourself on the social rather than the business circuit.

What about my hair and face?

In the affluent 1980s and 1990s you could reasonably expect the full treatment whenever you were invited to appear on television. A make-up artiste who was also a highly trained hairdresser and beautician would willingly trim and wash your hair free of charge and skilfully provide such make-up as was necessary.

Sadly those days have largely gone and in the austerity 2000s you may well simply be greeted and ushered into the studio without much advance pampering. If the crew turns up at your office or home, it will certainly be without a make-up artiste in tow. It is wise, therefore, to ensure that your hair is regularly trimmed if you are likely to receive media invitations and that you habitually carry a brush and/or comb. If you have fine, flyaway hair, invest in some hairspray – yes, even if you are male, as wispy strands of hair can once again reduce the impact of what you are saying. You may feel foolish carrying and using hairspray, but you will feel sillier when you see yourself with 'mad professor' hair detracting from your carefully reasoned arguments. Whether your hair has a tendency to be greasy or to dandruff, do ensure that it is washed before the programme, even if this means a dip in the hand-basin at work and a surreptitious application of your secretary's hairdryer. If you use it, keep hair gel to a minimum as it becomes more liquid under the lights and you could find yourself looking like a gigolo.

The heat from artificial lights and the nervous tension always tend to make even the most biddable hair limper and less manageable. As a last resort, a small aerosol of dry shampoo is useful. And always check the back of your head with a mirror as that may be seen on any over-the-shoulder shots. Always check your shoulders for spare hairs and dandruff, particularly if wearing a dark jacket.

If you have a fringe, check that it is not obscuring your eyes – if it is, either trim it or sweep it to one side. Check partings are straight and sideburns level, and if not a natural blonde, get your roots done regularly.

Next, though I broach this topic hesitantly, if you are 'folically challenged', can I urge you *not* to drape long strands of surviving hair over the areas from which it has long departed. On camera this looks even sadder than it does in real life. Come to terms with your baldness, and trim off those long strands bravely. And if any of you reading this is wearing a rug, toupé, wig or artificial hair aid – and we all know who you are – don't for one minute believe this will not be detected on television.

Now that you cannot rely on a highly skilled make-up artiste to enhance your appearance, it is worth having a critical look at yourself, preferably on video, and deciding if there is any room for improvement. This is another useful reason for undergoing some media training. Those with high foreheads and receding hairlines invariably become shinier under the hot lights of a studio. This not only reflects unattractively but it makes the poor sufferer appear more ill at ease than in reality they may be. A judicious application of translucent powder (Boots No7 is very good and much favoured by male MPs) will contain this shininess. If a make-up artiste does advance on you with a powder puff, let her do her worst, she knows what she is up to and is there to make you look better, not foolish.

Similarly, most of us, under artificial lights, and particularly in stressful situations, acquire shiny noses that can gleam like beacons on camera. The powder should be applied and repeated, as necessary, until recording or transmission.

Too pallid or too rosy complexions can be magically corrected by the judicious application of concealer. I found it strangely comforting when appearing for the second time on *Question Time* to find myself in Make-Up seated beside Sir Geoffrey Howe while he was being very carefully painted pale green by a make-up artiste, in order to tone down his florid cheeks before we went on air. If you suffer from very red cheeks, colour-correcting foundation and powder are economically available from all chemists.

Those with 'luggage problems' under the eyes can be helped by concealer too. Yves St Laurent's Touche Eclat is in the handbag of every actress over 40. If you look too exhausted on television, people worry about whether you are up to the job!

Even men with the lightest of beards should endeavour to shave just before appearing on television and it is imperative for those with a heavy beard. A 'five o'clock shadow' makes its wearer look slovenly and unreliable and the harsh lights will pick up even the faintest stubble. Similarly, I am frankly surprised in this age of increasing self-awareness and personal grooming how few men seem to bother to prune their eyebrows. The kind that beetle off in all directions or inexorably merge over the bridge of the nose in a monobrow, on camera give their owners a look almost indistinguishable from photofits of known villains – not the right signal for a lawyer to send out. Apply the tweezers (the best are made by Tweezerman) – or get someone close to you to do so – and the transformation to many faces is remarkable. It may even be necessary to apply them to your nostrils and ears to capture any stray whiskers, or to invest in one of the discreet little gadgets for nostril-tidying available from mail order catalogues. Trust me, it is worth it.

All this may seem wholly unnecessary to you, frivolous and superficial. But research has shown clearly that people who appear to neglect their personal appearance are also presumed to neglect other matters of perhaps even greater importance in their lives. Those, of course, who are thought to place too much reliance on appearance are similarly disliked.

Finally, before embarking on any television work it might be timely to check that your teeth are in first-rate shape. Cosmetic dentistry and tooth whitening treatments can transform a face seen in close-up.

Spectacles and contact lenses

Many people wear spectacles or contact lenses and feel vulnerable without them. Some professionals with short sight actually prefer to remove their specs before going on camera, as long as they are not having to use an autocue, as they find it less stressful when the technology and confusion of the studio blurs into soft focus. Others feel they cannot function efficiently without their specs or lenses securely in place.

The shape of spectacles is much more crucial on camera than off, as the entire face may fill the screen and the spectacle frames assume greater importance than usual. Try to check how your specs look on video first. Droop-sided frames often make their wearers look depressed and laconic. Too heavy or prominent dark frames can overwhelm their wearer. Some obscure the eyebrows and do not sit sufficiently high up on the nose, so that the eyes peer through the upper part of the frames instead of being centred. Bifocals look very strange on camera, as do half-moon specs in anything other than a drama production. When people become hot and sticky, as inevitably they will in a studio, their specs can slowly slide down their noses in a most irritating manner. Always check that yours remain in place, no matter how slippery your nose becomes. Regulars on television often have a spare pair of specs specially reserved for television because they sit firmly on the face and allow the eyes to look squarely through the centre of the lenses.

It is also possible to acquire spectacles with special non-reflective glass lenses that reduce glare. Spectacles with tinted lenses are rarely satisfactory on television, giving their wearer a rather untrustworthy air and often obscuring the eyes. Those with photochromatic lenses, which automatically darken as the light increases, are to be avoided at all costs, as they will darken totally in a studio. Although the wearer may be comfortably protected from the harsh lights, the audience will wonder why a lawyer is wearing sunglasses in a studio in winter. It really helps the viewer and interviewer to see the eyes of the person talking to them and anything that makes this difficult should be abandoned. Light, minimalist specs with virtually no frames are ideal as they form the most unobtrusive barrier between your face and the viewer.

If you wear contact lenses, whether hard, soft, gas permeable or coloured, you should experience no difficulties. Most are entirely invisible on camera but you may find that the strong lights cause you to blink more frequently than usual and can dry your eyes, and that lenses make this slightly worse. Eye-drops just before going on air can help. Coloured lenses can be very effective on television if you are vain enough to want to enhance or change your eye colour.

What about make-up?

If you are male, you may be horrified to find a make-up girl applying lipstick to you. This is designed to avoid your lips disappearing into your face on screen and should be tolerated. Women often find that professional make-up artistes use a stronger or darker colour lipstick and eye make-up than they would choose for everyday use, again in order to make the right impact under the strong studio lights.

Women applying their own make-up should guard against bright colours of eyeshadow – blues, purples and green look dreadful on screen, whatever you are wearing, and no matter what colour eyes you have or what make-up you habitually wear. Stick to safe autumnal tones and smudge any eyeliner you use to soften its impact. Lipstick should be a clear strong colour but not too bright, and pearlised lipsticks should be avoided. Apply your lipstick meticulously, with a brush, to ensure that it is absolutely accurate. If you must use a darker foundation than your natural skin tone, ensure that it is carried through to your neck and throat, if visible and does not end abruptly at your jaw-line.

Check your profile in the mirror for any tidemarks or irregularity of colour as this may be the way you are shot for much of the programme. If you like to use blusher, do so with caution as the strength of studio lights or those used by film crews can play strange tricks. If you tend to go pale when frightened, use warm tones of make-up to reduce viewers' anxiety about your health. If in doubt, use less rather than more but go for a slightly more matt, powdered effect than you may normally use, as the lights will make you shine.

What about my nerves?

Everyone, absolutely everyone, finds appearing on television nerve-wracking to a greater or lesser extent. I genuinely believe the old cliché that says that once the nerves disappear you should give up. The most experienced broadcasters often still react like novices in the few seconds before they go on air. As with almost everything, there are tricks and devices to help.

Unlock your voice

Nerves can grip your vocal chords in a vice and cause you to emit only strangulated squeaks instead of your usual firm tones. You can find your voice going up at least an octave, or acquiring a strange dry rasp you have never heard before. Your mouth can suddenly seem devoid of any saliva and you absolutely know that you will not be able to make a sound; or your mouth may seem worryingly full of saliva and you know you will have to swallow repeatedly if you are to get anything audible out or risk drowning. You may find yourself 'erring' and 'umming' much more than usual.

Breathing exercises can help and, however rushed you are, there is always time for a few.

Practise inhaling a big breath through your mouth, holding it for a slow, steady count of five and then exhaling gently through the nose. Do this three times. It will lower your heart rate and blood pressure and bring badly needed oxygen into your system. If the opportunity arises, blow hard a few times as if at an imaginary cobweb in a far distant corner. Again, this will help get your body working for you rather than against you.

Some tongue-twisters to get your mouth working

To exercise, repeat each phrase about three times, beginning with a whisper and increasing the volume through the second and third repeats. Do these exercises occasionally in order to increase the agility of the articulatory organs. Keep the words clear and sharp, avoiding both over-articulation and under-articulation when the words slide together.

- 'Twist the twine tightly round the tree trunks.'
- 'Did Dora dare to deceive David deliberately.'
- 'Kate Cooney carefully closed the kitchen cupboards.'
- 'Gregory Gartside gained good gradings in English grammar.'

- 'Naughty Nora has no nice neighbours.'
- 'Little Larry Lester lolled lazily on the li-lo.'
- 'Rosemary Wright was richly dressed in red corduroy.'
- 'Truly rural.'
- 'Peggy Babcock.'
- 'Red leather, yellow leather, red lorry, yellow lorry.'
- 'Unique New York, New York unique.'
- 'Fresh fried fish.'
- 'A cracked cricket critic.'
- 'Mixed biscuits.'
- 'Try tying the twine round the three tree twigs.'
- 'The seething sea ceaseth and thus sufficeth us.'
- 'Imagine an imaginary menagerie.'

Can you manage them all?

Cure those twitches

Nerves often manifest themselves in bodily twitches and spasms of which we were previously quite unaware. Hands clench and unclench, fingers drum on tabletops, feet tap spasmodically, twitches appear in our cheeks, we grind our teeth or clench our jaws unknowingly and we even develop stammers we never had before.

These are all our natural responses to fear – flight or fight. Constructive use of this surplus energy can ensure that these twitches are controlled and do not embarrass us.

First, on your way to the studio or while you are awaiting the crew, tense every single one of your muscles as tightly as you can. Clench your fists, screw up your face, clamp your jaw, curl your toes, tighten your buttocks (no one will know). Hold everything as tightly in check as possible for a slow count of five and then relax everything totally. Repeat this three times and you will be able to feel its beneficial effects. There will be a discernible lightening sensation and internal flutterings will be calmed. While listening to the studio countdown before you go on air, repeat the process with a couple of deep breaths and it will help to steady you. By burning off this surplus energy you will be able to appear steady and composed.

Be aware, however, that the ticks and twitches can return. So sit squarely and steadily in your seat, bottom well back and spine straight. If it is a swivel chair – don't. Adopt a posture that is relaxed and comfortable for you to maintain for at least 10 minutes, but does not look slovenly. If you are near a desk or table, it may be convenient to rest one arm on its top to anchor you.

Avoid folded arms, which look defensive. If you habitually use your hands when talking to illustrate points, feel free to do this – it looks natural and more animated than a static interviewee, but try to avoid waving too demonstratively in front of your face, which could cause problems for the camera crew and director.

Also try shaking your hands and arms by your sides to relax them before you start the interview as it ensures that there is adequate blood flow. You may feel foolish while you do all this – try to remember that all great actors go through a similar routine, often complete with exercises done lying on the floor, before attempting any performance. The buttock-clenching is particularly helpful as this can be done almost anywhere at any time and no one but you will know that you are doing it. It genuinely does burn off surplus energy discreetly.

Have water to hand – even if you do not use it it is reassuring to know it is there, and if you feel you need it, ensure that you have had a short drink of water before going on air.

Avoid tea, coffee and at all costs, alcohol. Their effects are respectively dehydrating and disastrous. For the avoidance of doubt, never ever drink any alcohol before broadcasting, even if the programme, such as *Question Time* and others, offers you generous hospitality beforehand. If you do, you will regret it.

When should I get to the studio?

Try to allow just enough time to locate the lavatory and familiarise yourself generally with the feel of the place. I have a tendency to be early for everything as I allow for all possible delaying contingencies and they rarely all occur. This is unhelpful, as you can then find yourself with too much time to kill, during which the nervous tension rises. The programme-makers will tell you when they want you to be there and you should aim for just 15 minutes earlier.

The 'hostility suite'

One of the few advantages of the increasing poverty of programme-makers is that the hospitality suite or Green Room is becoming a rarity. It used to be commonplace to be invited to turn up at the studios an hour or two before you were required to take part in the programme, so that you could meet the other participants informally and 'have a few drinks'. The drinks cupboards were well stocked, the nibbles enticing, the production personnel charming and hospitable, but the outcome of the hour in the Green Room could be lethal.

The effects of alcohol are visible to observers. It causes the eyes slightly to glaze, the colour to heighten, the speech to be slightly impaired and the thought processes to slow. Even one or two glasses, which the consumer feels have made no impact apart from relaxing him or her slightly, can seriously damage their performance.

If you are fortunate enough to encounter a programme like the showbiz chat shows where hospitality is still offered, stick to still mineral water or fruit juice until after the show, when you can do as you please.

A very few programmes make drinks available for the participants during the actual show. *After Dark*, which is returning to the airwaves, acquired some notoriety when its relaxed, post-dinner party, late-night formula gave rise to several of its guests becoming progressively more boorish as the programme wore on through the early hours. The late Oliver Reed's rendition of 'Wild One' on *Parkinson*, with beer mug in hand, has gone down in television history.

The secondary (or perhaps primary) purpose of the 'Hostility Suite' was – and sometimes still is – to create a valuable opportunity to relax participants so that the team could obtain additional information about the interviewees and possibly expose gaps in their armour. Innumerable stories are told by television professionals about indiscretions revealed in the Green Room that could subsequently be used to maximum effect during the programme. So, don't let your guard drop, no matter how beguiling your hosts and don't say anything to any member of the production team that you are not prepared to say to the interviewer or presenter or have repeated on air.

Microphones are there to help

In the television studio your voice will be picked up by a tie or lapel microphone, a stand mike or a boom mike, or a combination of these. If it is a boom then you have no worries as this hangs over your head and is controlled by an operator on a special motorised trolley and it will be adjusted as necessary to pick up your voice well. A tie mike, clipped near the knot of your tie, or on the neck of your dress or jacket lapel, is vulnerable to fingering – so leave it and your clothing strictly alone during the interview or the distortion will reverberate in the viewers' ears. For this reason shirts, blouses, jackets and ties made of stiff, shiny fabrics should be avoided as they can cause crackle on the mikes. A sound engineer will fit your tie mike when you are seated. Don't forget to remove your mike before you walk away from your seat once the interview is over, or you will be trailing an embarrassing umbilical cord, which could trip you up. To avoid trailing wires you may be given a battery pack, which is a small transistorised unit that usually clips to the back of your skirt or trousers and is linked to the mike. You are then free to move about but will still be amplified. The only danger with these is that they are easy to forget and while on will, of course, relay any comments you make to the studio gallery and even to the entire studio. There are innumerable tales of entire studio audiences being treated to the sound effects of a broadcaster's visit to the lavatory.

A stand or table mike should present no problems, as long as you avoid hitting it with your hands or kicking it when crossing or moving your legs. Any direct contact with a microphone produces a deafening noise for the sound technicians, and more importantly for the viewers and interrupts their concentration on your message.

If you are to walk on to present a programme, or move among an invited audience, you may be provided with a hand mike. These used to be attached to a long cable but are now usually battery operated. The technicians will give you guidance about the distance you should hold this from your mouth for maximum effect, but it is always further away than you think.

All microphones are designed to amplify the normal speaking voice, so don't adopt a special voice or try to 'project' or 'throw' your voice, no matter how large the studio is or how far away any other participants or audience have been positioned. Speak as you would speak in a normal conversational tone and the technicians will do all that is necessary to ensure that your voice is clearly heard.

Floor manager

The floor manager (FM) is the harrassed creature clutching a clipboard, with an earpiece jammed in one ear (like a hearing aid), a battery pack clipped to their belt, apparently talking loudly and often somewhat aggressively to themselves. At moments of extreme stress they seem to have some kind of seizure during which they make wild and inexplicable gestures.

The FM is in continuous contact with the director in the control booth or 'gallery', usually one floor above and overlooking the studio, and is there to ensure that his or her directions are communicated to the participants in the programme. The interviewer or presenter may also be wearing an earpiece and receiving the same talkback, or the director may have an additional facility to speak directly to the presenter during the interview. This is the way that additional questions are suggested or timings and running orders revised. The gestures are an international code telling programme presenters when to start speaking, how much longer they have left for their interview and when to stop. Ignore them.

What the studio looks like

It will almost certainly be a disappointment. It will be grey and scruffy, and the set, which may look quite glamorous on screen when you watched the programme at home, is revealed to be just a couple of hard-wood flats, propped up with metal stage weights. There will be cables everywhere, hundreds of lights suspended from the ceiling, strange gantries and catwalks and a considerable number of people who seem to have no clear function but who are saying and doing things that seem a complete mystery to you. Don't panic.

On air

Once you are in your seat in the studio, you will almost immediately see a television monitor positioned to be in the presenter's eyeline. Others may be dotted round the studio floor or suspended from the ceiling. Avoid looking at any of these monitors as it will undoubtedly distract you when your own image appears on them. Shifty sideways glances at your picture are destructive to an impressive performance and people have been known to dry up completely as they watch their own performance live. At best the viewer does not know what you are looking at and may conclude that for some reason you are unwilling to look the interviewer in the eye.

Equally, don't look directly into any of the cameras, and, as mentioned earlier, certainly don't try to 'work to the cameras' by turning to face the ones that have red lights on them. The director has carefully chosen camera angles, so let the cameras look at you. You should simply look at the interviewer and nowhere else. A good interview, remember, is an interesting conversation that is eavesdropped by cameras and microphones. If you are involved in an audience discussion, fielding questions from others, turn to address whoever is speaking to you as you would in real life and allow the cameras to accommodate this.

Maintaining eye contact with your interviewer and, if appropriate, others on the programme as you share the discussion, not only helps to create the impression of a conversation rather than a contest, but also enables the professional broadcaster to gauge your reactions more readily.

If you are coming to the end of a point you want to make, are desperate to intervene in a debate and make your contribution, are running out of things to say, have understood the point someone else is making, or are in danger of drying up altogether, this will all be signalled by your eyes before it is shown by your mouth. If you are looking directly at the interviewer it will make it easier for him or her to read these messages and react accordingly. It will also help you to achieve a more natural, conversational style. If you are talking straight ahead or, worse, to a camera, you will, quite subconsciously, adopt a broadcasting manner.

As with radio, aim for a friendly and relaxed approach. Establish whether first names or surnames are more appropriate but, whichever you choose, don't overuse. Smile in an approachable fashion at the start of the interview or when you are introduced (the camera may be on you even though the interviewer is speaking) and always ensure that you smile graciously at the end of the interview, no matter how challenging, unless it would be entirely inappropriate to do so.

Using notes on television

This should if at all possible be avoided. If you must use notes to refresh your memory about facts or figures, do so openly not furtively. But bear in mind that the use of notes can often be interpreted by your audience as a lack of knowledge of your subject. Don't under any circumstances arrive at an interview with a speech that is written out or previously learnt, or with examples of the questions you are prepared to answer. It simply will not work. Such an approach only clogs the mind, makes you less flexible and adds the 'will I remember it?' factor to nerves that are already likely to be quite tense.

It was interesting to observe on the few occasions when I took part in *Question Time* and similar current affairs programmes, that the Cabinet Ministers and senior MPs would all turn up with tidy ring-binders carefully stuffed with model answers to all the questions their officials and advisers had thought might come up. As if cramming for an exam, the poor creatures would thumb feverishly through the pages before they went into the studio, and then carry the file in, as if it were a safety blanket, only to be told to leave it unopened once we were recording. (In case you were wondering, you never have any idea what the questions are going to be until they emerge from the mouths of the questioners.)

Using pictorial material when on television

If you have photographs, captions, diagrams or statistical charts that you really believe will help illustrate the points you want to make, ensure that these are shown to the researcher or producer as early as possible, ideally before you get to the studio. They may need mounting, or loading on a computer or adjustment to be usable and producing them at the last moment will almost certainly mean they cannot be used.

During the interview

Try to relax. I know that all guidance about anything difficult resorts to this platitude. But unlike other activities, tension shows on camera and can get between you and those with whom you are communicating. Try to find a position that is comfortable but where you feel 'anchored' and secure.

If you habitually cross your legs, do so if space will permit, but watch that gap between sock and trouser and don't risk kicking the microphone.

If you want to use a table or desk to support an elbow, arrange yourself accordingly, but don't prop your head on your hands. Don't grip the arm of your chair till your knuckles whiten. Don't swivel or lean relentlessly in and out of shot. Try not to lean too far forward or backwards in your seat, no matter how heated the debate becomes, though some natural movement is fine and can be accommodated by the technicians. Whatever you do, don't bang the table, desk or microphone to emphasise a point, however sorely tempted you may be.

As a small degree of movement can be easily coped with by the technicians, remember that to show your passion and engagement with a point or issue, it helps if you move forward towards the interviewer or questioner. To show your scepticism or lack of conviction on a point, leaning backwards slightly your body language will reinforce your words.

During the interview, really try to settle into it and remind yourself that this is just one of many thousands of conversations you have had this month. Relaxing is hard in unfamiliar surroundings, in the knowledge that you are being questioned in front of up to 14 million people and certainly in front of your colleagues, many of whom will be watching and who may be your harshest critics.

But if you have done your preparation thoroughly and followed these hints, you will cope. You are certainly not going to be put down by somebody who has perhaps never heard of your subject until today, and provided you answer in an open, friendly manner the viewers will welcome you into their homes.

Once the interview is over, don't, whatever you do, breathe, however quietly 'Thank God that's over' or somesuch, as it may be picked up and transmitted. It could have the desired effect of ending your broadcasting career, but it will certainly expose you as a rank amateur and make you feel very foolish. Similarly, don't leap out of your seat and head for the exit until you have been detached from your microphone.

Demystify your language

Most lawyers, entirely unconsciously, use complex language and sentence structures that can be alienating and intimidating to a lay audience. On radio and television and when speaking to a journalist it is important to remember that those listening to you are rarely lawyers and it is most important of all to be understandable. Simplifying your language will help.

If you must use technical phrases, always try to explain them. Guard against legalese and the use of words such as:

- 'clients': use 'people';
- 'litigation': use 'court cases';
- 'judiciary': use 'judges';

- 'conveyancing': use 'the legal side of buying and selling your home';
- 'administration of estates': use 'putting someone's affairs in order after they die'.

If you have to use acronyms, translate them. The 'RCJ' means the Royal Courts of Justice to every central London litigator, but nothing to any member of the public apart from the perpetual litigant.

If you find you have lapsed into Latin, you are in deep trouble. There is no legal Latin that is not capable of translation into plain English. Some of it may seem longer and less elegant but if you really want your audience to understand what you are saying it is worth striving to use plain everyday English all the time. It will help in your daily contact with your clients too.

Can I endorse the Law Society's recommendation that you should check out the excellent and very comprehensive *A to Z Guide to Legal Phrases*, which can be found on the Plain English Campaign's website (**www.plainenglish.co.uk/legalaz.html**)? It translates literally hundreds of complex legal words and phrases into everyday language. It is also strongly recommended by the Law Society's new Client Charter.

Evaluating your performance

Whenever you receive the opportunity to appear on radio or television ensure that someone records that interview for you and make sure that you listen, carefully and preferably alone, to the interview afterwards. If you have objective colleagues whose judgement you can trust (as opposed to those who are fond of you but who may be less analytical) invite their feedback. It is really only by listening and watching yourself that you can learn. It may well be painful and difficult, but it is still the best way to improve your performance.

Discussion and panel programmes

These are rather different from one-to-one interviews, but most of the same rules and advice apply. The main difficulty for novice broadcasters participating for the first few times in a discussion with others in a panel format is ensuring that they claim their rightful share of the airtime.

We have all watched the political dogfight programmes and perhaps been wearied by the way that the two main opposing participants talked over each other, leant across each other, interrupted, heckled and disrupted. It is all too easy to be marginalised off the screen if we behave in our instinctive well-mannered way. Be assertive, not aggressive and if you feel that you have been given insufficient opportunity to put your case, say so quietly but firmly. Try to resist the temptation to score cheap points unless you feel braced to deal with the ire that may descend on you from your rival.

Many verbal devices are helpful, on television and radio, to draw the debate away from blind alleys. You can gently say, 'But, Mr Dimbleby, I suspect that what our viewers are more concerned about is . . .' or 'But surely the really important point for the audience here is . . .'. This is where lawyers excel. Our minds are trained into these tortuous hoops and once your confidence comes with practice, you will find dozens of ways of ensuring that your points are made. Watch out for politicians, though, who are rigorously trained and extremely well briefed. They often even learn how to lean over in order to obstruct the camera's view of their 'opponent'.

When there is an audience

This adds a quite different dimension and it is often hard to know whether to perform to the interviewer, to the audience or to the camera. Behave as normally as possible and, as you would in an ordinary group situation, speak directly to whoever is speaking to you or leading the discussion. Whatever the set-up, there will always be at least one professional presenter there to keep control. If you establish a comfortable rapport with the audience and even, perhaps, prompt them to applaud you at some point, this will give you enormous confidence and help the rest of your performance.

If you have been invited to participate in some kind of show with an audience, always try to establish just how the programme-makers select their audience. Some, for example *Question Time, V Graham Norton, Kilroy* and others are picked with care to provide a representative cross-section of the population or a group with specific interests and proclivities. Others simply come on a first-come, first-served basis by applying to a central ticket unit. For lively chat shows, the audience is often specifically selected with great care to contain only people with a vested interest in the topic under discussion. Usually, they have been screened for fluency beforehand and are expected to contribute or arrive primed to make a particular point. Some programmes particularly like audience members who can be relied upon to rant or weep. It is uncomfortable to be expected to confront an audience of disaffected people with a grudge about the legal profession or a legal issue, and you should be very wary of accepting such an invitation without some prior experience. It is regularly said that no one is invited on to *Newsnight* so that 'Paxo' can congratulate them.

If in doubt about any of these judgement calls, ring a media professional. Those in the business are always happy to give a few minutes of our time to advise and most of us know the benefits and bear-traps of participating in certain programmes.

When the cameras come to you

Frequently, to contain cost and give variety to the picture, programme-makers will choose to interview lawyers in their offices, chambers or outside courts.

Remember, it is legally permissible to film anything visible from a public highway, so the outside of your offices or chambers can be filmed from the pavement without your consent. This may remind you just to check how your office looks to a stranger from the other side of the road. Is that sign in need of repainting? Do those venetian blinds need replacing? Isn't it time that dead spider plant was replaced with a nice orchid or some fresh flowers? And are all those posters and stickers both up to date and relevant?

This apart, when the camera comes to you, you have slightly more control of events than when the interview takes place on alien territory. Most television people always seem to elect to interview lawyers in front of copies of law reports in a room that looks like an eighteenth-century representation of a lawyer's office or a law library. Your office may look like this and you may be happy to have it portrayed in this way. There are certainly many firms where little has changed in 20 years, apart from the more sophisticated technology used by their support staff.

If, however, you are striving to present a modern image, with information technology of the latest kind and best practice management standards and systems, you may prefer to ensure that a different story is told when your work environment is shown. Be aware and suggest, tactfully and firmly, where you think the interview would be best conducted. They may not always listen, but it is well worth a try, particularly if you can explain that their choice might well have extraneous noise and people passing through. Ideally offer a choice of two or three possible set-ups so that the director or producer can choose. Bear in mind the need for sufficient space to accommodate one or two lights, a cameraman with tripod and camera, a sound recordist, two chairs and an interviewer at the very least.

Try to show any aspects of your firm that distinguish it from others. Lovells' new offices in Holborn have 'client hosts and hostesses'. These are people with air cabin training and experience who are there exclusively to ensure that clients are well looked after when they visit the firm. In other firms, like Withers, the central atrium is filled with a modern café – like an ad agency – and these places are more like modern clubs than law offices. Some smaller family law firms always have toys in the reception area to amuse clients' children while the parent is consulting a solicitor. Think carefully and project the image you want.

If the interview is to take place at your desk, check that it and the surrounding area are as you would wish others to see them. I have noticed a tendency for the mountains of untidy files on lawyers' desks to vanish suspiciously when they are filmed these days, but instead there is an equally unconvincing totally empty desk. I suspect the files are all piled round the interviewee's feet while they believe they have presented a tidy and methodical image. In fact, I find myself wondering why, if they are expert enough to be interviewed, they haven't any work to do.

So, if necessary, cheat and 'dress the set' to make your work environment look as it ideally should, with some tidy files and neat reference materials and the appropriate tools of your trade if you use computers, calculators and time-recording light pens. Avoid out-of-date publications being visible.

Remember that most of the time the camera will be looking directly at you and the area of wall immediately behind you. Early on in my ill-fated political career I was interviewed at home. At the time I chaired a national organisation that campaigned to bring more women into politics and public life. In this particular interview I was at pains to distance myself from the strident feminism of which I had been accused. The row of exclusively feminist titles on the bookshelf behind me entirely undermined this stance, and was only noticed by me when the programme went out. You would think I had learnt my lesson, but years later, when at the Law Society, I gave a rather difficult interview on solicitors' charges to an investigative programme. My valiant efforts to defend my profession were somewhat discredited when the camera picked up a 'Thatcher card' a friend had sent me pinned on the wall behind my desk saying, 'In the event of my being involved in an accident, please ensure that Mrs Thatcher doesn't visit me in hospital'!

The snatched interview

As cameras are now so portable and news so much more immediate, we see each day more interviews that have been 'snatched' without any prior arrangement.

These happen on the court steps, as individuals emerge from a crucial meeting, outside clients' homes or lawyers' homes and offices. While it is reasonably easy to assess which cases and events are likely to have media attention, it is impossible always to know whether there will be a camera there or not. It is hard to prevent, though, since, as mentioned above, it is permissible to film from the public highway, as long as this does not cause an obstruction.

My advice, somewhat predictably, is to be prepared just in case. There are few things more unsettling than emerging from a courtroom with your client, with your thoughts in turmoil trying to formulate appropriate things to say to them, to be confronted by an abrasive journalist with a hand-held camera and a request for an instant reaction.

'No comment' simply will not do unless there are legal reasons preventing you from saying anything. A very short simple sentence will often suffice. 'My client is understandably very disappointed and I am sure you will allow her to return to her home without any more stress' is a good technique. Or, if you are prepared to provide an interview, but at a later time when you have collected your thoughts, then say, 'I'm sorry, ladies and gentlemen, I haven't had an opportunity to discuss this properly with my client, but if you like to come to . . . at . . . I'll then be able to help you.' On the whole most clients are not equipped to deal ably with media interviews immediately after court hearings or momentous meetings and should be protected from having to do so.

The counsel of perfection is to have thought carefully of the two or more likely outcomes of the case or the meeting, whether it goes for you or against you, and to have formulated alternative responses, depending on the result – the 'win or lose statements'. These should be only a few sentences long and, ideally, committed to paper. If you have time, it is always appreciated by the media if you have spare copies available for those unable to take down your statement. If you find yourself reading a prepared statement on your client's behalf to the assembled press on the court steps, hold the notes up, read the statement slowly and calmly, keep your head up and try to ensure that more than just the top of your head is visible to any cameras.

It is crucial to ensure a few things with these court steps' statements:

- Start preparing win and lose statements early and have them ready for the first day of the hearing, just in case the hearing collapses or a verdict is given earlier than anticipated.
- Arrange for someone back at your office, or for a consultant, to support you in case the statement needs to go out to the newswires or newspapers quickly, while you are still at court.
- If the client feels strong enough, it is always preferable for them to make their own statement. Sally Clark, with quite extraordinary courage and dignity, read her own statement after her successful appeal. Her husband, Steve had his arm round her while she did it and I stood by her side, but it was her statement and so very much better that she should make it, not me.
- Always make the statement as if from the client: it is their case and their statement, not yours. So it could start, 'Mr James would like to say. . .'.
- Always check that your client is comfortable with every single word you intend to say on their behalf. When the statement is controversial I have sometimes asked the client to sign a copy of it to provide me with protection, but this is rare.
- If counsel is advising or advocating the case, ensure that they are also happy with the proposed form of words and specifically that they do not jeopardise any subsequent appeal.

- If you want your statement to receive the widest coverage, as well as uttering it outside the court, e-mail a copy of it to the newswires (see earlier) and have spare copies available to hand out, put in the High Court Press room or fax to the media who were not at court.

Down-the-line interviews

Sometimes, having agreed to give a television interview, you will find you are expected to do so from a small scruffy room, with an earpiece jammed in one ear, a camera pointing straight at you and just an uninterested technician nearby. No interviewer, no audience. Just you.

These interviews in small remote studios are often the hardest to bring to life as there is no one to gauge a response from, no dynamics or sense of the mood of the interviewer apart from their voice in your ear.

Always look right through the camera lens, if necessary imagining yourself addressing a broadly sympathetic and interested person in your circle of friends, to soften your expression – which is probably initially one of discomfiture, if not fear.

Put the earpiece (or ask the technician to put the earpiece) in whichever ear you instinctively use when using a telephone. Check it is in securely and is as comfortable as it can be. Radio studios usually use 'cans' – large, padded earphones that sit outside your ears with a band across the top of your head. Down-the-line interviews and others tend to use a single earpiece, like a hearing aid either straight in the ear, or with a plastic piece round the back of the ear to keep it in place.

Speak as if in a conversation – the technicians will adjust the volume level as necessary.

The aim of the game

Your objective when participating in any television programme should be to allow your real self to show. Become familiar with your own personal strengths and weaknesses, play to one and minimise the other. If you have a nice dry wit, use it and allow a smile to show as frequently as feels right. If you have a rather formal, crusty exterior, practise loosening up a little and attempt to soften your style. It is hard to learn to be yourself in such artificial and potentially alarming situations, but the more naturally you can behave, the more convincing your performance will be and the more readily your audience will absorb what you are saying.

The more you do, the better you will become, and the more your confidence builds, the more your enjoyment will be contagious.

7

Media relations for marketing

This chapter aims to help you understand the role of media relations in the marketing mix. It is targeted primarily at 'marketing professionals' – all those from a marketing or media relations background – and 'the marketing amateurs' – those who are legally qualified but now tasked by their firm, chambers or colleagues with marketing responsibilities.

Marketing principles

Whenever professional marketing consultants start defining what are the essentials for effective marketing, they seem to fall back on the four (or even the seven) 'Ps':

- price;
- promotion;
- product;
- place;

and

- people management;
- processes;
- physical evidence.

This book is really only interested in the second, 'promotion' – but I suspect I should just counsel that without the others, it is unlikely to succeed.

Whether your firm is opening a new office in the regions, looking to expand an existing office or impress a merger partner, or is just aiming to attract new recruits or clients, positive media coverage is an invaluable addition to your strategic business development arsenal. The media provide the most effective ways to bring your practice to the attention of new clients, bolster its value in the eyes of existing clients, interest laterals in joining your firm, increase internal morale and encourage new or existing referral sources.

That said, those used to working with American journalists and others abroad, like Richard Levick, are clear that British journalists are the hardest in the world to incorporate safely into a marketing strategy. They are famous for their determined independence, their fast-moving investigations, their imperviousness to overtures of mutual back-scratching, and are ruthlessly competitive with their rival publications.

In the United Kingdom, legal journalists focus much more on law firm mergers, personnel movements and gossip than American journalists do. Many are under pressure from their publications to dig up information about firms that the firms in question would greatly prefer them not to find. The reduced loyalty within many firms, with movement from firm to firm throughout a legal career now much more common, means that journalists can exploit the gossipy leakiness of firms to their distinct advantage.

Some UK-based legal journalists have the power to build individual lawyers up to 'guru' status and also the ruthlessness to tear them down again at the first hint of vulnerability. There is something quite bizarre about journalists in their 20s causing panic in senior lawyers in their 50s, earning 20 times the amount the journalist is earning, when the lawyer realises the journalist has hold of a story the lawyer hoped would never see the light of day. While journalists are delighted to enjoy the lavish hospitality of the lawyers and their firms, and can party to Olympic standards, no matter how splendid the feast or numerous the drinks, very few UK legal journalists will produce a feature story about how strong your firm is nationally, or how cutting edge your medical negligence practice is, in return for your generosity to them.

Many of the legal journalists working in the United Kingdom today have been reporting legal matters for a decade or two, and their research skills have improved enormously over these years. To use the media to market your practice requires a mix, says Levick, of honesty, openness, wariness and an understanding of the rules that govern the media playing field (see Chapters 2, 5 and 6 for guidance).

Guidance from professional bodies

Since the relaxation of rules relating to advertising by law firms, almost anything is allowed by the Law Society, provided it complies with the reasonable requirements of good taste – often a subjective matter.

Henri Brandman's controversial posters inviting unhappy husbands to consult him and 'Ditch the bitch', though deemed acceptable by the Society, horrified some, not least the Solicitors' Family Law Association which encourages a non-aggressive approach to the practice of divorce law. He reported smugly, however, that the media fuss the posters caused produced a considerable number of new clients for his divorce practice, and as he is now described in legal journals as 'celebrity lawyer', he is presumably entirely satisfied with the result achieved. He recognised that the shock value of the ad copy, together with his availability for interviews and his unrepentant stance, made his bucks go a great deal further than anticipated.

Solicitors and those marketing their firms are advised to familiarise themselves with the relevant sections of the Solicitors' Practice Rules 1990, Rule 2, which relates to publicity. This is available on the Law Society's website (**www.lawsociety.org.uk**) and is updated from time to time, so is worth checking regularly.

Consider, for example, a minor, but important point, which several firms seem not yet to have picked up: the transitional provision allowing private practitioners in England and Wales to postpone putting 'regulated by the Law Society' on certain items of stationery expired on 31 December 2002. This statement must now appear not just on all letterheads but on fax headers, press release sheets and the like to comply with the Publicity Code 2001.

The Code not only sets out the professional obligations with which all marketing activities must comply, but covers the following specific topics:

(a)   misleading or inaccurate publicity;
(b)   clarity as to changes;
(c)   nature of firm;
(d)   unsolicited visits or telephone calls;
(e)   addresses to the court;
(f)   international aspects of publicity;
(g)   practitioner's responsibility for publicity; and
(h)   application.

It also provides detailed guidance on the vexed issues of introductions. See Appendix 1 for the code.

The Bar Council has produced its excellent *Practice Management for the Bar* guidance, section 2 of which covers 'Strategy and Marketing', with the subtitle 'Recommended Standards and Implementation Advice'.

The document should be in every set of chambers, and as more and more sets are appointing either chambers directors and managers with marketing in their job specifications, or are using external advisers to help market their barristers' services, it is unsurprising that this document is a great deal more comprehensive and sophisticated than when the first edition of this book appeared in 1994.

The topics covered include:

- creating a strategic business plan;
- producing a marketing plan;
- an explanation of professional services marketing;
- guidance on marketing materials;
- advice on marketing activities such as seminars, client entertainment;

- a section on press relations and advertising;
- information about chambers' websites;
- a model conditional fee agreement;
- questionnaires to be used to assist the planning process;
- topic guides for client satisfaction;
- a checklist with which to plan a client seminar.

Some pragmatic gems to give the flavour include:

The legal profession as a whole is currently subject to such extensive changes that a five-year plan may well be over-ambitious. If it is impossible to antici-pate the shape of the profession in five years' time, it follows that a plan will be of limited use in setting out anticipated actions. A three-year plan can strike the right balance of being sufficiently forward-looking, yet limited to a practical timescale. It is a good idea to have a detailed plan for the coming year and less detailed for the following two.

or

It is obvious, but worth stressing, that different skills and different styles are required in writing promotional literature compared with drafting legal documents.

or

The simple distinction [between press relations and advertising] is between what chambers pay for and have control over and editorial comment, which can be more persuasive but less reliable. It is worth remembering that jour-nalists are interested in stories and not simply information, such as changes in chambers' addresses.

I commend it highly as a practical, realistic document, written by pro-fessional marketers with a real understanding of the constraints that often put a brake on their work in the traditional environment of chambers.

Have a strategy

'Strategy' is an overused word, and often taken as an excuse to write wordy papers rather than get on and do something. But without a plan and a coherent approach, most marketing media relations will be a conspicuous waste of time, paper, electricity and energy. Any marketing activity should always be part of an agreed approach designed to achieve specific business objectives. Otherwise, it is simply about flattering egos and attracting attention and may not be a sensible use of resources.

Understanding the role of media relations in the marketing mix

Be aware of the tensions that exist between the two professions, lawyers and marketers.

First golden rule

Manage the expectations of your partners and fee-earners; make sure they understand what is realistically achievable in media relations. All in the firm will hopefully believe it is an excellent firm. It takes a great deal of work by everyone and hard facts to demonstrate this to the outside world.

Second golden rule

All media relations should be part of a planned approach to the marketing and business development strategy of your firm or chambers, or your client's business.

Harsh truths

1. However well your marketing media relations go and however much coverage you achieve, your paymasters – the lawyers – will be dissatisfied and will believe that you could do more.
2. Most lawyers, in their innermost hearts, believe that if only there were enough hours in the day, they could write advertising copy, produce articles, draft marketing strategies, conduct media interviews, schmooze journalists, design brochures, buy media space and time, organise events and commission print and photography as well, if not better, than any marketing or PR person. This gives them the right to challenge and criticise others' efforts in a way that few other professionals ever will. Never forget, either, that the structure of equity partnerships means that the partners all jointly own the firm and therefore have the right to a say in everything that affects it, unless they devise a more workable way of managing themselves.
3. Most journalists think most marketing and PR people are rubbish – unless the marketing people can repeatedly prove to the contrary. The journalists will always prefer to talk to the people in the front line, (i.e. the lawyers), not those in the press or marketing office or in the consultancy. Sadly, many PR and marketing people do not know what they are talking about, substituting process and contacts for careful thought. And many lawyers, while hankering for profile, prefer to clock up the chargeable hours rather than invest time in talking to journalists.

4.   Most lawyers believe that they are much cleverer than most journalists – this is not always true.
5.   Most fee-earners and too many marketers appear to think that a flurry of media attention will have a tangible impact on their business. It will not: building the profile of a practice or an individual takes time, often years, never days. The turnover in marketing teams can often be attributed to the disappointment on the part of the firm or chambers in what they see as inadequate results in a reasonable timescale – or the marketing people just get weary pushing water up a hill while wearing roller skates in the rain. Often the perpetual change of approach and personnel explains the limited effectiveness of media activity. Ask any of those handling media relations for the 'Magic Circle' firms and they will tell you that several concentrated years of effort are required to heighten the awareness of the firm and its particular expertise.

So, if you are a marketing professional, learn that you will never receive the plaudits from your paymasters for which you hanker and that you must accept that many journalists will want to talk to the experts, your qualified colleagues or your bosses, not you. Recognise that you will rarely know as much as they do on the topics, and your primary role will be to work out the strategies, identify the opportunities, open the doors, facilitate the exchange of information in the most effective way, advise the spokespeople in your firm on the messages and help them to build a case.

First imperative

Message-building and case-making are essential, even for the most pedestrian story or topic. Many people just knock out a news release, or pick up a phone to a journalist and start selling in the stories, without having checked they are approaching the right target, being clear whether it really is a story, or knowing what they want to achieve, what is the case they want to make and what will help persuade the journalist to run it in the right way. 'Engage brain' before picking up phone or hitting the keys.

Next, segment your media

The broad categories are:

*   print;
*   broadcast;
*   online.

Be clear about the many sub-categories.

Print

See Chapter 4:

- national;
- regional;
- sectoral/trade;
- consumer/lifestyle/personal finance/legal affairs;
- daily, weekly, monthly;
- freesheets;
- letters pages;
- opinion pieces;
- advice columns;
- City and business pages;
- feature articles;
- diary and gossip columns;
- the publications of relevant other organisations and introducers (CBI, TUC, Federation of Small Businesses, *Which?*).

A whole other issue is the enormous range of marketing brochures, newsletters and other publications produced in great quantity by most law firms.

Broadcast

See Chapters 5 and 6:

- national;
- regional;
- news/current affairs;
- consumer/personal finance/lifestyle;
- advice programmes and phone-ins.

Online

See Chapter 3:

- newswires/agencies, PA, Reuters, Bloomberg;
- *Lawyer, lawzone* and the other online legal outlets;
- other websites (e.g. law.com, rollonfriday.com);
- e-briefs, viral marketing;
- *BBC Online, Sky News*, CNN and the others;
- your own firm's website;
- scurrilous gossip sites like *popbitch*;
- discussion groups and chatrooms.

Avoid using just the one news release for all these categories/sub-categories. Target and focus.

What works perfectly well for a legally qualified specialist legal editor on a national newspaper simply will not work for a young reporter compiling a gossipy webpage for a consumer audience to surf. One sweeping generalisation is that there are fewer experienced journalists working for online offerings, and it is much more usual for copy generated by firms and their professional marketers to appear unedited online than it is when working with the traditional media. The immediacy of the medium is also alarming. On the last high-profile case on which I was working, my press statement appeared, entirely verbatim, on the *BBC News* and *Sky News* homepages less than 10 minutes after I issued it electronically.

Harnessing on the media for effective marketing

* Always remember that any media relations undertaken as part of marketing activity are meant to raise profile, heighten awareness of expertise and ultimately *generate business*. Your budget and its renewal or increase will be directly related to the perception within the firm about whether the expenditure has achieved a return. Your own job security may be influenced by this too. Always, therefore, be clear to target the audience from whom work will come, and not just the professional community in which you operate and your competitors.
* Set up systems to benchmark and evaluate the effectiveness of your work. If one intended result of media activity, for example, is to attract lateral hires to the firm, it is easy to see whether it has succeeded. It is harder to assess if the objective to develop the firm's practice in IT/telecoms has been met without keeping a careful eye on all new instructions to that practice group.
* Read voraciously and listen and watch widely – never target a publication, programme or website with which you are unfamiliar.
* Don't be a media snob – remember the circulation and audience figures and be up with the tabloids and popular media as well as the broadsheets and professional press.
* Do thorough research before you make contact: see recent editions, get tapes of programmes, check the websites and follow links, all to get a feel for the issues covered and tone and style.
* Target carefully – each medium and each outlet requires a different approach, tone and style.
* Be clear about all relevant deadlines and respect them.
* Always ensure you provide timely communications.
* Ensure everything you write passes the 30-second read test.

Regional media

The regional media are often the most relevant for firms interested in building brand awareness for their regional offices. Court them assiduously, including the local radio stations and the freesheets, and ensure that the lead partners/fee-earners actually meet the journalists on the local papers, the producers at local stations and remain accessible to them by phone and e-mail. Local radio ad campaigns have produced great results for some firms. Don't let the big firms hog all the opportunities. But be clear, your qualified colleagues will have a distinct preference for coverage in the national and legal media rather than a piece in the *Shropshire Star*. If their office is in Shropshire and their clients reside there, the latter is likely to generate real business whereas the former will simply give them a smug glow of satisfaction. For a year I contributed to a local radio programme quite late at night in Surrey. For a year it generated more leads than the Surrey office of my firm could handle, even after the dysfunctional and inappropriate potential clients, wedded to green ink and violet notepaper, had been gently turned away.

Building relationships and knowing your sector

Never restrict yourself to communicating just with the legal media if you are serious about marketing. If your firm aims to build an awareness of its banking expertise, then you should familiarise yourself with the range of publications read by bankers and those in finance and target them in preference to the mainstream legal and business press. A slot on BBC Radio 4's *Moneybox* programme will reach millions, including many lawyers and possible private clients, but will also position the interviewee and their firm as expert and influential. (You will find you are in competition with sharp-elbowed accountants who are all now keen to demonstrate that only they can explain wills, probate, tax and a range of topics in which lawyers are also expert.)

If your firm seeks to expand its private client or SME base, then a feature in *Director* might help. If it is the divorce practice you want to build, then the plethora of women's magazines can be invaluable as 70 per cent of divorces are initiated by women, though family law firms, whose topics are always of interest, have often already secured regular slots in many of them.

With the proliferation of publications, virtually every sector, no matter how obscure, will have its own specialist publications, which you must get to know. Lists are available on software programs such as Media Disk, which reveal the extent of the range.

Courting journalists for effective marketing

Invest time in building relationships with individual journalists, broad-casters and programme-makers. Read and listen to their work, and without being sycophantic, comment occasionally on their columns and programmes, even though they may not be referring to your firm. *Never* rely on faxing news releases or bulletins to the news desk or e-mailing them to a central account.

If time permits, it is always best to telephone to alert the particular recipient of anything you are sending before despatching it.

A few facts of life about journalists:

* Journalists are often pressured, stressed and sometimes lazy.
* They change jobs often, never telling you where they are going and if in a new post may be very inexpert in your sector.
* Alternatively, they may have a legal qualification, as well as years of journalistic experience and know more about the law game than most of your partners.
* Helpful, accessible and reliable sources are returned to over and over again by journalists in preference to having to make new contacts every time.
* They will have views about your firm, chambers or lawyers that may not be right.
* Journalists are extraordinarily good at getting inside information, often from the most junior in the firm.
* If you make yourself impossible to dislike you are more than halfway there.
* One inept spokesperson can scupper a firm's chances of ever getting a decent profile – only field reliable spokespeople who give good quotes.
* One failure to deliver copy or information on time can ruin a long-term relationship.
* Most journalists are cynical about marketing and PR professionals, though often reliant on them – demonstrate in all you do and say that you are a committed professional.
* Most journalists have had personal experience of instructing a solicitor – it has not always been a happy experience.

Getting to know journalists takes time, but is the currency of your work. Lunches, drinks after work and regular chats by phone or e-mail build the relationship over time, and increase their trust in your reliability and in your understanding of your sector. Empathise with their work, and take an interest in the pieces they write on other issues/firms.

Planned media relations for marketing

Build three media lists:

- national media;
- non-legal trade or sectoral media;
- legal trade press.

Each of these sectors has potential, but you must identify your priorities dependent on your marketing objectives.

Get to know all the key journalists in all these sectors as people as well as professionals: try to get face-to-face with them all, and at the very least with all the lead ones; show an interest in their careers and the challenges they face; refresh the relationship regularly.

Introduce them to your lead spokespeople, and those in your firm who you believe represent its most appealing aspects.

Have a structured media contact programme so that the key people in your firm get to meet the relevant journalists and programme researchers and producers for one lunch a month (or whatever) and keep to it.

Find out their preferences in terms of information, timing, mechanisms: some welcome short e-mails, some hate them; some like long discursive chats, some get irritated by them. Be clear about their publication/programme's remit, tone and style.

Never waste their time with stories that have no merit. Be tough with your paymasters about what is realistically going to be of interest and what isn't (getting it wrong degrades your own credibility as well as the firm's).

Keep it short – phone calls, conversations, meetings, documents. Be available 24 hours a day: give journalists your home and mobile numbers and if you have one, a pager number too. Have properly prepared spokespeople similarly available at short notice. Return calls and e-mails promptly.

Always thank them when they do something helpful. Notice and comment when they do good work, even if it is not immediately of benefit to you or your firm – showing an interest in what they do is not just flattering, but pays dividends in the longer term.

Identifying and packaging stories and selling them in

A few guidelines to help identify stories:

- Think like the consumer, client, reader, listener or viewer, not like the lawyer or marketing professional, unless you are writing or broadcasting for a specifically legal or marketing audience.

- Ensure your story is both relevant to the audience and right for the publication or programme.
- Does it answer the 'so what?' test?
- Is there something about it that is new or adds to the coverage already given to the topic?
- Will achieving coverage for the story meet the business development objectives of your firm, chambers or the relevant practice group and fee-earners?
- Does it sit comfortably with the overall communications strategy of the firm or practice group? Does the tone and style of the work reflect the culture of the firm?

Packaging the story

If you are aiming to get the journalist to write an article on the topic or make a programme, quoting or interviewing someone from your firm, here are a few guidelines:

Consider how best to communicate: depending on your objectives the story can be designed for widespread exposure or tightly targeted – this will influence which mechanisms you employ. Always remember, 90 per cent of news releases issued each day are binned unread. The same percentage of electronic ones are deleted as soon as the sender or first line is seen. All good journalists soon know which firms and marketers send out worthwhile releases and which do not; ensure you are in the former category, and if your firm is not rated, make real efforts to demonstrate there has been a sea change.

Be clear in your own mind why the story is of interest and be clear which audience(s) you believe will be interested.

Ensure you are able to communicate any technical details sufficiently clearly. If you can understand it, then it should be possible for the journalist, and through them, the lay reader or audience to understand it. If you do not really understand it yourself and are reliant on a lawyer to explain it, you will find it hard to sell it in convincingly and the journalist may choose not to bother with it.

If using a news release, keep it short, punchy, non-technical and use it as an appetite-whetter; tell the whole story in the first paragraph; keep quotes short; make clear the role of any spokesperson and treble check grammar, punctuation, spelling and relevance (see Chapter 4 above).

If using an e-brief, use a wholly different style – it should be shorter, punchier and accessible quickly and easily, with all the key information in the first sentence. Strip out unnecessary graphics that will slow it down and congest the screen (see Chapter 3).

If targeting a particular journalist or programme, depending on their preference, ring them and talk the idea through, send them an e-mail outlining the story, offer to provide more information once they have expressed interest, but don't deluge them too early.

Research as a PR platform

This is one of the oldest tricks, but invariably still works, as does regionalising aspects of the research:

- Only ask questions to which you think you know the answers.
- Only ask questions that will give rise to interesting and PR-able answers, e.g. interesting articles that can easily be communicated, or an eye-catching news release with a surprising fact or two.
- Ensure the research is conducted by a credible organisation unless you are just trying to get some cheap and cheerful insights, in which case you may undertake the research yourself and should say so.
- Consider undertaking online research among your clients – it can often provide illuminating findings and signal your interest in their business or wishes.
- Try to include a question or two that will provide a regional dimension, if your firm has regional offices.
- Remember to let the polling company see a copy of any release you produce that includes their research findings *before* it goes to press – it is easy to misinterpret findings and the company may also take press calls and need to be aware of the angle you are taking, so that it can reinforce it.

Placing an article by-lined by someone in your firm

Never write uncommissioned: it is wasteful of time and energy, unless the publication is so prestigious that you and your colleagues are prepared to take a 'punt' and invest the time in the hope of inclusion.

Establish interest from the targeted publication by sending through a short outline of the proposed piece, with bullet points; if the publication/commissioning journalist is interested, establish the word count, deadline and style they require.

Always read several editions of any publication to which you or one of your fee-earners is expecting to contribute or ask for the style guide – it can save hours of editing – and ask for a few back numbers, or obtain them through the library.

If the piece refers to a client, obtain their permission to refer to them first.

Watch the language and vocabulary like a hawk – cut out all jargon. It is rare for a piece, even for a national broadsheet, to be rejected for being too straightforward; it is commonplace for pieces to be rejected for being too complex. If fee-earners are writing the piece, allow sufficient time to edit and translate their prose – few lawyers write well for a non-professional audience.

Ideally, send the piece through ahead of the deadline with the offer of polishing it further if necessary. Always deliver before the deadline without having to be chased.

Always check the by-line or credit to make sure the job title, spelling, etc. are correct. Provide an appropriate photo or arrange for the author to be photographed, if necessary.

Placing an opinion piece

Getting your firm's leaders recognised as 'thought leaders' or 'opinion formers' in their chosen profession is a useful part of building awareness for the firm or chambers and their individuals.

Consider identifying hot professional and political topics on which your lawyers feel strongly which would make an interesting piece(s) and then offer the idea to the relevant publication or programme, identifying not just your own lead spokesperson, but others in the sector who could also contribute.

The kind of things currently attracting interest include:

- multidisciplinary partnerships (MDPs);
- limited liability partnerships (LLPs);
- complaints handling, the impact of the new Ombudsman and the possible demise of self-regulation;
- costs of litigation including conditional fee agreements (CFAs);
- impact of external regulation on professional firms;
- governance of firms and professions;
- probity of advisers in the light of Andersen/Enron;
- conflict issues as more big firms merge;
- the increasing globalisation of the legal profession;
- survival in an economic downturn;
- work–life balance;
- pro bono/corporate social responsibility;
- the number of women achieving partnership;
- the legal exposure of non-executive directors and other corporate governance issues;
- business school and management training for all managing partners of law firms.

You must have a lead player who is expert in his/her field who is prepared to articulate a firmly held, interesting view on the topic, and who will not equivocate.

Selling stories in

Its the standard phrase and I use the word 'selling' expressly to emphasise that much of effective marketing media relations requires salesmanship. Be under no illusions – one of the many reasons lawyers were so late in embracing marketing and its techniques was because of their natural abhorrence for anything that smacked of having to sell. The true professional still believes they should be sought out by their eager clients and not be obliged to tout for business. Indeed, when many of them first qualified, touting and all active promotion of a firm and its lawyers were prohibited. Commercial survival required change. Today, however, with every publication receiving innumerable news releases and faxes with potential stories, and every programme-maker invited to feature a range of issues of interest to their viewers and listeners, to get your story or issue noticed and reported requires you to convince the media that it is of greater interest than others that have been sent in.

A few guidelines:

- Start early enough – better to identify interest and have a journalist holding space than be trying to place something after they have filled their page.
- Respect the pressure the journalist or programme-maker is under (they may have a dozen calls from people like you each hour). Start each call with something like 'Is this a good time for you?' Be persistent but not irritating.
- Be realistic about the amount of editorial control you are likely to achieve – very little unless you have an exclusive and newsy story and a long-standing relationship with the editor. Ensure the fee-earners understand this as they are often prone to ask to check copy and are rarely able to do so.
- Have at least one alternative if your chosen outlet rejects you; have more than one angle to the story to offer – if the first does not work for them, try the other.
- Have an authoritative spokesperson available to comment, provide 'colour' to the story or help with technical detail.
- Be clear why you think the story is right for that particular publication or programme; show that you are familiar with it, read it/listen to it regularly and know what issues have been covered recently and why your story is a natural fit.
- Take no for an answer – be gracious when rejected. Make the one story work hard by considering how to sell it in to a range of different outlets that are not in competition with each other.

Creative use of photography

You will know the cliché about a picture being worth a thousand words. It is true. You know yourself that when leafing through a publication you will certainly not read every word, but you probably will glance at every picture and dwell on those that catch your eye.

Professional services firms are getting more adept at supplying imaginative photographs with their news releases and copy. Try to avoid the predictable head and shoulders shot and the rows of men in suits, if at all possible, but guard against anything too staged or desperate.

Also avoid the endless photos of charitable initiatives with eager young lawyers stripped for some fund-raising sporting challenge – these are becoming too commonplace.

If, for example, the practice area you are trying to promote is media law, then consider having a photograph taken in a client's studios or factory, rather than in your offices. If your firm's specialism is the construction industry, use a photographer who works in this sector and take the lawyers to a site.

Always be aware of the impression photographs can give subliminally. If your firm is intent on demonstrating it is inclusive, equal opportunity-oriented and young, ensure that accompanying photographs are not just of white, middle-class, middle-aged men.

Keep apace of developing technology. Most photographs are now required in digital format and are exchanged online. This gives you great freedom and many firms are finding that investing in their own digital camera can be useful to capture potentially newsworthy moments. Ensure that the shots are only taken by someone who has an eye for a well-composed picture.

Like everything you do, view the photographs dispassionately from the perspective of the viewer and ask if they meet your objectives for them.

Follow-up

Ensure you track all your efforts and capture all cuttings and broadcasts in which your firm, colleagues or matters were mentioned (see Chapter 3). Bring the successes to the attention of all the relevant people in the firm or chambers, by circulating them, but remember the constraints of copyright as regards press cuttings and ensure you have the necessary licence if you are distributing your cuttings round your firm.

Thank the journalists or programme-makers who have been helpful and let them know that your colleagues were pleased, if they were. If the piece was spiked and did not appear, gently enquire why so you can be better prepared next time and explain what happened, if asked.

Merchandise favourable coverage: both within the firm (to other fee-earners and practice groups who may not read the relevant sectoral press) and also consider obtaining run-off copies from the publications in question and sending them, nicely packaged, to key existing and potential clients, with a suitable personal note from the relevant contact partner.

If yours is one of the increasing number of firms that keeps its press cuttings in a folder in reception, to be flicked through by existing and new clients and visitors, check that they are all properly reproduced, well mounted and sealed in acetate and up to date. I regularly visit firms where these books have not been updated for months, and again it speaks volumes about the efficiency of their systems, or the frequency of their media mentions.

Exploiting technology to promote your firm

In Chapter 3, we touched on the development of the Internet and online media relations. One device employed by several firms, and particularly those with American head offices and London presences, is the cybercast seminar. I was involved in the first, organised by innovative American law firm publicist, Richard Levick of Levick Strategic Communications.

He advised an American client law firm with a subsidiary office in London, which was anxious to attract recognition, to hold a round table seminar on the vexed issue of multidisciplinary partnership. The aim was to generate global media coverage and professional interest to demonstrate that the firm was global and at the cutting edge of law firm thinking.

The guests were invited, drawn from the ranks of prestigious law firms, general counsel in client companies, legal organisations and knowledgeable legal commentators. Legal Network Television agreed to direct broadcast the event, which was the first cybercast/satellite broadcast ever in Europe on a legal issue. A live audience was invited to observe the discussion at the firm's London offices, but many hundreds – or even thousands – of others were assembled around the world, at their computer screens, by invitation. The discussion gave rise to four different articles in international legal publications, to contemporaneous online debate with members of the audience whose e-contact details were captured for following up, and a videotape was recorded of the debate and mailed to those too Luddite to participate or observe online. As part of the media relations of the exercise, Levick pushed the event to 160 reporters worldwide who had been covering MDPs as an issue, and turned their computers into virtual televisions, where they could either read the transcript of the discussion or watch the broadcast at their convenience.

Another initiative, used by several others now as well as Levick, capitalising on smart use of new technology, is the online press conference. In 2002 two members of the Austrian royal family visited the United States in the hope of reclaiming some of their country's treasures, which had been confiscated under Hitler's regime. They aimed to raise awareness on the part of the Austrian government of their concerns, by visiting the United States where many of the artefacts are now in private ownership. Levick's company aimed to provide a way for journalists not located in Washington, where the single press conference was to be held, to participate in the event by making it available via the Internet. Many journalists were contacted ahead of the event and encouraged to submit questions for the Archdukes to answer before the event. A website was then created to broadcast the event in RealAudio format, designed to permit journalists to access the discussion and hear the answers to the questions they had put in.

In fact, one of the elderly Archdukes became too unwell to hold the planned news conference, but having alerted the journalists to the event, it was easy to contact them quickly about its postponement, and much enthusiasm and curiosity about the event was identified. When one of the Archdukes returned to the United States a number of high-profile interviews were arranged, publicising the issue to what Levick believes is up to 37 million people.

As mentioned in Chapter 4, I very rarely recommend the use of press conferences these days, but this use of the technology may provide a clear alternative. It all makes the faxed news release look rather superfluous, doesn't it?

Award-winning marketing

The law is full of competitive people and nowhere is this more evident than in the annual publication of the two legal directories, *Legal 500* and *Chambers*. These, after assiduous research by an army of legal journalists and researchers, provide league tables of law firms, and identify leading practitioners – solicitors and barristers – in the various practice areas. They are launched at lavish parties, where those attending feverishly fumble through the pages of the latest edition to establish whether they or their firm have risen, slipped or plateaued. Each year, at frenetic dinners in the ballroom of a large London hotel, the *Lawyer Legal Business* awards are doled out to the firms and lawyers who panels of judges declare to have been the best in their field in the past year.

Many hundreds of hours are invested in drafting the submissions for the directories and the awards, extolling the distinctive merits of the firms. Important clients are invited to give testimonials, profit figures are massaged and disguised, deals are puffed and promoted, and front pages of legal journals, published by the same companies that publish the directories, are devoted to the smallest change in the pecking order of firms. It is all rather incestuous, but is an exercise that most in the large and medium-sized law firms and chambers take remarkably seriously. It remains debatable just how many actual decisions to award major legal mandates are influenced by these things, but it is certainly confirmed by many general counsel, heads of legal and private individuals appointing law firms and lawyers for the first time that the comfort factor of finding them rated in the directories can be influential.

One or two firms (notably DLA, the first) have courageously declined to play this game any more, trusting that their reputations will survive, despite their absence from these expensive tomes. They remain tight-lipped about the impact, if any, this decision has had on their income. Many of the lawyers in these firms, though, complain bitterly that they are no longer rated among their peers in the way they once enjoyed. I have yet to encounter a lawyer who isn't thrilled when he moves up the tables, or isn't desolated when his position in the tables slips. The editors and researchers know each year to brace themselves before publication for the welter of letters and calls from aggrieved lawyers or their marketing staff, challenging the wisdom of decisions made.

I recommend that the submissions to the directories and the relationships with their researchers and editors should be handled primarily by professional marketers, who will hopefully not only be able to produce appropriately drafted copy, but should have established relationships with those compiling the directory entries and a clear idea of what works best. Access should be given so that they can talk directly, if they need, to the relevant lawyers, but the drafting of the submission and its supporting materials is a task for which lawyers are not trained or equipped.

Martha Sellers Klein, the feisty American lawyer who formerly edited the monthly legal glossy, *Legal Business*, and is now editor in chief of *Legal 500*, one of the two legal directories, recently provided the following guidance at a legal lunch for law firm marketers on how to win a *Legal Business* award:

- satisfied client endorsements clinch awards;
- assembling the same team of lawyers to work on a client's behalf, after they have been working apart for some time, impresses;
- overcoming time constraints (fast work wins);
- influencing your competitors so they speak about your firm approvingly;
- making an overall contribution to the legal marketplace (by devising new approaches, finding an innovative deal structure or creative approaches to the law);
- overcoming obstacles that could scupper the deal;

- obviously dominating the sector or the marketplace (being regularly named and top-of-head does pay off);
- submitting a clear, impressive presentation;
- bridging the gap between partners and journalists most effectively;
- taking the trouble to meet the researchers and journalists working on the nominations, legal journals or directories;
- staying away from journalists when the deal, the firm or the team are in difficulties.

Marketing advice from a senior partner

Leslie Perrin, the senior partner and former managing partner of well-known national firm Osborne Clarke, with offices in Bristol, California and the City, knows more about branding and smart use of the media to build the profile of a firm than many. His was the first firm to appoint designers to rebrand it in a way specifically to get it noticed by the business sectors from which it wanted instructions, such as innovative and entrepreneurial technology companies. (I must declare an interest as I was a director of the consultancy that handled this branding.) Its quirky orange cat and distinctive accessible, witty media style invented in 1996 meant that it attracted an entirely disproportionate level of interest for a firm of its size when it opened its City and Californian offices. It also gave rise to closer scrutiny than was comfortable when the firm was obliged to downsize, as the impact of the 2002/3 recession hit it hard.

A few gems of wisdom from Perrin:

> Lawyers tend to find things interesting that are only interesting to lawyers. For example, a fascinating piece of law giving rise to a decision in the Court of Appeal, or the acquisition of a new cappuccino machine for the firm, are the things that lawyers tend to think are the bread and butter of legal PR. They're wrong. The only thing interesting about any law firm is its people and you have to be prepared to tell the story all the time.
>
> The media profile of a law firm is vital. As well as promoting the firm to the in-house lawyers who hire it, it influences the view potential recruits take of the firm.
>
> Our cat logo was something different, and gave rise to widespread admiration that a law firm had managed to achieve something like this. It has acquired strong internal affection, but now the clients no longer comment. Our competitors, though, still comment and it's been very useful as we built our network of European affiliate offices, which have all adopted the cat.
>
> It's essential to explain internally what your strategy is. You must have worked out and written down what the big, top level business objectives are. It may be something as simple as OC's, which is 'to serve our clients and give our people interesting and rewarding careers'. But it must also include setting

out the business objectives and the rate at which you intend the profits to grow. It should include your people values – in our firm we expect everyone to be treated with consideration and respect, which is hard to stick to when the going gets tough and you have to let some of them go. Your senior managers must be visible, available and talking, and all have to have instilled in them what the essence of the firm is. All firms have an essence and a history, it comes from their founding fathers, and then evolves, but they all have their own stories to tell. But that essence must also be communicated to those outside, or it's worthless.

Media savvy lawyers are on 'transmit' permanently, not only just when they have something interesting to say. Our four senior managers are all coached in how to deal with journalists. If they are phoned for comment, they know to be helpful and appreciate that the journos are just doing their job. If you're helpful, they will come back for more and you will become a source of authoritative information. If the information is reliable, the journalists will believe it and write accurately about your firm and its matters. Never forget that legal journalists are, on the whole, very knowledgeable. But don't make the mistake of thinking that they're your friend, even if you eat, drink and even dance with them. Ultimately they just aren't as interested in your firm as you are. But think of them as professionals and almost none of the time you spend with them will be wasted. You should eventually establish a relationship of trust and confidence, but it takes about five years.

Always be truthful and follow the thread of truth about your firm. You will forget the lies you told, and will be caught out, but you can always remember the truth.

But as OC found, that open, truthful style is tricky when times get hard. The firm admitted candidly in 2002 that it was obliged to make some equity partners redundant. It was the first firm to go public on this, though others were doing it by stealth. This news led one of the legal journals for a week and the atmosphere within the firm changed perceptibly when the news got out. It was also no longer possible for the senior managers to be as candid with their people or the journalists as they had previously been while they planned the new structure and made the tough choices. As so many clients of the firm also read the legal media, it was crucial that their confidence in the firm was maintained while this restructuring took place.

Some unhelpful headlines caused internal morale to plummet and hackles to rise. But doggedly the firm's managers continued to talk to the legal journalists, explaining with commendable candour the difficult decisions they were being obliged to make and the strategy that underpinned them. Slowly the more accurate and positive coverage returned. When one legal journal ran a piece that was not entirely correct and caused more angst within the firm, the firm's managers took deep breaths and then arranged a meeting with the editor of the publication to brief him comprehensively and then saw a more accurate piece emerge the following week.

While the bad news is always riveting to the journalists and to the firm's rivals, much of the legal daily grind just isn't. Leslie Perrin concedes an unavoidable truth: 'Some firms are just deeply boring, and it's hard for them to find something about themselves, which makes them more interesting'. If you are in that kind of firm, then you may well find that there is limited scope for media relations and a range of other marketing activities will be required.

Perrin is clear that for Osborne Clarke, timing was everything:

> The regional law firms' movement was interesting – about six firms decided there was a new way of doing things. The 'magic circle' firms had benefited for too long from the mystique surrounding them, but there were new kids on the block from Leeds, Birmingham, Manchester and Bristol. These realised the major benefits of being seen as alternatives offering unusual legal solutions, and they started re-defining how the business of law was done, how much it costs, and the role of the client in setting standards. I think it was a defining moment in the law – we were able to seize the opportunities and capitalise on them, both to grow our business and to raise our profile – the two were inextricably linked.

Marketing advice from a legal editor

Tom Freeman has edited the monthly legal magazine, *Legal Business*, for the past couple of years, having been a journalist on the publication for some time before that. His large-format glossy is read avidly by the very people who have the largest legal mandates in their gift. He has probably been subjected to more law firm hospitality, schmooze and charm than most.

I asked him for his views, and though some simply reinforce comments from other journalists and my own advice, they bear repetition.

On news releases, Tom, like everyone else in the media, receives more than he and his colleagues can ever use. To make yours count, he advises the following:

> Avoid big titles, big graphics and superfluous 'headlines' – a total turnoff, journalists are vain and want to find the angle themselves, not be steered by something that has gone out to their rivals.
> If there's something to report, say it. If not, don't. Why risk making the recipient of a press release cynical about their usefulness?
> Don't bow to the whims of publicity-seeking partners. Take control of the PR strategy, particularly if that's your job. If your employers or colleagues don't understand that, educate them. If that fails, go to a place that does.

On the use of e-mail, Tom, like virtually all the journalists with whom I am in touch, prefers this means of communication. As he says, 'if you want a paper copy, you hit "print", but it doesn't interrupt in the way that phone calls do, and it reaches the right desk each time, which is far from the case with faxes to a busy newsroom where fax machines are always shared.' This increasing reliance on e-mail can eliminate some lawyers from the communication loop. I still meet those who dictate their e-mails, defeating the purpose of their speed, and completely changing the tone and style of this means of communication. Lawyers, particularly older ones, still seem convinced that typing is done by less intellectually well-equipped life forms, who are invariably female. They do not deserve the media attention they often crave. Two lines saying, 'Can I interest you in a short piece on an interesting decision about privacy due to be decided on Thursday?' takes seconds only to type and send and does the job more effectively than a two-page release on fancy paper.

Given a chance, all journalists will sound off cheerfully about what really irritates them about their work. Tom Freeman is no exception. He is maddened when the lawyer or publicist shows no signs of having understood the needs and character of his particular publication. He also is not impressed when the callers show signs of being harassed, saying 'we're all harassed – we might as well conduct ourselves with good cheer'. I often glance at the time of his e-mails and know the hours he works.

Tom also does not warm to those with no sense of humour and a good joke will almost always get through his defences.

I asked him, if he had the unenviable task many of us have probably had at some time, of trying to interest a publication or journalist in a firm that had nothing very distinctive about it and was not really very interesting, how would he go about it. In true *Legal Business* style, he thought he would probably start by 'gossiping about the firm's rivals – always a good start'. More seriously, he suggested that as his magazine has a considerable amount of management analysis, the publicist should look for an angle from that perspective. 'Many law firm managements dream of being less distinctive than fate has made them.'

Earlier I made the point when counselling against patronising or dismissing journalists as unqualified, that many are themselves lawyers. Tom Freeman is not, but his publisher (and the former editor of *Legal Business*) is an American lawyer with years of commercial practice under her belt. Two of the team of 20 or so on his magazine are fully legally qualified. While he gets many applications from lawyers looking to transfer into legal journalism, he comments that the pay levels are usually a disincentive. He adds that ex-lawyers often approach legal journalism with an air of reverence and ingrained risk-aversion, which simply does not work. His particular magazine is about personal and business dynamics taking place in the legal market, not about the law.

Like all journalists, given the choice between talking to the lawyers and talking to their marketing and public relations people, Tom and his team would prefer to talk to the lawyers.

They're our readers. But a PR with the confidence of his or her partners can save time all round, providing crucial background, context and spin – and focusing both parties' minds on the key issues at hand. But being overbearing is wearisome.

Both from personal curiosity and because so many firms and chambers now employ marketing professionals, I invited his views on the PR and marketing people in the legal game. He was unequivocal:

Those who have the partners' confidence, facilitate the flow of information to the benefit of all concerned. Those who don't, hinder it.

One of the most common complaints by those in marketing and communications roles in law firms and chambers is that they are excluded from the top level discussions, are not taken into the confidence of the firm's leaders and are not empowered to speak authoritatively on its behalf, yet are expected to raise the visibility of the business and its lawyers. As an adviser to so many firms and individual lawyers, I observe this disconnect daily. The firms that are flourishing, that have a well-understood and visible place in the legal market and are attracting both clients and recruits satisfactorily, tend all to have experienced marketing or business development professionals in senior positions in the firm, working in close collaboration with the firm's managers.

Finally, I asked Tom Freeman, when almost all transactional legal work is very similar, and most firms have many common characteristics, what is it that makes one firm or group of lawyers more interesting to a legal publication than another. His reply was predictable:

Personalities among the partnership, and the emergence of a fussier breed of corporate client. The development of the latter places more emphasis on the qualities or otherwise of the former.

Certainly, I have always been clear that while the practice of law is a sophisticated people business, and the structures within which we all operate are statutes, precedents and processes, all the buying decisions made by clients and staff are informed by their view of the people within the firms. If the clients were able to assess accurately the varying degrees of technical competence within similar firms, they would probably be less likely to need lawyers at all. In reality, whenever I ask general counsel, heads of in-house legal teams or private clients – let alone journalists and commentators – why they chose one particular lawyer or firm in preference to another, their answer is almost always based on the simple fact that they liked or rated one person or group of people better or more highly than another. Identifying the interesting personality traits of the lawyers and allowing them to be visible, where appropriate, is usually the trick to profile-raising and effective law firm PR.

Finding and appointing a marketing or PR consultant

From much that I have said already you will probably have gathered that I strongly favour lawyers restricting themselves to the legal practice for which they were trained and best suited and leaving much of the marketing and media relations to support their work to others who have trained and acquired a different set of skills and experiences. While it is imperative that all in the firm, company or chambers own and support not just the strategic development of their collective business but also the activities agreed to achieve its delivery, I am convinced that most firms benefit from the objective advice of external advisers. But I would say that, wouldn't I – I'm a consultant.

Few relationships are more important or trickier to get right than the one between external advisers and organisations, and lawyers are notoriously difficult as clients.

There are a number of routes to find a consultant or consultancy to help you.

The **Institute of Public Relations** (IPR) is the only body that trains, accredits and speaks for the trade, profession or industry of PR. It provides a useful PR toolkit and some helpful publications. It has also provided some guidance on evaluating the effectiveness of PR activity. Many law firm marketers are among its members. It is based at The Old Trading House, 15 Northburgh Street, London EC1V 0PR (**www.ipr.org.uk**), phone: 020 7253 5151; fax: 020 7490 0588; e-mail: info@ipr.org.uk

Alternatively, public relations consultants can choose to belong to the smaller **Public Relations Consultants Association** (PRCA). It also has a free referral service, but most of its members are the costlier end of the market. It is based at Willow House, Willow Place, London SW1P 1JH (**www.prca.org.uk**), phone: 020 7233 6026; fax: 020 7828 4797. For some time there were discussions about merging the two organisations, but though talks continue, the merger does not.

Hollis Directories have invaluable contact details. You can make contact at Harlequin House, 7 High Street, Teddington, Middlesex TW11 8EL (**http://hollis-pr.com**), phone: 020 8977 7711. Virtually all the consultancies of any size or repute, both London-based and throughout the United Kingdom, are listed.

But if you are not London-based you may prefer to find a regional consultant or a freelance individual consultant, and virtually all of them now have their own websites. Simply searching on 'public+relations +region' will produce a long list and their specialisms, clients and credentials can all be quickly assessed from their sites.

While *PR Week,* the weekly journal of the PR world (published by Haymarket Publishing, phone: 020 8943 5000), is available on newsstands (but not fully online), it rarely focuses on professional services marketing. It does, however, contain advertisements from many PR consultancies each week.

Another way to identify some of those experienced at working with professional partnerships is to join and become involved in one of the professional services marketing networks.

Professional Services Marketing Group (PSMG) (**www.psmg.co.uk**) is a membership and support organisation for those in all sorts of professional partnerships. As well as law firms, its members work with accountancy, architecture, civil engineering and other practices. Like most organisations of this kind, it produces regular mailings, largely electronic, it organises workshops, training sessions and a big annual conference and its members report that it provides a valuable network, not just in which to empathise about the problems of lawyers and accountants, but also to share best practice and new tactics.

Professional Marketing Forum (**www.pmint.co.uk**) is run by Richard Chaplin. It organises and produces some of the same things as the PSMG, including *Professional Marketing,* a magazine published quarterly for members, a conference, a series of training and updating workshops for PR and marketing practitioners of all levels of proficiency and a subsidiary recruitment consultancy, Strategic Marketing Connections.

Many qualified lawyers, accountants and other professionals have found membership of one or both of these groups is useful and brings them into contact with professional marketers, PR practitioners and others grappling with the same issues in professional partnerships.

Suggested process when recruiting a consultant

1. Never approach just one consultant or one consultancy, unless you have worked with them before, or have received the highest personal recommendation from someone who has done so recently and can be really sure they are exactly what you want and need. Even if you are minded to hire the agency recommended or used before, just ensure you are up to date on their latest work and that the team they will field are the ones you want. The movement within the industry means that people flit from consultancy to consultancy, giving rise to variable quality.

2. Always invite at least two or three promising sounding people or companies to come and present their preliminary ideas to you. Even when you receive strong recommendations from others, check out any consultants or consultancies by visiting their websites, perhaps ringing and asking what relevant experience they have and doing all you can in advance to establish that they appear skilled, congenial and competent.

3. Be clear precisely what the budget is that you have available each month or year for this appointment or project. While you may not wish to disclose the exact amount that has been allocated by your firm or chambers until you have decided which consultants to appoint, preferring to invite the consultants to indicate what they

think the work they are proposing to undertake will cost, you should at least be prepared to give a 'ballpark' figure and have thought through whether you are anticipating this being an annual spend, with a contract for two or three years, or a specific project with which you need help for a finite shorter period.

4. Work out carefully exactly what you think you need external help with and commit it to paper. The act of writing a proper brief as part of the tendering process should help you all understand just what you are seeking to achieve and how you propose dividing the roles between your own in-house colleagues and staff and the outside advisers. (See below for a bit more help on this.) It is rarely cost-effective to ask consultants to do things you have already retained staff to do for the firm. The real strength of consultants is their external objectivity, their contacts and experience of working with others in your marketplace.

5. Send out the brief with a comprehensive covering letter to all those you have invited to pitch for the work, setting out:

   • when you propose inviting them to come to present to you, the duration of the proposed presentation, and
   • the timescale before a decision about the appointment will be made or the contract will start.

   I always recommend indicating in this covering letter your willingness to be available to answer any queries on the phone, or to have a pre-presentation meeting, if they wish. Any consultant who does not take advantage of a phone conversation or a meeting with you when this offer has been made does not deserve to get hired. Watch out for the organisation that bids to present last – the oldest trick in the world, based on the presumption that the last to be seen leaves the most lingering impression.

6. Although information about your firm or chambers will be available from your website and perhaps by a trawl of the Web for press mentions, provide some additional information in the pack that goes with the brief and invitation to pitch to the consultancies. If part of the task you are setting them is to update and upgrade your firm's marketing materials, they need to see just what you are currently using and base their presentation on their improvement. Discount any consultants who do not do pretty rigorous desk research about the organisation by which they are hoping to be hired.

7. Arrange the 'beauty parade' or 'pitch'. This is when the competing consultants or agencies are invited in to present their ideas to you. A common mistake is to schedule all the presentations on the one day, back-to-back without providing any time for the home team to reflect on the presentation they have just seen, grab a bite to eat or field calls. As the day wears on, particularly if there are four or more consultancies to be seen, the audience for the presentation becomes progres-

sively more jaundiced and the differences between the various presentations begin to blur. Teams should be advised to ensure that the presentations should last no more than 40 minutes (remember one of the tasks of all working with lawyers is to reduce their verbiage, not expand it) and that a maximum of 20 minutes should then be allowed for Qs and As. Then take a quarter of an hour break, perhaps to score the presentation on a prepared sheet, maybe to grab a coffee or have a quick debrief. This avoids collisions in your reception area if the schedule slips. Take a break for lunch and don't let the presentations trail on too late into the afternoon.

8. Consider getting a marketing or PR professional to sit in with you to help you make the final decision. When appointing people to work with us, we inevitably all make our decisions on whether or not we like and respect them as people. This is vitally important, particularly when anticipating a long-term working relationship. It often helps to have someone sitting in on the presentation to help check the technical competence of those presenting and ask the questions that may not have occurred to you.

9. A few areas to probe in the Q and A session:

- What is the piece of work they are most proud of recently?
- What is the piece of work they most disliked having to undertake?
- What is the average monthly fee they receive? (They may decline to tell you.)
- If it is a team presenting, how will they manage the team? How much involvement will there be directly between you and the team leader? (Probe this: it is commonplace for agencies to field their most senior directors, who are their most able presenters, ensure you fall in love with them, and hire them, and then fob you off with a much more junior consultant who is your point of contact on a daily basis and actually undertakes the work. Ensure that the ones you meet and like will be the ones who will work with you throughout.)
- How realistic do they think your objectives are from what they know of your firm, or the marketplace already? (I always warm to those who are robust and candid. At this stage I do not want obsequious 'brown-nosing', and the merit of using an outsider is their objective take on the firm. But rude is different.)
- How do they propose evaluating and benchmarking the work they envisage undertaking?
- What overheads do they charge and what mark-up on suppliers' charges? (See below for an explanation of this bear-trap.)
- Do they have any difficulty if you use your own designers, webmaster, printer, and will they be comfortable working alongside them?

- What direct practical experience have they had of working in your sector?
- Can you ring existing or former clients of theirs for a reference or two? (If they are wary of this for any reasons other than client confidentiality, probe further. Always try to talk to at least one of a consultancy's existing or previous clients before finalising their contract.)
- Which journalist on a particular publication in which you are keenest to appear do they know best? (If they are claiming close and congenial relationships with lots of journalists, it pays to try to check this out a bit. The names are all easy to find, the relationships are much harder to establish. I am always impressed if a consultant can indicate they know some personal detail about a particular crucial journalist, thereby evidencing they are in regular contact with them.)
- How frequently do they think you should meet to review progress? (Some consultancies largely clock up their time charges by having the most junior member of the team produce elegant weekly progress reports, timetables, charts and materials. Others just get on and do the work. You need something that fits your needs somewhere in the middle.)

10. Ask yourself whether these people had enthusiastic, easy, accessible personalities. Did they impress you with both their intellects and their attitudes? Would you find it pleasant to spend quite a bit of time in their company, particularly at difficult, pressured times, or could you, on further acquaintance, find them quite tiresome? It is important, this chemistry.

The brief

I have received briefs in all shapes and sizes, from lengthy documents, beautifully colour printed and acetate bound, to rather unfocused conversations on the phone, during which I scribbled frantic notes. I rather arrogantly have chosen not to pursue a relationship with those firms or consultancies that cannot differentiate between 'practise' and 'practice', who describe law firms as 'companies', who clearly do not understand the first thing about the dynamics of equity partnership, who struggle with different ways of describing the structure of their organisation coherently or who appear to be deluding themselves about their real place in the market. That can rule out quite a few law firms, a lot of chambers and far too many PR consultancies.

Make yours a model brief, if only to ensure that you impress the people you are inviting to pitch for your work, and encourage them to want to work with you. If they are horrified by the amateur approach you take to this process, at some point they may feel compelled to say so and ultimately it could be damaging.

The components of a good brief are:

- Description of your firm, chambers or company, its structure, its people (including its in-house marketing and PR personnel), its clients, its expertise, its culture. Expect them to do Web research, but include a selection of all your latest marketing materials, and perhaps a bundle of press cuttings if you are already in the media.
- An honest assessment of where it is in its sector/league, including any accreditation or awards (Investors in People or Best IT team).
- A brief description of where it aims to be in the short and longer term, including expansion plans, if not confidential.
- A short SWOT (Strengths, Weaknesses, Opportunities, Threats) of the firm, candidly outlining what it does well, and less well.
- Details of any research you have undertaken or are considering commissioning – if the findings are confidential, say so clearly.
- Details of the project(s) or objectives for the PR activity with which you are looking for help. What are you hoping to achieve? Have you undertaken a similar exercise before? Have you used consultants before? How was it? (Go carefully here if you are inviting existing consultants to repitch: ensure nothing is in the brief that you have not already said to them directly.)
- If you really need help managing a tricky issue (recession-driven downsizing, an international merger, a rebranding), but cannot reveal this in any detail at this stage, at least provide an indication of the challenges the project will involve and the specific expertise you are seeking.
- The duration of the contract and its renewability, e.g. three years, reviewed annually; or six months with an option to renew for a further six months; and any onerous terms or conditions you impose (e.g. conflict checking: most specialist consultants working with law firms have several on their books already, but if you particularly need help promoting your banking practice, you may want a consultancy that specialises in and has media contacts in this sector).
- An indication of the budget, for both the consultancy fees and any implementation costs. Are you proposing a monthly retainer, if so within which parameters? Is there an annual consultancy budget allocated already? If so, give some indication. What additional resource is available for design, materials, printing, upgrading the website, mounting events, providing hospitality to the journalists, etc.? Be clear about the charges you will find acceptable over and above the consultancy fee. Many agencies charge for every fax, phone call, photocopy, courier and even, in some cases, e-mail, and add a handling charge of 10 per cent or more on top of any charges by

suppliers they appoint and with whom they liaise, whereas others just charge their out-of-pocket expenses such as travelling to and from meetings. And forgive me for teaching you to suck eggs, but don't forget VAT. While freelance sole operators may not be VAT registered, all consultancies of any quality are and 17.5 per cent will be added to the monthly fee they intend to charge, but may have to be found from your fixed budget, even if recoverable.

- Require them to show how they intend to allocate their time to your work. Like lawyers, most consultants charge for their time by the hour, but can also calculate a 'price for the job' or a monthly fee. All, however, will be based in some way on their hourly time charges and their necessary profit margins. These can range as widely as they do in the law. In a small provincial town a sole practitioner working from home may charge herself out (it is usually a woman at this rate, sadly) at £150 a day, which works out at something like £21.43 an hour, if she takes a break for lunch. That's about as cheap as it gets, and is probably the average hourly rate for a London PR practitioner. In the top central London consultancies, the likes of Sir Tim Bell are famed ('the most expensive but the best') for having charged at least £500 per hour for some years. I reckon that my hourly rate is about what it would be were I still in private practice as a solicitor, with some 20 years' post-admission experience under my belt, operating in central London, but it always causes my legal clients to suck their teeth, before reaching for their cheque-books. All lawyers clearly believe that theirs is the superior skill set. Just be clear, though, that as with a team of lawyers allocated to a commercial transaction, the medium and large consultancies have a mix of experience and hourly charges among their teams and need to make healthy profit margins. If you are looking to retain them at £2,000 per month, then for the consultancy to make your work profitable for it, you may be getting something like eight hours of a fairly junior consultant's time, five of a middle ranker and just one of a really senior player. Ask yourself whether you would rather have more time of the senior player and less of the junior and can the consultancy accommodate this wish?
- A clear description, with organogram, if necessary, of how the relationship with the consultancy will be managed. Reporting lines in law firms are notoriously hard to grasp. The collective ownership of a business means that some operate rather like a hippy commune, apart from the suits, while others are now structured in a way that is almost indistinguishable from a limited company. Spell out to whom the consultants will be reporting, and the frequency and mode of the preferred reports (face-to-face at least monthly), show the status of any in-house marketing professionals and whether they are part of the management team of the firm, or simply regarded as support staff.

- Give clear guidance on your, or a colleague's, availability to field any further questions, when the presentations are to take place, their duration and format, whether you are expecting visual aids and when the appointment decision will be made and notified. If you are in a position to appoint consultants to handle a long-term, high-budget contract, consider holding a session for all to give preliminary presentations and then call back a couple of shortlisted finalists to address the issues in greater depth, as the decider.
- If you require them to provide some original design work, it is usual these days to make some contribution towards the cost of the materials used in its production which are expensive.

Sole practitioner versus big agency

The decisive factors are very similar to those of lawyers. The sole practitioner usually has low overheads, a less demanding work schedule and is untrammelled by any need to liaise with colleagues. But they will often be spread pretty thinly if anything untoward happens to any of their clients, their domestic life falls into turmoil or their health fails. For smaller, particularly publicly funded law firms the freelance, self-employed consultant may be the answer, if the skills and personalities fit.

It is unlikely, though, that someone operating on their own would be able to provide a comprehensive enough service to a firm of 20 partners or more, unless that firm also had an in-house individual or small team to help with the implementation of all marketing and PR plans.

The very large glitzy agencies have all the same overheads and pressures as the large glitzy law firms. They should fit comfortably together.

The key decider, though, should be the experience and intelligence of the advisers and their ability to be able to mobilise the lawyers into co-operative action. A few hours of a senior consultant's candid advice and time may be much more valuable than many hours of a well-meaning but inexperienced and unfocused junior consultant. Much like the law, really.

Housekeeping arrangements for the beauty parade or pitch

1. Ensure that *all* the equipment the presenting team will need is available. Be worried if they do not ring and check this well in advance: it indicates they are sloppy in their planning. Nowadays most presentations are done by Powerpoint from a laptop, but the necessity for a blank wall or a screen and a compatible projector can still make it a logistical nightmare. One of my least fine moments was being found by the senior partner on my hands and knees under a boardroom table in a 'Magic Circle' firm, with my bottom in the air, trying to plug my projector into a socket that had been craftily hidden from sight. My favourite presentations are where I just take a disk

and someone else slots it in and makes it run! Ideally, those presenting should ask if they can set up their kit ahead of the presentation itself. An advantage of going first is that this is more likely to be possible. If the setting up must be done in front of you, observe how the consultants handle this. If they deal with it with charm and humour, they are likely to cope well in a crisis and you are much more likely to get on than if they appear harassed and ill at ease.

2. Schedule the presentations as suggested above – and do allow comfort breaks and ensure there are refreshments, for both the reviewing panel and those presenting. How your potential consultants deal with the 'tea ceremony' can be another good pointer to how they will interact with you and your colleagues, as well as with the journalists and others they will be talking to on your behalf.

3. Ensure all mobile phones and land lines into the room are switched off. If a pressing business matter does cause an interruption, it is preferable for a messenger to come into the room with a manuscript message, rather than allow a phone to ring, with the attendant confusion that will follow.

4. Even if you are bored to distraction with what is being presented to you, be courteous and supportive throughout. Public speaking, even in just small groups, is one of the most terrifying things, even for those who have to do it for their living, and the junior members of consultancy teams are often up most of the night, finalising the slides, rehearsing what they are going to say and sleepless with worry. Their careers can be influenced by how they perform and the success of the presentation. You can afford to be charitable. Please stay awake, suppress yawns and remember how little you like giving presentations yourself. When giving feedback, try to be constructive, and rather than saying something like, 'I'm afraid you entirely missed the point of our wish to expand our personal injury practice', say something like, 'If you had emphasised more our keenness to build awareness of our PI practice, I think it might have worked a bit better'.

5. Don't forget that those presenting will have invested time and effort in the presentation, however inadequate you think it is, and, if unsuccessful, will not receive any payment for the work expended.

6. As soon as those who are making the decision about the appointment have done so, telephone all who presented. Ring the successful consultants first and tell them what it was that influenced your decision (it is so helpful to know), and also ring the unsuccessful candidates, and advise them, with generosity and warmth, where they went wrong, or why the victor won. Please don't delay for days or even weeks before doing this – consultants are all incentivised and on performance-pay and will be on tenterhooks till they know the outcome. Also, offer a comprehensive debriefing on the unsuccessful presenta-

tions if you have the time, either over the phone or even better, face-to-face. These people may just be 'ships that pass' today, but one day they could be the MD of a client company.

7. Follow up your calls with polite letters, being honest with the losers, and formalise the contractual aspects with the successful consultants without delay. There are few things more frustrating than investing a lot of time and effort in a pitch, getting all fired up to perform well, winning the business and then having an energy-sapping hiatus while the new client sorts out the procedures and the work actually begins.

8. Set up an early lunch or drinks session to bond with the new team on a personal basis and celebrate their appointment. These people could be crucial for your business. Forging a strong working relationship at the start is imperative.

The voice of experience

Finally, I asked Fenella Gentleman for her advice. She is probably the most experienced law firm publicist in the United Kingdom, now director of public relations at international law firm, Lovells, and formerly a colleague:

> Lawyers understand as well as anyone that their firm's reputation, and indeed their own, is a hugely valuable asset. But they don't always have much of an instinct for managing it.
>
> You have to get the firm's name known by the right people and for the right things, whilst preserving trust between the firm on one hand and clients, colleagues and the media on the other. Long term, it isn't worth being economical with the niceties where a client relationship is at stake. It doesn't do much for team work if the person briefing the press gets all the glory, and you'll get nowhere at all if your firm fails to safeguard its credibility with the press.
>
> Understandably, what seems elementary to PR practitioners may be somewhat counter-intuitive to the lawyer, whose professional priorities are so different. Most lawyers appreciate guidance on spotting stories and dealing with the press. They may imagine that the media are interested in the minutiae of what they are doing for clients or what's going on at the firm: not true. Journalists are after a story, and that may just as often be found in the lawyer's feel for the market, which equips them to give expert comment on the legal and regulatory environment and on wider business and professional issues.
>
> Lawyers also tend to look for unreasonably quick results. They should think again. Building a relationship with a journalist is much like courting a business prospect, except that what journalists have in their gift is coverage rather than direct legal instructions. Both parties need an incentive to invest in getting to know each other. Even if the lawyer's credentials and the journalist's need for copy are understood and a personal rapport has been established, the payback comes only when their interests coincide.

PR people can be expected to have a nose for the news and for the potential media stars. But it isn't always easy to explain what this amounts to to a City lawyer and to get them on side.

At Lovells our media training includes an exercise in which small groups of lawyers are charged with finding a PR opportunity for the firm in the day's papers, selling that idea to the firm's Press Office and handling the resultant press interview. They learn a lot from hearing each other struggle to identify the kernel of their respective stories, to communicate it effectively and to answer questions on it from someone whose agenda is not necessarily their own.

It is rather more tricky explaining tactfully why some lawyers are just not going to cut it with the press. The nuances usually give the game away: an inability to see the big picture, so the real story is overlooked, or an edge of patronisation in the voice, which will rile just about any journalist. That's pretty personal. So giving a few examples, citing very different personalities who are good at this, is often the best way of getting the point across. You need a store of anecdotes about the enthusiasts with a bit of flair, who will uncover something newsworthy in the most unpromising raw material and in a brief chat will capture the attention of the most sceptical of journalists. The real pros are easy to recognise.

8

Litigation support

To some this phrase means the range of people or equipment that supports a team of litigators in a law firm when they are handling a complex court case.

In communications terms, it is now taken to mean the role that communications professionals can play to support the lawyers or the client on one side or the other involved in a complex piece of litigation. It is accepted by some that if well done it can enhance the chances of a satisfactory outcome to the litigation.

This work can be described as 'building a favourable climate of opinion' or 'advocating a case in the court of public opinion'.

It can be a controversial area as some feel – entirely understandably – that it is inappropriate for any skills other than those of the lawyer to be used to influence the outcome of a suit, particularly if the ultimate decision must be one made by a judge or jury in a court of law. But since the essence of litigation in this country is evolving case law to keep apace of the times and inquisitorial advocacy, our cases are inevitably influenced by the decision-makers' perceptions of the very people and the issues about whom they are deciding.

Now that police habitually sell stories to the papers, the victims of crimes consult publicists and newspapers before reporting the crimes, speculation about the guilt or innocence of an accused runs for months before a matter comes to trial, court artists capture the features of those being tried and giving evidence, and newspapers devote front pages to the opening speeches by the prosecution (but not always by the defence), I would argue that it is perfectly proper for those involved in cases that are likely to attract media attention to seek to have their interests protected by appropriately experienced professionals. Appendix 4 provides some information about campaigning and lobbying on miscarriages of justice.

If the Attorney General's consultation commenced in April 2003 puts an effective end to 'trial by media' this need will reduce and many of us concerned with access to justice will be delighted; but while we operate in the current environment, I believe more and more clients will expect their lawyers either to have these additional reputation management skills themselves, or to know someone who has.

I learnt an enormous amount about the power and importance of thoughtful media relations while advising Sally Clark and her family pro bono. After many years of working on high profile cases and endeavouring to help lawyers fighting to remedy miscarriages of justice, this was probably the case that attracted the most media interest and the work of which I am proudest.

Sally Clark, a young woman solicitor, was convicted of murdering her two baby sons and sentenced to life imprisonment. Her solicitor husband, her father (a former divisional commander of police) and a small team of friends, most of whom were legally qualified and gave their time without charge, worked tirelessly for three years to get her convictions overturned. I offered to raise awareness of her plight, draw attention to the concern many had about the safety of her convictions and support the work of the lawyers as they prepared an application to the Criminal Cases Review Commission, having been unsuccessful in persuading the Court of Appeal that Sally had been wrongly convicted.

On 29 January 2002 I had the privilege of standing beside Sally and Steve Clark on the steps of the Royal Courts of Justice while Sally, free after three-and-a-half years of wrongful imprisonment, with enormous self-control and dignity, read a statement to the world's media.

As the *British Medical Journal* reported, in the space of three years Sally Clark's case had been turned in the media from that of a *bête noire* to a *cause célèbre*. Her family is clear that media relations played a major part in that transition.

Sally's own comments appear later in this chapter (p.227).

How to identify cases with potential media interest

It is simple – they are either human interest cases or ones involving large numbers. All cases where human beings have got themselves into difficulties are potentially of interest to others, and commercial cases where large organisations are at risk of losing or winning large sums of money also attract attention.

Often the clients and the lawyers advising them are very clear that despite the newsworthy nature of the matter on which they are engaged, they have no wish to see it trawled through the national or regional media. Curbing that interest, however, may be difficult and controlling and managing the process may be the best that can be hoped for.

On the other hand, it is sometimes the case that in order to campaign on an issue, to raise awareness of a perceived injustice or to emphasise how an individual or business has been wronged, some carefully orchestrated media coverage can be invaluable in alerting public opinion to the issue as it heads for adjudication.

We should never forget the public's fascination not just with people in trouble, but with the glamour and mystique of the courts. Think of the number of television programmes and films set in courtrooms, with stereotypical casting showing dramatic exchanges between exotic be-wigged lawyers, dusty judges and struggling jurors, witnesses and defendants. Think of the number of photos you have seen over the years of people going into or out of the Royal Courts of Justice, or campaigners with placards stationed patiently outside, of the number of journalists who started their careers reporting their local magistrates' courts, and the riveting television that the OJ Simpson trial made.

While the vast bulk of legal work is detailed, dry and decidedly dull, most of us at some time in our careers find we are dealing with something that would be of interest to the wider world. Sometimes we find ourselves handling a case that attracts an unprecedented level of interest.

The topics that currently are guaranteed to get the journalists and programme-makers salivating include:

- almost anything to do with the private lives of celebrities;
- marital or sexual strife, particularly if infidelity or violence is involved;
- same-sex relationships (we still live in a surprisingly homophobic country);
- child abuse and most other matters relating to small children;
- rich businessmen or politicians being caught out;
- 'David v. Goliath' stories, i.e. 'little people' taking on and beating large organisations;
- defamation suits;
- anyone in a position of influence or authority who is caught in breach of the law, e.g. captains of industry, MPs, vicars.

There are many more, but they are almost always 'people' stories, and even when commercial litigation involving City deals and large institutions is concerned, the media interest is in the chairman, chief executive and board members, or the member of staff bringing the claim against their employer.

The guiding principle

Even if the media handler or adviser is legally qualified, it is imperative that all media relations undertaken to support litigation should ultimately be approved by the lawyers who have the conduct of the case, and must complement the legal process – decisions can never be driven just by the media. Ideally, a close and harmonious working relationship should be established by the two teams of professionals and there should be open access to each other's materials and strategies. The media relations strategy must assist and strengthen the legal strategy, and never overwhelm it.

That said, while I was advising the National Grid on the reputational challenge it was facing from class action litigation brought by families claiming that their children had suffered leukaemia because of exposure to electric and magnetic fields generated by the Grid, the relationship with the law firm instructed was so close that as we headed for trial, we all used one Intranet. This enabled me to make amendments to some of the pleadings, to ensure that if they ever came into the public domain the language was appropriate and made it clear that we never lost sight of the fact that infant lives were at stake; equally the lawyers felt able to tinker with press statements to ensure they accurately reflected the technical accuracy of the pleadings. It took us over a year to work seamlessly as a team, but I believe the closeness of our working relationship provided the client with the very best service as a result.

Before embarking on any litigation media work, absorb Chapter 2 on the rules and guidelines and thumb through *Media Law* by Geoffrey Robertson QC and Andrew Nicol QC of Doughty Street Chambers, so that you are clear about what you can and cannot do.

The practicalities

Most of the necessary guidance has already been provided. The key thing, apart from offering advice but ultimately allowing the lawyers to dictate the pace and activity of any media relations work, is to be fully on top of the detail of the case. Without really understanding what the objectives of the litigation are for the client, the possible outcomes of the case and the potential disadvantages of providing the media with information, it would be negligent to embark on any media relations work.

While the objectives of criminal justice cases are rarely hard to grasp, those in civil matters can be enormously complex and if the matter has taken many years to come to court, with cabinets full of papers to absorb, you will be very reliant on the willingness of the lawyers instructed to provide you with a clear précis of the matter and access to the pleadings.

None of this should be attempted unless you have a genuine familiarity with the civil justice process.

Trial by jury

If the matter in which you or your clients are involved will come before a jury, the advocates (and you) will be primarily addressing a very specific and small audience of 12. Despite attempts to widen the mix of the backgrounds of jurors from 1972 when the age and property restrictions were lifted, the types of people who have become jurors have clearly changed, and it is now often said that the average jury is comprised of 12 people not bright enough to get out of jury service, or that there are usually more shoplifters than shop-owners on today's juries. To remedy this, more professionals will be expected to undertake jury service soon.

The first beneficiaries of the change in 1972 were said to be the pornographers, when younger and more broad-minded juries repeatedly acquitted them in obscenity trials. After *Inside Linda Lovelace* was acquitted in 1977, the DPP decided to mount no further obscenity prosecutions in relation to the written word. In 1985, an Old Bailey judge gave the final push to the discredited section 2 of the Official Secrets Act 1939, acquitting Clive Ponting, despite the fact that he was obviously guilty of breaching the Act by supplying a Labour MP with secret information that falsified government statements about the sinking of the *Belgrano*.

In 2000, juries were still sympathetic to honest radicals and acquitted demonstrators who destroyed genetically modified crops and attacked nuclear submarines. Government law officers are reluctant to put journalists and publishers in the dock of a criminal court for fear that a modern jury will acquit them.

In essence, though, as Robertson and Nicol point out, the role of trial by jury as a guarantor of free speech is limited in practice to protecting the speech of defendants who are *likeable personalities*. Unpopular artists, allegedly responsible for utterances or actions that shock or disgust remain targets for jury prejudices. Jurors' susceptibility to media influence is therefore considerable and great care must be exercised if generating interest in a case prior to trial to avoid any allegations of prejudice. How papers portray those involved in trials in their copy and their photographs can create impressions that lodge in our minds, without our being fully aware of the impact they have made and the views that we have subconsciously formed.

In the past year, without the matters ever coming to court, we have seen popular daytime television presenter, John Leslie, lose his job (about £350,000 a year) and reputation as a result of inadvertent comments linking him to an allegation of rape made in a book written by another television personality, who throughout declined to name him. We have seen Matthew Kelly vilified and then exonerated when the charges of paedophilia against him were found to be unsubstantiated.

In each case, there was real doubt that there could ever be a fair trial because of the level of prejudice already suffered by these personalities in both the traditional media and on the Internet in the months following their names first being connected with the allegations made. It remains to be seen if the Leslie trial can be fair.

Three procedures can be used to bypass a jury where it is thought that media coverage is prejudicial:

- obtaining interim injunctions, where claimants (particularly the government) prevail on judges to ban publication for the 'interim' period before trial on the grounds of confidence or copyright; suppressed information soon becomes stale, and the case is not worth the cost to the media defendant of fighting a trial a year or so later;

- creating media offences only triable in magistrates' courts, where breaches of restrictions on court reporting, for example, which carry fines of up to £5,000, are not triable by jury; in such cases, magistrates are much more likely to convict;

- prosecuting for contempt of court, where the penalty is a maximum of two years' imprisonment; it is the only serious crime in England not triable by a jury. Here judges are judges in their own cause and have convicted in many cases where juries would probably have acquitted, such as Harriet Harman for giving a journalist access to documents to read out in open court, and *The Independent* for publishing extracts from *Spycatcher* at time when the government was trying to stop the British public from reading it although it was for sale elsewhere in the world.

A blatant example of government attempting to avoid the right of jury trial or involving High Court judges in creating media offences occurred in 1981, when it was made a criminal contempt punishable with two years' imprisonment for journalists to interview jurors about their deliberations after a trial was over. This was excused by MPs at the time as necessary to preserve the jury system.

The media as a litigation tool

Sometimes the threat of media exposure can bring a recalcitrant party to the negotiating table and be a powerful weapon in the tactics of modern litigation, particularly in these post-Woolf times.

A carefully crafted letter intimating that one of the parties to a suit might be obliged to brief the media if the other obstructs the progress of the action much longer, can achieve more movement in the matter than had been the case for months. Many have found that casually mentioning that a letter of complaint would be copied to *Watchdog* has brought an unco-operative retailer or holiday company to heel.

An example is cited by Richard Levick of Levick Strategic Communications, which gave rise to 40 stories in less than 48 hours. The mid-western office of an American intellectual property law firm represented a local bookstore in a lawsuit against one of the leading Internet retail providers. The lawsuit alleged that the Internet giant had knowingly infringed the bookstore's trademark. The bookstore claimed that it had continuously used its name as a trademark since it was founded in 1970. It also claimed that the Internet giant was causing confusion among its customers as to its affiliation and the source of its products.

The bookstore's lawyer did not want to go to trial and a strategy was devised to focus enough attention on the lawsuit to put pressure on the Internet giant to consider settling with the bookstore. A copy of the complaint was shared, details of the lawsuit were reviewed and a media strategy was then developed. Three succinct messages were prepared and the bookstore's lawyer was ready for journalists' enquiries. The plan was simple: to be available for interviews, respond to the media's questions, and adhere to the messages developed.

The bookstore's lawyer was advised to adhere to the details of the complaint when speaking to the media. No extrajudicial statements were to be made to jeopardise the relationship with the judiciary. The bookstore owner was prepared by the publicists so that she would deliver the same messages as her lawyer.

The global nature and growth of the Internet has created similar trademark disputes and so media attention to the issue has also increased. By tracking the news and identifying all the reporters who had previously written about similar trademark disputes, a targeted press list was created, a brief news alert was prepared and sent to the broadcast media and phone calls were made to notify print journalists.

The story generated great interest among reporters, and the profiles of the lawyer and client were heightened. The allegations against the internationally known Internet giant by the local bookstore (a classic David v. Goliath case) created a buzz and became big news, attracting the attention of local, national and trade press, reaching as far as the United Kingdom.

In less than 48 hours, the law firm and the bookstore's lawyer had appeared in 40 separate news stories. The Associated Press ran the first story and both the lawyer and the client were on all the local television news programmes. Print coverage was also considerable.

Not only did this flurry of activity enhance the profiles of the bookstore, its owner and its lawyer, it influenced the opposition and brought about a settlement.

The partner's experience

I recently worked alongside Nick Cunningham, defamation partner at Wragge & Co., Birmingham, on a high profile child abuse case, which gave rise to the highest award of damages for defamation. Although the judgment ultimately went against our mutual clients, Nick is convinced that the level of our preparedness and the speed with which we jointly handled the media interest helped minimise the damage to our client's reputation. His comments may be helpful:

I think the media coverage of a case may affect the judgement of a jury, and there must be marginal circumstances in which a trial is allowed to proceed but the media coverage has had some effect. It is perhaps difficult to distinguish in some instances from the public policy aspects of sentencing when the media are reflecting public opinion on contentious issues.

It is definitely right to bring in outside advisers when the case is bound to attract a high level of media interest. Most lawyers and most of their clients only get occasional media attention, if that, and will not know what to expect, what the media want, how best to handle them and what can realistically be achieved in particular circumstances. Outside help may come from inside the client's own organisation, if they have an experienced PR team, but even then that team may not be experienced in dealing with the specific issues which arise in litigation, or with the degree of attention a case may attract.

Your decision about which advisers to appoint should be based on their experience and track record and on personal qualities, such as their ability to get the best out of the client.

The external advisers can add value to the legal team by bridging the gap between the client's own staff, who are responsible for the proceedings, and those who have to face the camera. They can support the client's own PR team. They can support the external lawyers, who may also be nervous about the scrutiny they will find themselves under. They can provide focused attention on what may seem to be a secondary issue at the time, but will become a primary issue the moment judgment is given, if not before. They can help the client to formulate realistic PR objectives and devise effective strategies to achieve them. They can make introductions and assist with communications directly with the media.

The things to guard against when using external advisers to help with the communications on a high-profile case, are that their activities don't cause any distractions. To ensure this, the advisers really need to understand the detail of the litigation and the client's best interests. It's not a good idea to prejudge the outcome of a case and put out material on that basis. I have been on the other side when media advisers put out material which built a contextual awareness of the issues ahead of judgment. It was irritating to our clients, and showed a tactic that only a media insider would have come up with or been able to implement.

From my recent involvement in this last high-profile case, where the PR adviser required me to be one of the lead media spokespeople, I learnt that the media are more handleable than one might suppose, but that certain skills are needed, which can be developed with a bit of training, and that it helps a lot to understand what the media want and what will be of interest to them. It all taught me to be generally less worried about the media, provided you had put in the work needed to be well prepared (I found preparation was everything when you had to think on your feet).

I found it enjoyable to receive last minute media coaching in withstanding difficult interviews. I also found it reassuring. I was pleased that some of the people in my client's team also had much the same response. It enhanced my firm's standing with the client organisation that we brought in high-quality

PR input, and I know that the client's own PR department much appreciated the very experienced assistance and advice that was provided.

The client's perspective

It is very rare for a solicitor to be the defendant in a criminal trial and as a result under the media spotlight. It may help you to understand how media scrutiny really feels to its subject, and enable you to empathise with your clients, if you hear from Sally Clark, to whom this happened.

After being wrongfully convicted of the murder of her two babies, Sally served three-and-half-years in prison. Throughout she maintained her innocence while a small team of lawyers with her solicitor husband fought for her convictions to be overturned. After the Solicitors' Disciplinary Tribunal declined to strike her from the Roll and the Criminal Cases Review Commission ordered the reopening of her case, her second appeal was successful. She was released in January 2003 to be reunited with her husband and surviving son.

> To be honest, I read very little of the press coverage of my case during my trial or immediately after my conviction. During the trial emotionally, mentally and physically it was enough to get myself to court each day and home again in one piece without having the additional trauma of reading about myself in the newspapers. I was so focused on what was being alleged and said about me each day in court it was as if the outside world did not exist.
>
> Looking back, I was completely naïve as to the extent of the public interest in my situation. I had no idea about the level of media scrutiny it would attract. Also, and again with hindsight naïvely, when you know you are innocent of the charges laid against you, you believe that your innocence is glaringly obvious for all to see, notwithstanding what the prosecution says about you.
>
> Towards the end of my time in prison, I had a meeting with my two barristers. One of them said to me, 'you must have been prepared for a guilty verdict once the statistic of 1 in 73 million had been given in evidence'. I had absolutely not been. If you are innocent it doesn't dawn on you that you could be found guilty. So to all intents and purposes you believe it is irrelevant what the papers are saying about you, because you are convinced the truth will shine through. If comments were made that were inaccurate or misleading, then I personally initially just found they irritated rather than angered me, as I felt sure that the truth would prevail and these inaccurate commentators would just have to 'eat their words'.
>
> Following my conviction I was protected from the majority of what was written about me. It was harder for my family who weren't. I have read some of the coverage since and there is no doubt that much of it is very hurtful. Friends and family who know me well have commented that they did not recognise the 'monster' that was described. From my perspective it was not so much the crime that I had been accused of that I found upsetting, because I

felt sure that one day the allegations would be found to be false. It was rather what I call the 'ancillary lies', used somehow to validate the prosecution case against me, which I found the most distressing.

I guess that there are all sorts of matters that tabloid journalists thrive on, but these are the accusations which have remained with me for the longest time, had the most long-standing effect on me, and are making it hard to move on: it was reported that we were born with silver spoons in our mouths and enjoyed a champagne lifestyle; that I was a career woman who never really wanted children and only agreed to have our sons to placate Steve; that I was a perfectionist who looked upon babies as irritating and disruptive; that I was obsessed with my appearance and upset when I put on weight in pregnancy; that I had no friends and was a depressed and lonely alcoholic. These views were formed without talking to me, or the people who know me, and though none of them is true, they will remain with me forever.

I completely understand that the majority of journalists are only earning a living and doing their jobs. After all, a good story sells newspapers and mine was a good story. I feel, though, that the reporting could have been more balanced and less sensationalist. I understand that the press reported the prosecution's opening speech in full, but then most journalists left the court, only to reappear when the verdict was due. There was only scant coverage of the defence arguments and indeed little attention was paid to the substantive part of the trial between the prosecution opening and the verdict, apart from the now infamous flawed statistic, which was introduced by the prosecution. This, as I understand it, was the headline of every major newspaper the day after it was given in evidence.

It may be interesting for you to know that it was the judgment of the first Appeal Court that this statistic was a 'side show' and did not influence the jury. At the original trial the judge told the jury not to discuss my case outside the confines of the court, or to read newspapers or watch television reports of the trial. Yet as I came to court one morning, I passed a juror with a copy of the *Mirror* carrying that statistic, tucked under his arm.

To this day my family, friends and I remain very hurt by a lot of what was said about me in the media, even though my father tried hard to counter some of the worst untruths, and we all tried to excuse the journalists as just doing their jobs. It was particularly galling to compare these reports and headlines with those that were written the day after my release. There were few hints of an apology at what had been written before. Even more irritating were attempts on the part of some papers to imply that they had always believed in my innocence and felt that my case was a miscarriage of justice, and they had somehow now been proved right. There are a few journalists who have some justification for feeling this way, but none of the newspapers can claim to have fought a campaign to secure my release.

There is absolutely no doubt in my mind that more sympathetic and investigative journalism, following the failure of my first appeal and, in particular the decision of the Solicitors' Disciplinary Tribunal, was instrumental in changing public opinion about my case and speeding its progress through the judicial review process. This was the case from the time when we had professional help with our media relations. But be in no doubt, it is a risky business to hand over evidence to a few well-chosen journalists and let them make up their own minds about one's guilt or innocence. We were advised we had nothing to hide and everything to gain. I believe journalists are a strange breed and require careful handling – we were lucky to have the advice and guidance of a media expert, which was always spot on and second to none. But it goes against the grain to feel that you have to manage the press and 'play the game'. For a long time I was uncomfortable with this and still am to a certain extent. Why should anyone have to present an image and choose their words carefully when they have nothing to hide? But I now recognise, before my world was turned upside down I was somewhat naïve, and have had to do a lot of growing up. In the world we now live in, the media is hugely influential.

High Court cases

One final tip: if you are in a high profile case in the Royal Courts of Justice in the Strand make yourself known to the journalists who are habitually based in the Press room by the door to the cells at the back right hand side of the main hall. The Press Association and other agency reporters are based there with full technological support and are always grateful to know you are prepared to help them.

No photographs can be taken within the court building, so all filming and photography is always done immediately outside. There are several entrances to the court building if you want to help your client to evade the press, who are usually at the front or back entrances.

9

Crisis management: not making a disaster out of a crisis

Crises can take all manner of forms, from a secret merger leaking to the media at a crucial stage, to the personal impropriety of a senior lawyer; from terrorist action destroying an entire building to a professional negligence suit. I define it as whenever an action or an event causes damage to life, property, a business or a reputation. How the situation is reported in the media and thereby communicated to the wider world can influence dramatically the impact of the incident and the recovery process required.

Even in the best-managed work environment things can and do go wrong. A client finds that despite their best endeavours a lawsuit they are facing is in the media and threatening to destroy their business. Law firms discover to their horror that one of their partners is less than honest. In-house lawyers have to cope with their employing company experiencing financial difficulties, announcing redundancies, producing a defective product. The spokespeople for the Office for the Supervision of Solicitors have to cope with an Annual Report showing a rise in the dishonesty of solicitors, despite measures to curb its increase.

In the past year or so a few of the incidents that have attracted wide media interest have included a law firm discovering that its head of probate had been systematically stealing from his clients' accounts over many years; the largest law firm in the world finding itself facing a memo from its most junior lawyers complaining vociferously about the way the firm was managed and implying that they were encouraged to pad their fees; a gay MP finding his private life over five pages of the tabloid press; a major law firm finding its finance director had been arrested and was likely to be charged with downloading child pornography from his home computer; a major public school undergoing internal restructuring, which needed to be carefully communicated if the parents were to maintain their confidence in the school; a casual e-mail exchanged by young lawyers about one's intimate life, being circulated globally to the embarrassment of the firm that employed him; and a law firm obliged to downsize unexpectedly which had to retain staff and client loyalty through the process. In each case, to the organisation or individual, the event constituted a disaster or a crisis, and in each case they turned both to their lawyers and to their communications professionals for help in salvaging the situation.

Risk analysis

Few organisations, and virtually no individuals or their advisers, invest much if any time in analysing what risks *could* impact on their businesses, what crises could paralyse them or ruin their reputations, but in the small hours of the night we can all envisage them.

Increasingly, it is an essential part of corporate management, particularly with increasing globalisation, for all major companies to be required by their insurers to invest senior management time in a risk analysis exercise, which in turn leads to a proper risk management strategy being formulated and laid down.

This can involve for an oil company, for example, thinking through the very worst case scenario of a major fire in an oil field with multiple deaths and injuries, or for a banking institution, the destruction of its head office by a terrorist bomb. It was invaluable that the Law Society had undergone a similar exercise when terrorist bombings were decimating the City of London and a controlled explosion had to take place at one of its Chancery Lane sites.

No organisation, however small, and no senior business person or celebrity is immune from actual or reputational damage. Quite often the destructive force can be internal. Some time should be devoted to identifying just what could go wrong, and what steps should be taken to manage and communicate about the situation in order to return the enterprise to normal as quickly as practicable. It will then become clearer what should and can be said to the media and the organisation's other audiences.

Admittedly, if most organisations put this in hand I would find myself unemployed, as these days most of my work comes as a result of ill-prepared organisations or people finding themselves unexpectedly facing challenges and needing help to manage the process.

Excellent books exist on crisis management and some are recommended in Appendix 5.

This chapter deals mainly with news management and assumes that others are responsible for the management of other aspects of the crisis.

Preparing by planning

Reputations – those of firms, clients and individual lawyers – take years to build and seconds to destroy.

Planning for all eventualities is never achievable, but preparing for possible problems ensures a less damaging outcome. Innumerable law firms ring for advice while a camera crew waits in the reception area, or lawyers call on the morning judgment is to be given in a newsworthy case when they have received the first media call. Most lawyers believe if they are able advocates their skills will transfer seamlessly to media interviews. Many clients assume their lawyers have a full understanding of how to mobilise media support for their case. All are *wrong*.

Do:

- consider what could go wrong and give rise to media interest: fraud or negligence within the firm, high-level departures, a dissatisfied client, a rumoured merger, sexual impropriety of one of its lawyers, a high-profile client case;
- take advice from the Law Society and crisis experts *before* it's too late;
- prepare a plan of action for each situation;
- allocate spokespeople;
- put them all through intensive media interview skills training;
- rehearse the scenario, to ensure all understand their roles;
- prepare holding statements, key messages and questions and answers;
- consider involving professional issues management consultants;
- contact external advisers early;
- keep all appropriate personnel within the firm suitably informed, including switchboard operators, receptionists, security staff, secretaries;
- speak up and speak up fast – be open and accessible;
- exhibit your humanity – say you are sorry (if you, your organisation or your client is at fault) and empathise with any suffering caused.

Don't:

- delay in the hope that the problem(s) will go away;
- lie – ever;
- speculate;
- be defensive;
- blame others;
- say 'no comment' and go to ground;
- assume that the most senior person is the most able spokesperson;
- hide behind a bureaucratic exterior.

Examples of competent crisis management

The managing director of Vauxhall Motors countered the BBC *Top Gear* Satisfaction Survey, showing the Vectra as the most unsatisfactory car of the year, by taking same-day advertisements in national newspapers explaining that the concerns had been incorporated into the recent models and the car was now the most popular fleet car.

Paddy Ashdown's well-managed press conference, called by his solicitor, to confess to adultery with his researcher, 24 hours before the story broke, gave rise to an *increase* in his popularity in the polls.

Examples of incompetent crisis management

These include:

- the handling of Camelot's chief executive's unfortunately candid admission that most people now were cynical about their chances of winning the Lottery;
- much of the news management of the Iraqi war;
- the initial response of Clifford Chance to its associates' memo revealing their discontent, which implied accusations of fee padding;
- initial response from the Royal Family to the death of Diana, Princess of Wales.

First reaction

When things go wrong, the instinctive response is to remain silent and to avoid, wherever possible, contact with all who might ask awkward questions, particularly the media.

This reaction is triggered by one or more of the following factors:

- 'Common sense': the idea that reasonable people (and particularly lawyers) must have sure, specific data that has been checked before they make any pronouncements; the more serious the situation is, the more sure of yourself you feel you must be before saying anything.
- The manager's sense of responsibility: you don't gamble lightly with the reputation of your firm, your chambers, your client; you only speak when you have a mandate to do so, on the basis of a document that has been discussed and approved.
- It is never pleasant to have to announce or deal with a serious or potentially serious problem.
- Describing a potentially grave problem can heighten your own sense of disorientation: when you have to explain the danger or problem in public, it becomes more real and worrying to you personally, and could impact on your family.
- Making any announcement can be worrying to the speaker – haunted by the panic myth, we think 'Why not wait before we get everyone upset?'
- When someone speaks out, that person becomes one highly exposed individual, whereas if everyone remains silent, the failure can be blamed on the structure or the system.
- There is always the hope that no one on the outside will notice that anything is amiss if you don't say anything to draw attention.

So, you wait. You wait to know everything before speaking up; you wait for permission or confirmation before giving even a few facts. This is a recipe for further disaster.

Speak up and speak up fast

The experts in the field of damage limitation, disaster recovery and news management always counsel: in almost every case it is vital to communicate without waiting.

These are the reasons why:

- Other people will fill any information vacuum – these people may not be in the best position to give correct information. Above all, they may be promoting their own interests.
- A filter immediately falls into place to determine the trust placed in your communications. If they are insufficient at the outset, you will suffer for it throughout the crisis. Those who remain silent are automatically assumed to be guilty or worse.
- Those who have had to handle the media management of real crises say: 'The scene is set in the first 48 hours. This is the stage on which the coming weeks, and months will be played out – it will be almost impossible to modify.'
- Almost certainly the press will obtain some information about the crisis, problem or difficulty early on and once they have the information, however skeletal, it will get into the public domain.

To ensure that you take some control of the issue, and ensure that your side of the story is told, apply the following rule: **take the communication initiative immediately**.

It is one of the keys to the survival of your organisation or your client's reputation in a crisis situation. You should tell your story and tell it fast.

This advice may send chills down your spine and panic into your heart. What should you say? When should you say it? To whom? And how? Wouldn't getting it wrong compound the problem? Wouldn't acknowledging there is a problem confirm your liability and expose you to litigation? Won't people start blaming you for the mess? But remember, not knowing is not an evil in itself, it is a normal condition in a crisis. What no one can accept is absence, a refusal to comment, an apparent lack of interest, or the presumed incapacity to react – not just in civic but in human terms.

A few fundamentals of crisis communication

Communication is more than a verbal exercise; as we have seen, it also comprises gestures, underlying attitudes and physical presence.

In what are often dramatic circumstances, the psychological disturbance can drive the person in charge of communications to take refuge in well-defined frameworks, such as professional jargon or legal restrictions. For lawyers, it is particularly easy to fall back on obscure language (a safety blanket for us when times get difficult) or to rely on implying or saying openly that we are legally prevented from saying as much as we would like.

Some instinctively avoid any statements showing personal sensitivity when in fact it is because the individuals are genuinely personally distressed that they hide behind a withdrawn and insensitive attitude. This can lead to bitterness on the part of those suffering from the crisis and additional uneasiness, thereby making the decision-makers' task even harder.

Those in charge of managing the crisis should also ensure that they never let the idea take root by anything they say that the victims of the crisis are yet another problem that must be dealt with. Even if this feeling is camouflaged by carefully drafted statements, the truth will emerge. You cannot trick victims and any trickery is devastating for those who try to carry it off, and strips them of all dignity. In those circumstances, what was merely a crisis can be turned into an all-out war between the victims and the alleged perpetrators.

So should we communicate for communication's sake?

No. There is one reservation about this plea for openness. In the event of difficulties that have caused no damage or loss and pose no imminent danger, the most urgent task is clearly to remedy the situation and not to undertake a massive media campaign. Do not confuse prompt post-accident communications with systematic public self-flagellation. If nothing is happening, and you may well be able to manage the situation without it receiving external attention, you should prepare to communicate just in case, but not go rushing into the limelight.

If the issue causing concern is a sensitive internal one, it would clearly be unwise to turn a searchlight on it yourself if there is a real likelihood it will not attract external attention.

There is, though, a dilemma here. It is always recommended that things go better if the eventuality of a problem has been raised beforehand. Some regret not having insisted more on a detail made public but not played up sufficiently by the press. A few months later, the issue resurfaces and can be presented as a shameless cover-up. There is no easy way to dispense with these complications once and for all. The contradictions and ambiguities that mark the terrain of crisis resist all defences, including the natural one of naïvety. In a crisis, however it may unfold, nothing can replace a capacity for evaluation and good judgement. And here lawyers score, because these are the very skills our training helps us to acquire.

But it can also be invaluable to bring in skilled external advisers who will not only have handled and survived other major difficulties elsewhere, but will be able to advise on all those tough judgement calls that must be made quickly, without being in any way emotionally involved with the organisation, its people, its finances or its future. Often my job is to ask the most senior people in organisations in trouble the most difficult and direct questions, in order to enable them to confront issues that they have otherwise being trying to bury. An outsider is sometimes the only one who can do this.

When not to communicate

Do not overlook the fact that in the case of certain threats (not imminent risks), especially terrorism, immediate communications can have negative consequences:

- Silence is a communications strategy: the decision not to inform must derive from a specific analysis of the risks run and those avoided, rather than from a classic reflex to cover up.
- The decision not to inform must be seen as an exception to the basic rule, which can be justified by overriding motivations.
- It should be understood that this intentional lack of communication may become public knowledge at any moment. You must therefore be in a position to offer convincing explanations about opting to remain silent, on both technical and moral grounds.

The rules of crisis management

The following seem to apply in all but the most exceptional circumstances.

1. Work out and *commit to paper your communications strategy* and a plan for its implementation. This should include your aims and objectives when communicating and the mechanisms by which you propose to do so.
2. Name a *high-ranking spokesperson*, ideally someone with technical as well as communication competence, who has been fully prepared for communication with the media, rather than a communicator who has only rapidly been filled in on the technical questions.

3. Make sure you are the first to supply information.
4. *Provide full and accurate information on a very regular basis*, keeping close to developments in the crisis rather than just handing out the occasional news release.
5. Give out this information from a *well-identified press centre*, in order to pin down and control media demands.
6. *Take account of media deadlines.* Treat different forms of media differently, as they all have their own specific needs (as we have learnt).
7. *Use communication material prepared in advance.* For yourself, this will comprise lists of correspondents, and statements and answers to all the trickiest questions, which have been prepared in advance in respect of a certain number of possible scenarios and checked and approved. For the press, it will include outlines and reference data (e.g. on the firm, the law, the previous problems in this area).

All this preparation and advice are geared to aid just one thing: that you should become the best source of information, or at least one of the most reliable sources and therefore rapidly the most credible and the one with the largest audience. If you follow these rules, you will keep a foothold in the competitive area of communication.

A few negative principles

1. *Never lie*, for as soon as your lies are spotted (and they will be) you will be permanently discredited.
2. *Never just say 'no comment'.* If you do not want to reply to a question because you judge that the information cannot be made public, you must give reasons (e.g. 'For obvious security reasons, it would be irresponsible for me to tell you which strategy the intervention teams are going to follow in this hostage-taking'; 'this concerns matters that are *sub judice* and I'm afraid I really can't speak about them yet'; 'The police are carrying out an investigation and we are not allowed to give out any specific details at this stage'; or 'The families have not yet been told, so you'll understand if, out of respect to them, I don't give you the victims-names at this time').
3. This does not mean you have to pour out wild speculations about the worst possible developments.

Example of a company's media rules

Dow Chemical of Canada has the following long-standing instructions to cover all disaster news management:

1. The public must be informed frequently, accurately through the media, from the outset. This must be done by one or two highly credible senior spokesmen who understand the situation and can explain it calmly and clearly in lay language. The first 24 hours of a crisis are critical.
2. If this is not done, a public information vacuum probably will develop rapidly – and be filled by rumours or alarms far worse than the real situation.
3. Silence in the midst of a crisis implies guilt, whether justified or not.
4. It is not enough merely to assure the public that everything is OK and there's no reason for alarm. To be credible, we must provide details of how that conclusion is drawn.
5. It is vital to realise that reporters face deadlines hour by hour. Information must always be correct, consistent and current, even if all the answers aren't immediately available.

A few key points to remember

1. Recognise and remember that you must regard the demand and the need for information on the part of all different publics as entirely justifiable.
2. An organisation does not only exist through its activities and results, it also lives through its relationship with its environment. You must take just as much care in responding to these publics as you would when dealing with your organisation's other activities. (You will then find it easy to abandon the reflex of arrogance that always comes over people in charge when they come under attack both from the crisis and from their public when they learn of the crisis.)
3. Information and communication roles should therefore always be given proper recognition in any organisation. This means that the people in charge of communication should have direct access to all the strategic echelons, even in crisis situations. It is worryingly common to observe the director of communications absent from the summit meeting when the crisis strikes. S/he is a pivotal player. The communication dimension must also be taken into consideration when major options are being decided during the crisis.
4. The role of communication must be accepted by all within the organisation, from the switchboard operator or receptionist to the senior partner. Journalists making legitimate enquiries must not be regarded as a time-consuming nuisance and treated accordingly. It must be understood that they and their listeners and readers have a right to the information they are seeking and must be assisted in acquiring it.
5. Candour is essential with those tasked with helping the recovery process. Those in charge of communications in organisations often report that they experience as much difficulty obtaining information *within* their own organisation as journalists have from the outside!
6. Make sure you do not tackle communication in too fragmented a

way. The goal is not to juggle with an avalanche of details and anecdotes to be unleashed without a thought.

7. If people start chasing insignificant details, it is mostly in order to
    make up for a lack of more essential news. When it comes to infor-
    mation, people do not want to follow all the turns the crisis takes.
    Instead, they want to know why you have chosen a particular
    approach and why a particular assessment has been made. They
    want to understand the general attitudes giving meaning and direc-
    tion to the decision-makers' responses. Once they have been satis-
    fied, pressure will ease considerably, giving you more time to make
    your messages more relevant and show more consideration towards
    the publics concerned.

8. You will find it easier, when handling the communications sur-
    rounding a crisis, if you cease to believe that the crisis is an incur-
    able failure on the part of you and your colleagues and that the crisis
    can only be dealt with in a covert fashion. The shift in emphasis
    from guilt and abdication to responsibilty will result in more fruit-
    ful responses showing greater respect for the facts and the people
    involved. You will then be able to anticipate problems and abandon
    a purely defensive stance. This is important, as failure in communi-
    cation is still possible, not because of any hiding of facts or an
    inability to respond, but because of the simple 'absence of initiative
    in the information field'.

9. Lastly, it should be stressed yet again that you will not be able to do
    anything in a time of crisis if you have not made thorough
    preparations beforehand.

Who can I turn to for help?

Never feel you are required to struggle through unaided. When a crisis
strikes – or better, well before it looms on the horizon – may be the time
to approach external professionals to help. You are, after all, a lawyer or
a marketer and not a public relations expert specialising in crisis management. If you have your own in-house communications professionals
or retained consultants with real issues management experience (very few
marketing or business developments have this experience) involve them
and work closely with them from the first sign of trouble.

If in doubt about your (or their) coping ability – get help. Many of the
larger public relations consultancies have entire departments devoted to
this kind of work with extremely skilled specialists on board. If it is a law
firm in trouble, or a legal case under scrutiny, do ensure that they are
familiar with the dynamics of equity partnerships and do not just have
experience of working with corporates, which are so very different, and
be confident they understand how the legal system works. Ensure they

are ready, willing and able to provide '24/7' support – if not they may not be available to you at the very time you need them most. Invite them to outline the strategy they would adopt to help you through this difficult time, so that you are confident they understand the imperatives and will support you properly. Be clear about the financial basis of their engagement: when consultants are working through the night, consultancy fees can clock up fast and you want to be absolutely certain you can afford their services, if necessary for the long haul.

If you communicate well and effectively to the media, it can provide a timely channel of communication for you to many of your audiences and external help can maximise this opportunity. Time may be of the essence if you are also involved in the management of the issue, as well as its media handling, and having help to get a simple holding statement out to the media may be vital, may reduce the work you have to undertake and speed the recovery process.

If you fail to communicate well to the media, and it is rarely possible to prevent them getting wind when something is awry, their speculation can compound the uncertainty and anxiety experienced by your staff, clients and commentators, and make your own tasks much more difficult. This could be too risky to embark on unaided.

The crisis toolkit

Your communications professionals, whether in-house or external advisers, should be able to help you establish your own customised crisis toolkit.

I recommend that at the very least it should include:

- the written communications strategy setting out what are the objectives in communicating and the process by which the strategy is to be implemented (never assume this is all known and understood subliminally – write it down and share it);
- a telephone log book, or several, ready ruled and clearly laid out so all incoming and outgoing calls concerning the issue being managed can be neatly logged with timings, contact details of the callers or recipients of calls and responses (it is actually faster to use the old-fashioned manual system when time is of the essence, than to do it electronically);
- several copies of a basic press pack, with core details about the firm, biographies of its senior managers, contact details for its press managers, some statistics about it and, if appropriate, a copy of its latest marketing materials;
- an up-to-date media list with contact details of all the relevant print, online and broadcast media, national, legal, regional and sectoral, together with their publication/news deadlines;

- a full contact list for the 'crisis team' with all their out-of-hours numbers, home e-mail addresses, and even details of relatives with whom they sometimes spend time at weekends or in the evenings – crises rarely strike conveniently during office hours;
- contact details, including outside office hours, for the organisation's premises managers, including insurers, fire station, police, IT support, security personnel, etc.

Preparing by questioning

A standard device employed by all familiar with issues management is to prepare for any media or other attention by 'bottoming out' rigorously the details of the issue. This is most effectively done by drafting all the very trickiest questions that in the deepest darkest moments of the night the senior people in the organisation most dread being asked. Unless they, and the business, are required to confront honestly and openly the extent of the enquiries that could be made and work through what form of answers they could provide if these very questions came up, the preparation will be inadequate and incomplete.

Undergoing this kind of interrogation can be a revealing and bruising experience for those who have never been subjected to it before, particularly if outside advisers are those raising the questions and the exercise is being undertaken against the clock so there is little time to mince words. The areas that have to be explored range far wider than the business or court case or issue giving rise to the likely media scrutiny. The private lives of those in charge of it, or involved in the situation, should also be scrutinised and every single possible skeleton lurking in any cupboard should be identified and looked at squarely.

I have had to ask senior partners of firms to reveal to me their precise annual incomes from their firms and the level of the expenses they draw. On innumerable occasions I have had to unearth infidelities and embarrassments in the private lives or families of people under the spotlight. But these are the very questions any good investigative journalist may ask. If you prepare carefully, for example, to deal with any questions on a firm's merger, but are unprepared for a question about the amount the senior partner stands to make from the change, you can be confident that will be the very question that comes up. This does not mean that you should give full disclosure if to do so would not be proper, but you should at the very least have a form of words you can easily use that will close down that line of questioning.

If you are unaware that your client whose white-collar crime is about to be adjudicated also left his third wife just before he was arrested, you will be unable to help him deal with the interest this will inevitably attract over and above the reports of the verdict.

I recommend that a long and intrusive list of questions is prepared as early as possible. The appropriate person within the organisation who has answers to most of them should then provide candid responses. It is then the task of the communications professionals to convert these answers into appropriate ones for onward transmission to the media, clients, staff or any other audiences if it proves necessary. The answers should not be untruthful, or artfully spun, but should put the most positive slant on the situation, while remaining accurate. The objective should be to close down difficult avenues from further probing. The final version of the answers should then be checked and approved, if necessary, with any lawyers advising on the matter in hand before they are made available.

It is not usual to distribute the actual questions and answers in written form, although sometimes attaching a sheet of FAQs (frequently asked questions) can be a helpful device to pre-empt repeated questioning on some obvious topics.

The final Qs and As will be an invaluable guide for the spokesperson when they are briefing the media, talking to staff or others, and fielding their questions. They are also enormously useful if it is proposed (or there is time) for the spokesperson to undergo media coaching, as they can be given to a media trainer/interviewer as the basis of the role play interviews they will take the spokesperson through, and can save much time in bringing a newcomer to the situation up to speed with the bear-traps ahead.

Selecting your spokesperson

To comply with all the above guidelines and communicate appropriately and effectively at a time of crisis inevitably takes some skill. It may well be that the appropriate person to deal with the media and communications in a crisis is not necessarily the senior partner, head of chambers or managing director. It may well be someone else in the chain of command who has the right manner of calmness, accessibility and credibility.

To have any impact in public communications, you have to be one of the best sources of information. This means, at the time when you are perhaps busiest and under the most pressure, you must be prepared to field enquiries and patiently answer questions. For this reason too, it may be right to identify someone who does not have to manage the crisis resolution, but who can be free to deal with the communications aspects alone.

A spokesperson is often only as good as the information they have to communicate and before going public you must ensure that high-quality information has been collected. The public, via the media, will not be taken in by illusions. Both private individuals and the media are quick to cross-check information and decide which spokespeople are trustworthy. Judgements are quickly formulated, on a scale with the level of shock and anxiety.

That gauge I used earlier of 'likeability' is a useful one when deciding whom to use to speak on the issue. Ideally your spokesperson should be senior in the organisation, candid and unafraid in their communications style and someone whom others instinctively warm to and trust.

However able a public speaker or senior the spokesperson selected may be, they will always benefit from some media coaching. Even if the issue is unlikely to be covered by the broadcast media and all that must be done is to explain it clearly to staff and a local newspaper journalist, it can be invaluable to have rehearsed aloud the statements and answers to questions that you have decided may be uttered.

Several excellent media training organisations exist around the country, which at very short notice can provide a studio to replicate a radio or television environment with a professional radio or television presenter who can take the spokesperson through all those difficult questions they may have to handle. Observing themselves dealing with such a grilling, while initially daunting, can provide the spokesperson with most effective and rapid training available. Even an address to a group of staff can be improved by a rehearsal on camera first.

Things to avoid saying in a crisis

All the following phrases have been uttered in the heat of the moment. None of them has made the situation any better.

- 'Nothing is wrong, everything is under control' – when in fact no one is really sure and the situation is changing constantly.
- 'These systems were supposed to be fail-proof, everything was done correctly' – when in fact no system is ever totally perfect. At the same time, it is constantly repeated that 'it is impossible to exclude all risk' – thereby confirming what the accident has shown: that the system does have weaknesses.
- 'We have the best system in the world – just look at our record' – when death or injury or loss has just been announced.
- 'There are no deaths, only injuries', or 'There are no large losses, only small ones' or 'There are only a few redundancies' – all these responses are offensive to those bereaved, suffering loss or made redundant and indicate that the employing organisation or spokesman is uncaring.
- 'Everything will be back to normal by tomorrow evening' – when the actual duration of the episode and its implications have yet to be assessed.

Avoid boisterous declarations that can back you into a corner. Communicating effectively at this difficult time does not mean just saying anything in order to demonstrate your media-friendliness. Sometimes when decision-makers abandon their cultural references and instincts (i.e. keeping silent, in this case) they run the risk of demonstrating that the new standards to which they are being subjected are potentially absurd and dangerous. This risk is especially high for those who have no preparation for the openness they are called on to practise in a highly turbulent situation.

Actively managing the media

Once you have completed as much preparation as possible, if you have decided to try to pre-empt questioning or are being asked for a comment, you should make the agreed statement you have prepared available to the media, after you have had it cleared, if necessary, by lawyers and indemnity insurers. Putting it out electronically to the newswires would be appropriate if you were dealing with a matter of national media interest. An event that is lower key would obviously attract a different level of interest and your statement would be despatched appropriately.

A major national crisis could merit a press briefing being convened and advice about this appears earlier in Chapter 4.

If you are not making your spokesperson available to brief a number of journalists at the one time, but are putting out a statement, there may well be many follow-up calls and it is important that this media interest is carefully and properly managed.

All incoming media calls to the firm, or direct to the individual in difficulties, should ideally be routed through one media professional or press office, who should have an agreed strategy for dealing with them. Adhere to the advice in Chapter 4 by ensuring that no caller is put through to an unprepared spokesperson, but that all calls are politely taken, callers are carefully identified and their calls returned.

So what should you say?

Before you speak to anyone, you need to be very clear what can and cannot be said. Often you will be dependent on legal advice on this, and lawyers are often very bad at taking advice from other lawyers. If, however, you are a family law practitioner and your family law practice is in jeopardy, your insurers and a professional partnership or negligence specialist lawyer will be best placed to guide you. Don't rely on your own judgement, but seek that of an appropriate expert.

While you may well be advised to say nothing that could be construed as admitting liability, you can and must acknowledge others' pain or distress; you can exhibit empathy without admitting guilt; you can use humane language rather than hiding behind professional phrases.

Unless you are a natural communicator, now is the time to place some reliance on either your own in-house communications professionals or professional advisers. The actual words, when and how they go out and whom they go to, can be crucial at this time.

Your initial communications strategy in any crisis should be to strive to say as much of the following as is truthful and appropriate:

- We are aware of the problem, and we have taken charge of all its aspects (technological, organisational, human and social).
- Many unknowns remain, but the situation is under control, or everything is being done to acquire additional information and to handle the situation: the emergency plans are being enacted, and here is how they work.
- More information will be provided, readily, just as soon as it is available.
- If people are injured or worse: we are distressed/sad/concerned/sorry that people have been hurt/killed and our thoughts are with the families of those concerned. Efforts are being made to . . . .

Before considering putting out any statement, go through a careful 'planning by questions' process and jot down, or expect that your advisers will, all the tricky questions that could come up once your statement has been seen and read, and think through how you would answer this. This will influence what you can and cannot say at this time and prepare you for subsequent questioning.

Maintaining the media competence

Once you have opened up the channels of communication, you must keep this up throughout the duration of the crisis. Many think they can put out one short statement and then go to ground and decline to take further calls. Your vigilance must not flag, even after getting through the initial shock caused by the announcement that the event has taken place.

While all organisations, naturally enough, experience considerable difficulty when reacting to the initial wave of media attention, it is the second wave that can be the most dangerous. This unfurls just after the first has crashed down on the organisation, when everyone is looking forward to a breathing space. The media return in force, this time armed with real questions, just when you are least expecting them and when everyone is recovering from the initial ordeal. It has been said that 'the accident after the accident is what kills the company, not the first accident'.

The legal editor's viewpoint

Fiona Bawdon, editor of the legal aid lawyers' journal, *Independent Lawyer*, firmly advises:

> Don't insult my intelligence. When something goes wrong, admit it (albeit putting a positive gloss on things, if you want). Nothing is worse than being given a load of bull about, say, how the departure of an entire team of lawyers to a rival firm, or losing a major no win, no fee case is Completely Fine. What's wrong with just saying, 'yes, we are very disappointed, but that's life – we always knew there was a risk', etc., etc.
>
> A brilliant example of this was when Martyn Day at Leigh Day lost the big tobacco case. His response was totally straight and honest. He admitted it was a big financial (and personal) blow, but that they would live to fight another day.

Fiona goes on:

> If we (the journalists) get something wrong, let us know. If you are the person I spoke to, *you* should phone me up to put me straight, not your PR. Tell me what you're not happy about. Don't phone up and be Mr Angry, assuming a conspiracy, rubbishing all journalists, and behaving as though we all have it in for you. Let's have a conversation about it. It may be just a different interpretation of events or the hack may have made a genuine mistake. If the journalist is any good, they will welcome this kind of feedback. I always do. I would much rather know if I've screwed up than be left guessing that the person is fuming about something when they no longer return my calls. I don't do that classic lawyer thing of getting Carter Rucks to send a heavy (expensive) letter demanding the moon/costs/front page correction/head on a plate, when both the complainant and I know that, at best, the matter merits a small correction or letter published setting out the position. The people complaining will only look foolish and have missed what would otherwise be an opportunity to develop a good relationship with the journalist, if they don't deal with it in this sensible way.

To recap

In every situation, the aim should be to be open, accessible and truthful and to endeavour to help enquiring journalists as much as is possible, provided it is in the commercial interests of the firm, its staff and its clients to do so. The tone and style of all utterances should be sympathetic, non-aggressive and should acknowledge the concerns or distress of observers.

Your spokesperson should aim for a lightness of touch, which signals confidence not defensiveness. To be ready for all eventualities, at the very least the following should rapidly be put in place:

- agreed communications objectives;
- agreed holding statement;
- key messages;
- if appropriate, preparation of a news release or briefing, agreed internally;
- a letter for the firm's affected clients and those likely to be concerned by the news, agreed internally and ready to go out under the managing partner's hand;
- internal communications strategy (who will be firm's spokesperson, how will incoming enquiries be handled and routed, etc.);
- the key spokesperson should be rehearsed through the delivery of the messages, and if necessary media trained;
- all relevant personnel within the firm, and any external communications advisers, should be clear how the issue is to be handled and by whom, and kept informed as the situation develops, so that the strategy can be refined as time goes on.

Examples of legal crises

The departure of the tax team in its entirety from a law firm

If I am advising the managing partner, the primary objective would be to preserve the reputation of the firm, play down the importance of this departure and avoid being drawn on the personal difficulties between the two lead lawyers (the head of the tax team and the managing partner – it is fair to assume if they get along perfectly and share a vision for the future, the former would not be leaving). The credibility of this approach will be influenced by the percentage of the firm's work handled by the tax team, if the departing team is going to an accountancy practice or another rival law firm, whether the firm intends to rebuild a new tax team, or if the firm accepts that this will not be a service it will be able to offer in future or for some time. Successful communications will be easier if the firm is full service and the tax department was only one part of its offering.

If this tax team is recognised as being the foremost in the City, the damage will be harder to limit than if it was just one of a number of practice areas within a firm with a reputation for excellence in other areas.

The main audience for messages should be the existing clients of the departing tax team, and other existing and potential clients of the firm. The secondary audiences will be other partners and staff within the firm, and those who make referrals to the firm or supply it with assorted services. The primary media focus should be the publications it is thought the key clients will be reading, not those read just by rivals, although preserving the firm's reputation in the legal marketplace via the legal trade media will be important. The primary publications to ensure accurate reportage in, if interested, will be the *Financial Times*, the *Daily Telegraph* and *The Times*. The accountancy press should also be kept informed, particularly if the departing team is joining an accountancy firm.

The managing partner should pre-empt any inaccurate press coverage by taking the journalists' calls, once the line has been agreed, and actively contact those relevant journalists who have not already rung. S/he should be as candid as possible. S/he should avoid denigrating the departing partner and team, or being drawn into personal comments, and should be guarded in commenting on their difficult relationship. Messages should include:

- 'We will miss Mr X, he was a very talented lawyer.'
- 'We are, of course, sorry that his colleagues have chosen to go with him, but that is happening increasingly often in the competitive legal environment in which we are all operating.'
- 'My primary concern is to ensure that all our clients are kept fully informed – we will not, for the time being, be able to look after their tax concerns so anticipate that they will elect to follow Mr X or look elsewhere for advice.'
- 'We are very sorry for any concern or inconvenience this may cause our valued clients – we shall do all we can to keep this to a minimum and for this reason intend to co-operate fully with Mr X and his colleagues in the transfer of files, rendering of final accounts, etc. You will appreciate, we have a lien over our clients' papers until we have been paid for work undertaken for them by this firm, but are confident that this can be amicably and speedily resolved.'
- 'No, it wouldn't be appropriate for me to comment on my own relationship with Mr X – we have worked together successfully for . . . years; you will know how volatile the legal marketplace has become with people moving firms more often.'
- 'Although we are of course disappointed to lose a team of good lawyers, this will not make any major difference to the success of our firm – we have, as you know, considerable strength in corporate finance, utilities, . . . and are entirely confident that the many very prestigious clients who chose to use these practice groups will want to continue to do so. Tax, as I have said, only represented . . . per cent of our business.'
- 'It's really too early to say whether we will be looking to replace Mr X and his team. We may do so, but you can be sure whatever we decide to do will be influenced by what we believe to be in our clients' best interests.'
- 'Thank you for your interest in our firm. If I can tell you any more in a day or two, I'll ensure someone gets in touch.'

Medium-sized firm's finance director absconds with funds

The communications strategy will be influenced by whether the finance director has been caught, arrested and charged, or is still on the run. If his case is coming to court, an awareness of the rules of *sub judice* and contempt will be required. The lawyers providing the firm with legal advice should be allowed to drive the communications and media strategy as the criminal law will be of relevance.

As before, a crisis communications strategy should be prepared. Additionally, the firm should put its indemnity insurers on notice, if there is likely to be a claim. It should, of course, also notify the police and press charges. The primary objective, though, should be to reassure clients that any funds the firm is holding in client account will be secure and that no client will suffer financial loss as a result of this theft.

If the story is to break in the national media, all the clients of the firm who have money handled by the firm will require reassurance as it is possible that there has been financial irregularity for some time, prior to the finance director's theft.

The partners will also require reassurance from the managing or senior partner that their own capital interest in the partnership will be protected. Salaried staff and support staff will want to know they will be paid at the end of the month and that their benefit packages are safe. Those who provide the firm with referrals and suppliers who may be owed money by the firm will also all be anxious.

The senior or managing partner of the firm should issue a press statement and be assisted in getting this exposure, rather than waiting for the press to run a half-baked or inaccurate story without the firm's co-operation.

Key messages should include:

- 'The finance director was an administrator, not a lawyer, and all our lawyers continue to act, as they always have done, with complete probity.'
- 'We are fully insured and all our clients are fully indemnified; law firms are the only profession that is required to have limitless liability insurance cover so none of our clients or staff will suffer loss as a result of this unfortunate affair'.
- 'We are frankly horrified by the finance director's apparent behaviour. We have, of course, immediately contacted the police and are co-operating fully with them. They appear to be confident that he will be brought to book soon.'
- 'We have no reason to believe there are any other financial irregularities prior to this' [if true], or 'We are, of course, undergoing a complete audit of all our financial procedures to ascertain the full extent of the loss.'

- 'No, we had absolutely no indication that the finance director was contemplating any such action, although we do understand he has been under some personal pressure of late [if true]. . . No, it would not be appropriate for me to comment further.'
- 'No, it is entirely unconnected with the nature of some of our work here, we are sure. Just because we represent some accused of [or the victims of] white-collar crime, does not mean that any of our staff or partners can be assumed to employ practices that have featured in court cases they have been involved in. It would make a very nice story for you, but I do not believe it has a grain of truth' [if true].
- [If the theft copies a recent high-profile case in which the firm was involved] 'On the face of it there do seem to be some similarities – we all hear about copycat crimes. It's far too early for me to comment.'

Legal charges by a law firm for work for a popular charity or well-known figure's trust are thought to be too high

The last time this happened it was agreed the communications could have been handled better, but legal fees are regularly complained about in the media and generally perceived as unacceptably high by those who do not know fully what work is involved.

If the fees are accurately reported, and particularly if an actual bill has already got into the hands of journalists, all that can be done is damage limitation. If the figure being bandied about is inaccurately high, it is easier to reduce the potentially damaging PR. It is important to portray the charity's board or trustees as having acted honestly and with probity, and as united and unconcerned about the fees, or it will be hard to safeguard the reputation of the firm and the partner responsible.

As before, the plan and toolkit should be formulated. Ideally, the spokesperson should be one of the trustees, preferably someone not a partner in/connected with the law firm involved, as third party endorsement in this situation would be helpful. They should be encouraged to speak openly to the press rather than waiting for the journalists to call, in the hope of containing the escalating interest in the story, and with the aim of damping it down.

Whether a trustee unconnected with the firm or its senior or managing partner is the spokesperson, his/her messages should include:

- 'Yes, I agree these fees do appear to be on the high side, but they are entirely in accordance with the fee agreement negotiated between the trustees and the firm before work even began.'
- 'You must understand that a complicated enduring trust of this sort requires a lot of work to set up. It involves tax planning, public interest issues, and careful research to ensure that its beneficiaries are those which [the celebrity] would have wished. This helps to explain

these seemingly high costs in the first year. Thereafter, having been professionally established, the trust will be able to operate for very many years with much lower legal fees being incurred' or 'You should appreciate we have been administering a very complex trust with an £ . . . million fund for some . . . months/years. It has involved . . . of donations and bequests . . . The work throughout has been supervised by a senior partner of . . . years specialist experience.'

- 'All the trustees are aware that many hours of time invested by the firm have not been charged, and that the charges incurred have all been no higher than the standard charges for a firm with this specialist experience.'

- 'All the trustees have a responsibility to ensure that the fund is well managed and the donations accumulated are not dissipated unnecessarily in legal fees.'

- 'You will know that the firm undertakes a considerable amount of work on a pro bono basis, is a Member of the Solicitors' Pro Bono Group and a supporter of Business in the Community [if true]. It is unreasonable to expect the firm to do complex work of this nature without appropriate remuneration at the fair market rate.'

- 'It is unfair to claim that this firm is staffed by "fat cats" – our partners and assistants do not receive more than is commonplace in most law firms of this size and stature, and indeed its commitment to continuing to undertake legal aid work and pro bono work [if true] would indicate that it is also aware of the importance of providing access to justice.'

A public figure's private life attracts tabloid media interest, which puts his job in jeopardy

It pays to try to stay one jump ahead if you are tasked with protecting your client's interests. A tough call I regularly have to make is whether to volunteer uncomfortable information to the media in order to dictate the agenda and control the issue, and thereby risk drawing attention to something that might never otherwise be covered, or whether to wait in the hope it does not appear, aware that if it does you will be on the back foot fire-fighting with the media dictating the agenda. On the whole, I always favour candour and control, but clients are sometimes nervous about this approach, preferring to do impersonations of ostriches.

In a recent case, a Member of Parliament was photographed on holiday with his much younger same-sex partner, when he had not come out openly to his family, his constituents or his local party as a homosexual.

It was clear that at least one tabloid paper was likely to 'out' the public figure and in so doing would reveal some unfortunate aspects of his companion's past and their relationship. Working closely alongside his solicitor, we arranged a rapid interview with the most trustworthy of the

MP's local journalists and within a few hours the MP had effectively outed himself in a candid and upbeat interview, for which he had been carefully coached. Our angle was that he knew there was press speculation about his sexual orientation and as he was coming up for reselection, he wished to be open with his constituents and was speaking to the highest circulation local newspaper in order to do so. True and credible.

The article, which contained all the messages we had rehearsed, was inevitably picked up by the nationals and ran a day later, quite visibly in all the tabloids and most of the broadsheets, with one paper accompanying its article with the anticipated snatched holiday snap. By admitting and dealing openly himself with most of the issues on which the MP knew he was vulnerable, much of the impact of the national tabloid stories had been diluted. The story ran, as these things do, for several days with new revelations tumbling out, particularly after the boyfriend had been paid to part with some more information and a few snaps of his own, but the MP kept his job and maintained his constituents' support, which had been our objectives.

The senior partner's viewpoint

Leslie Perrin, senior partner of national firm Osborne Clarke, is experienced at dealing with difficult issues with journalists. He is better equipped to do so than most as his first career was as an actor and he is acknowledged to be a very able communicator:

> Unexpected or tricky issues attracting attention might take you into the realms of journalists who are strangers with whom you have no established relationship – which makes it infinitely more dangerous. Lawyers want to get out of contact with the media what they put in and with journos there is always refraction. With journalists who don't know you that refraction will be greater.
>
> It's always wise to use external advice, particularly as some advisers have a network of contacts and relationships with journalists that you can never have.
>
> If what you are dealing with is a serious commercial problem for a client, and there is potential for the media to be antagonistic you owe it to the client to ensure that the media dimension is well handled, and you owe it to your firm that what you are trying to achieve for the client is presented accurately.

Merger communications

Though a decision for law firms to merge should never be regarded as a disaster or crisis, if news of the negotiations leaks into the legal press at a crucial stage in the negotiations, it can scupper the whole process.

In terms of news, your main audiences (in order of priority) are:

- partners;
- fee-earners;
- support staff;
- clients;
- media;
- referrers/introducers;
- potential clients;
- suppliers.

Prior to merger announcement

The stages and actions in the communication process are as follows.

1. As talks commence, prepare holding statements, Qs and As and enquiry-handling mechanisms to ensure that any enquiries, from any audiences, are appropriately parried.
2. Ensure all documentation is kept totally secure and the project is only referred to by code name.
3. Ensure no faxes are sent without prior warning, no printers are left unsupervised and, if secretarial staff have to be informed, they know as little as possible and are pressed to ensure the security of documentation and information at all times.
4. Appoint one spokesperson on the issue. Be aware, the media and other contacts may make enquiries at all levels within the firm, and exploit friendships/relationships that may exist with the firm under discussion and others.
5. Manage speculation (internal and external) while preliminary top level discussions are going on, due diligence and disclosure taking place and the viability of the deal being explored.
6. Having told the core team in each firm, contain the information beyond this group for as long as possible until there is reasonable certainty the deal will proceed.
7. Fend off all media enquiries and speculation without confirming or providing any information that could lead to the story of the merger possibility naming firms; damp down interest; if necessary – without actually lying – aim to obscure the issue and throw them off the scent.
8. If any member of the informed core team reports rumour/speculation within the firm at any level, speak directly to the person believed to be speculating and press them to observe confidentiality for fear of jeopardising the deal.
9. Once the proposition is in a fit state to be put to the partners in each firm for approval, endeavour to organise simultaneous meetings,

prepare similar scripts for the presentations, prepare appropriate visual support and hard copy materials (to be left behind after the meeting), and endeavour to identify any likely dissidents, for advance canvassing.

10.   Prepare the following in advance of the meeting (ideally both firms should prepare identical support materials):

- fully accurate client/marketing database;
- photographs of the lead players together, taking care to ensure appropriate style of shot;
- letter to all staff;
- a letter to all main clients, to go under the hand of the contact partner;
- a draft news release with comprehensive notes showing clearly the advantages of the merged entity, the rationale behind the decision, the key practice areas and lead lawyers;
- full press distribution list;
- ideally, if a visual identity and name have already been developed by a branding consultancy the visual image can be used on the above and unveiled at this time;
- information to update the website immediately the deal is agreed.

11.   If the partnerships approve the proposition in principle, undertake the following actions on the same day and as immediately after the meeting as achievable:

- Issue the announcement to all staff (ideally in a large meeting or to everyone by e-mail). This should make clear (if true) that there will be no immediate downsizing, that jobs are secure, that remuneration will be unaffected or improved, that prospects for all are enhanced, and that individual counselling sessions are available for anyone who has any concerns, with a suitably qualified and informed individual at times to be identified. It should acknowledge that in the run-up to the merger going live all will be involved in additional work and the author of the communication appreciates their dedication and commitment. It should also include some guidance about enquiry handling on the issue – all enquiries to be routed to the key spokesperson and caller's details logged.
- Despatch the client letters: consider including a copy of the release so that the letter can make reference and say, 'we wanted you to see the information we have today released to the press'; sell in the most positive aspects of the merger from the clients' point of view and offer early meetings to discuss the impact on their business/relationship with the firm. Ensure messages about 'business as usual' are the primary focus of the letter.

- Distribute the news release to legal, national and relevant sectoral media on lines such as: 'P and X are delighted to announced that the respective partnerships last night agreed to merge the two firms and anticipate operating as a merged firm, to be known as . . . and continuing to operate from . . . , on . . . . The Senior Partner will be . . . , the Managing Partner will be . . . , and the firm will be governed by an Executive Board comprised of . . . '.
- Identify times when the lead spokespeople for both firms will be available for media briefings, if required.

After the announcement

Once the announcement is out, there will be reduced media interest, but much to be undertaken in a very short time. The more all staff, including the support staff, can be involved in the process, the better. Do not communicate solely with the partners and the lawyers. Make the process as inclusive as possible and encourage your merger partner to adopt a similar approach. Both firms should be operating during this phase in as similar a manner as is achievable, to ensure a smooth cultural fit on merger and avoid any interfirm territoriality, jealousy or discord. (Note: simple things like one firm providing free coffee for all staff and the other having pay machines can destabilise an entire merger.)

During this period before the merged partnership goes live, the following actions should be undertaken:

1. Produce a clear, punchy, business development strategy to which both firms' leaders fully subscribe.
2. Devise an organogram showing clearly how the new firm will be structured and governed.
3. Resolve all outstanding management and remuneration issues (it is crucial that none remain unresolved at the time of going live).
4. Appoint a small project team with representatives of both firms from various levels to drive the logistics of merger administration; appoint joint project managers with responsibility for nothing but the merger administration.
5. Establish a cross-firm communications group to lead on all communications matters (literature, website, staff and client communications, interior décor, house colours and style) in liaison with in-house and external professionals.
6. Complete the development of the visual identity, marketing literature, letterhead, signage and all physical manifestations of the new brand.
7. Ensure as much media activity as possible is undertaken by both firms during this interim phase to signal the excellence of their work

and deals, and make relevant reference to the pending merger taking effect. If possible, find transactions on which lawyers in the two firms can collaborate, and include that information in press briefings.

8. Design and trial a new updated website for the merged firm containing the best of both existing sites and upgraded (increasingly the modernity of a firm's website is seen as indicator of its overall approach to business). Ensure online recruitment applications, direct e-mail links to all key contacts, news releases on site and e-briefings established, as a minimum.

9. Set up meetings with all relevant staff to explain the new structure, remuneration schemes, career prospects, etc.

10. Hold an all-staff meeting, before going live, to enthuse, motivate and explain.

11. Arrange one-on-one meetings with all key clients (starting with those most likely to be disenchanted at the prospect of working with a larger firm).

12. Arrange meetings with or phone calls to all key introducers and suppliers.

13. Plan a final staff party to say goodbye to the old firm.

14. Plan an all-staff celebratory party shortly after the merger goes live.

15. Devise activities to ensure as many cross-firm meetings as possible to familiarise the lawyers and support staff with their new colleagues within practice groups (social as well as business-oriented: quizzes, seven-a-side, etc.).

16. Plan an early client celebration to celebrate the firms' merger.

17. Plan a press party to familiarise the relevant journalists with the new firm and its leaders.

18. Book a holiday!

Going live

On the day that the merger takes effect, if the firms are to continue to operate from their existing buildings it is important to do everything possible to make their offices look and feel different and to create some enthusiasm among the staff that things have changed and changed for the better. Apart from the signage, which should be changed overnight/over the weekend to ensure that both offices are rebranded by the start of business on 'Launch Monday', it is important to involve all staff.

Some of the things that can be done with forward planning and budget include:

- balloons, decorations or banners outside the offices or in the foyers/reception areas;
- string quartets for the first day playing in reception (if space);

- new mugs with the new name and logo on every staff member's desk before they arrive for work;
- new corporate umbrellas for all staff on their chairs on the first day;
- a booklet explaining the rationale and vision of the firm, with its new logo and mission, a 'rogues' gallery' of photos of all the key players, a 'Who Does What' guide and any other relevant information in the 'rough guide' format, on all staff desks.

Clients should also receive on the first day (despatched the previous Friday) an upbeat letter saying that the merger has now taken effect, and outlining what it will mean to them in terms of greater depth and breadth of service and, if relevant, any economies of scale. If media coverage of the merger announcement was extensive and favourable, a collage of the best coverage can be created for despatch with this letter to inform the clients about the reaction to the news in the marketplace and to signal your media awareness.

Ideally, one or more major deals should be kept back for announcement to coincide with the merger taking effect.

A comprehensive programme of media briefings with old and new media contacts and the new joint leaders should be established and actioned as soon as workable after the merger has gone live. A series of in-house lunches is most convenient, but devote time to this. It is important, and easy to ignore when management issues are paramount.

There should be continuous careful monitoring of all reactions to the merger among all audiences, particularly among staff, and meetings to take the temperature should continue.

If promises were made or ambitions indicated at the time of the merger announcement (e.g. 'By next year we hope the merged firm will be acting for . . . Top 350 companies'), and are fulfilled, particularly if ahead of deadline, trumpet this.

A few final tips:

- plan a celebration for staff and a further one for clients a year after the merger takes effect;
- consider a client attitude survey a year after the merger takes effect;
- consider a staff attitude survey;
- undertake a rigorous evaluation of the whole exercise and *learn from it*.

Appendix 1

Solicitors' Publicity Code 2001[1]

Code dated 16 November 2001 promulgated by the Council of the Law Society with the concurrence of the Master of the Rolls under rule 2 of the Solicitors' Practice Rules 1990, regulating the publicity of:

- solicitors, registered European lawyers and recognised bodies practising in England and Wales; and
- registered foreign lawyers practising in England and Wales in partnership with solicitors or registered European lawyers.

Section 1 – General principles

(a) Misleading or inaccurate publicity

Publicity must not be misleading or inaccurate.

(b) Clarity as to charges

Any publicity as to charges or a basis of charging must be clearly expressed. It must be clear whether disbursements and VAT are included.

(c) Name of firm

A private practice must not use a name or description which is misleading. It would be misleading for a name or description to include the word 'solicitor(s)', if none of the principals or directors (or members in the case of a limited liability partnership) is a solicitor.

(d) Unsolicited visits or telephone calls

(i)   Practitioners must not publicise their practices by making unsolicited visits or telephone calls to a member of the public.

(ii) 'Member of the public' does not include:

(A) a current or former client;
(B) another lawyer;

1. Last amended 13 January 2003.

(C) an existing or potential professional or business connection; or

(D) a commercial organisation or public body.

(e) Addresses to the court

It is not proper for practitioners to distribute to the press, radio or television copies of a speech or address to any court, tribunal or inquiry, except at the time and place of the hearing to persons attending the hearing to report the proceedings.

(f) International aspects of publicity

Publicity intended for a jurisdiction outside England and Wales must comply with:

(i)   the provisions of this code; and

(ii)   the rules in force in that jurisdiction concerning lawyers' publicity.

Publicity intended for a jurisdiction where it is permitted will not breach this paragraph through being incidentally received in a jurisdiction where it is not permitted.

(g) Practitioners' responsibility for publicity

A practitioner must not authorise any other person to conduct publicity for the practitioner's practice in a way which would be contrary to this code.

(h) Application

This section of the code applies to all forms of publicity including stationery, advertisements, brochures, directory entries, media appearances, press releases promoting a practice, and direct approaches to potential clients and other persons, and whether conducted in person, in writing, or in electronic form.

Section 2 – Professional stationery

(a)   The letterhead of a private practice must bear the words 'regulated by the Law Society'.

(b)   (i)   The letterhead of:

(A)   a sole principal must include the name of the sole principal;

       (B)   a partnership of 20 or fewer persons must include a list of the partners;

       (C)   a recognised body which is a company with a sole director must include the name of the director, identified as director.

  (ii)   The letterhead of:

       (A)   a partnership of more than 20 persons must include either a list of the partners,

       (B)   a recognised body which is a limited liability partnership must include either a list of the members, identified as members,

       (C)   a recognised body which is a company with more than one director must include either a list of the directors, identified as directors,

    or a statement that the list is open to inspection at the office.

  (iii) (A)   On the letterhead of a recognised body which is an unlimited company; or

       (B)   in the list of partners referred to in sub-paragraph (i) or (ii) above, if a partnership has an unlimited company as a member; or

       (C)   in the list of members referred to in sub-paragraph (ii) above, if a limited liability partnership has an unlimited company as a member;

  it shall be stated, either as part of the unlimited company's name or otherwise, that the unlimited company is a body corporate.

(c)   In a private practice, if the partners (or directors in the case of a company, or members in the case of a limited liability partnership) comprise both solicitors and foreign lawyers, the list referred to in (b)(i) or (ii) above must:

  (i)   in the case of any solicitor, identify him or her as a solicitor;

  (ii)   in the case of any lawyer or notary of a state (other than the UK) covered by the Establishment of Lawyers Directive 98/5/EC:

       (A)   identify the European jurisdiction(s) – local or national as appropriate – under whose professional title he or she is practising;

       (B)   give the professional title, expressed in an official language of the European state(s) concerned; and

       (C)   if the lawyer is a registered European lawyer, refer to his or her registration with the Law Society; and

(iii)   in the case of any registered foreign lawyer not included in (c)(ii) above, indicate his or her professional qualification(s) as a lawyer and the country or jurisdiction of qualification.

(d)   Whenever a registered European lawyer is named on the letterhead used by any private or in-house practice, there must be compliance with paragraph (c)(ii) above.

Section 3 – Interpretation and repeal

(a)   In this code, words have the meanings assigned to them in rule 18 of the Solicitors' Practice Rules 1990, except that:

(i)   'letterhead' includes a fax heading; and
(ii)   'solicitor' means a solicitor of the Supreme Court.

(b)   This code replaces the Solicitors' Publicity Code 1990.

Appendix 2

Guidance notes for branches of the Institute of Legal Executives (ILEX)

Favourable information about ILEX and its members can be placed in the columns of local weekly and evening newspapers, and on local radio/TV stations. This underpins the national PR campaign mounted by ILEX to promote awareness and understanding of legal executives. Promoting legal executives and ILEX locally can also stimulate interest by students and members to join their nearest ILEX branch.

To be effective, effort needs to be *sustained over several years*, to build up credibility with the news media and with the readers or audience. News is an ephemeral commodity and, to achieve repetition of the ILEX brand, it is important to plan your news releases evenly over the course of each year.

Most branches now appoint a press officer/press contact. For continuity, all communications to or from the media should be channelled through the local press officer.

Legal executives tasked with media relations are asked to liaise regularly with the ILEX Communications & PR Department, Tel: 01234 841000, and to remember to send the department copies of all press releases.

They are asked to report any contact with national or local media, and especially any requests to appear for interviews.

The approach technique recommended by ILEX

Establish a list of the news media in your area, including local radio stations (both BBC and independents), regional evening and morning newspapers, free distribution newspapers and regional periodicals covering business and/or social news.

Write to the media, introducing your branch giving brief details on legal executives. Address your initial communication to the editor. An example of such a letter of introduction follows.

The letters should be addressed to the individual by name. A telephone call to the publication can quickly establish the correct destination.

Contact the ILEX Communications & PR Department if you need assistance in compiling your list and/or contacts.

Once you have the name of an individual within the news media who will accept submissions for the news columns or programmes, make sure you always communicate with that contact. This saves time explaining your bona fides on subsequent occasions.

Suggested items for press releases

Appointments of branch officials or to the Council of ILEX: the appointment of officials can be of interest to local media, especially when accompanied by a clear print or digital photograph. The release should be no more than two or three paragraphs providing the full name and home address of the appointee (do not give the house number), name and place of business, and details of hobbies or local community work.

Annual dinner or major social occasion: a complimentary ticket must be sent to invited press. If the occasion is appropriate (i.e. a dinner dance) consider inviting their partner. 'This is a treat, we don't often get out together!'

Ideally, any press representative should be supplied with outline details, in writing or e-mail in advance, in case they wish to send a photographer. A copy of the speech should be available for any press representative attending, ideally ahead of its delivery and marked 'check against delivery', so that if it changes, the journalist is on notice.

Other events: seminars, training sessions, group visits, sporting events and other branch activities may warrant news coverage.

Charity events can be looked upon favourably by local editors. If the general public is being invited to take part, local radio will often make an announcement. Obviously, the more novel the event, the greater the news value. Make it clear that the local branch of ILEX is the organiser. For ceremonial handovers of money raised, bumper-sized presentation cheques may be obtained from branches of the major banks.

The news release

The story should be no more than an A4 sheet, typewritten in double spacing, with a wide margin on the left (see specimen news release below).

Choose a short title that describes the reason for the release.

The first paragraph should answer the questions Who, Why, What, Where and When.

As the sender, your name, telephone number and e-mail address should be prominently displayed so a reporter can contact you for further information or to check facts.

Ensure that any name used in the release is spelt correctly and forenames are provided as well as surnames. (Anyone mentioned or quoted in the release should be aware of the contents in advance of release.)

Avoid use of jargon and abbreviations.

Issue news releases promptly. An exception is undated material (such as new appointments), which may be issued at any time.

Always include the following 'positioning statement' (otherwise known as a 'boilerplate') which identifies and promotes the objectives of ILEX: '. . . the Institute of Legal Executives (ILEX), the professional body representing over 22,000 Legal Executives and trainees'.

Do not send photographs to radio stations. Whether sent by print or digitally, always ensure that a caption accompanies the photograph and is attached to the back as separate pieces of paper can get separated on a congested photo editor's desk. Give full identification of the subject(s) and your name and telephone number as a contact in case photographs become separated from the text in the newsroom. The quality of amateur 'snaps' is rarely good enough: ideally photographs should be taken professionally for media purposes.

Follow-up activity

If you have succeeded in generating publicity locally, please send an original cutting from the newspaper to the ILEX Communications & PR Department. Under Newspaper Licensing Authority regulations you are not usually permitted to take a photocopy, even if it is your news release that has been printed.

Do not pester journalists. If you have sent a release, correctly addressed to your contact, they will make up their own mind whether they will use it or not. Of course, it is permissible to 'progress chase' on invitations to attend dinners or meetings.

ILEX specimen introduction letter to local editor

Date

Mr S Brown
Editor
Bedfordshire Daily Planet
High Street
Bedford

Dear Mr Brown

Bedfordshire Branch of the Institute of Legal Executives

There are many Legal Executives and trainee personnel working as lawyers in legal practices in Bedfordshire. I have recently been appointed press officer for the Bedfordshire Branch of the Institute of Legal Executives (ILEX) and am writing to introduce myself.

ILEX is the professional body for Legal Executives and represents over 22,000 members nationwide. I would like from time to time to send you items of local interest concerning the appointments of officials, details of our professional training giving opportunities to local students or social/charity events in the area.

Can you please let me have the name of the individual to whom this information should be sent to so I can ensure any future communications are correctly addressed.

Thank you in advance for your co-operation. Please contact me if you require any further information on ILEX or its activities. My telephone number is . . . and my e-mail address is . . .

Yours sincerely

John Smith
Press Officer

ILEX specimen news release

Date release sent out

LOCAL LAWYER APPOINTED CHAIRMAN OF ILEX LEEDS BRANCH

Mr David Smith has been appointed chairman of the re-launched Leeds Branch of the Institute of Legal Executives (ILEX), the professional body representing over 22,000 Legal Executives and trainees in England and Wales.

With a law career spanning 21 years and a Fellow of ILEX, Mr Smith is Head of the Crown Court department at Highfield Solicitors, High Street, Leeds.

Commenting on his appointment and re-establishment of an ILEX Branch in Leeds, Mr Smith said: 'I am confident that the branch will be enthusiastically supported by local members of ILEX. As chairman, my task will be to listen locally and action nationally through the ILEX Headquarters in Bedford.'

Mr Smith, married with two children, lives in Acacia Street, Leeds. He is extremely active in the local community and is a member of the church committee for St Michael's Church, Leeds.

For further information contact:

Name of contact	John Smith
	Press Officer
	ILEX Leeds Branch
Issuing Branch telephone number	Tel: . . .

Notes to Editors

The Institute of Legal Executives (ILEX) is recognised as the third branch of the legal profession alongside solicitors and barristers. Legal Executives are lawyers who have qualified by studying and working at the same time. They work in law firms, government departments and private companies. Their day-to-day work is similar to that of solicitors, although the training and qualifications are different.

Appendix 3

Law Society's Commerce & Industry Group media relations guidelines

The Law Society Commerce and Industry Group (C&I) does not issue a media relations policy for members who are not part of the National Main Executive Committee. All press and publicity enquiries regarding C&I are handled through a central communications/press office. If an individual C&I member wants specific media relations advice (and this does happen from time to time) then the C&I National Office would endeavour to assist.

The 10 basic guidelines followed by C&I's National Executive are as follows:

1. Always involve your company's internal press office in relation to any media enquiry.
2. Do not underestimate the importance of accepting specialist media relations advice or media training.
3. Do not allow yourself to be caught off guard – offer to call the journalist back if you are not prepared.
4. No matter how tempting it is to give a teaser of information to a journalist before an embargoed release, do not!
5. Be well prepared for interviews – have an approved press release or press statement in front of you and a hymn sheet of other key points to refer to.
6. Don't deviate from the question.
7. Adopt an open communication style, i.e. not guarded or defensive.
8. If additional information is promised then ensure this is followed through.
9. First impressions count. Treat each and every media opportunity as important and valued.
10. Portray a consistent, transparent and positive approach to the media at all times and recognise that editorial control/licence always rests with the journalist.

Currently all press and publicity enquiries for the C&I are handled via Sue Blake Media Relations on 020 8891 2203 and sue@sueblakemedia.co.uk

Appendix 4

Campaigning on miscarriages of justice

The following is advice provided by Conviction, a voluntary organisation set up to help those – not just lawyers – campaigning on behalf of people thought to have been wrongfully imprisoned. I am not responsible for these notes but believe they may contain some useful guidance.

If you are helping someone you believe to have been wrongly convicted and sentenced to imprisonment for a serious crime, you should demand help in order to overturn their conviction. You don't need to have educational qualifications, or to know about the law, or to write letters that have perfect spelling or grammar, in order to contest your conviction: but you do need to be very determined, and to know where to get help, how to persuade people outside prison to help you, and to check that the help you are getting is being given you in the best possible way. These notes attempt to give you some initial leads and guidance in making best use of the help that is available.

There are circumstances in which your friend or relative may be innocent, but can do nothing to overturn their conviction. The quickest way of getting out of prison may be to do whatever is necessary to obtain parole (or release on licence for those with life sentences). We wouldn't want to give prisoners false hopes that justice will always triumph and the truth will come out in the end. But it is possible to obtain release on parole without admitting guilt. What parole boards should be concerned with is whether you are likely to commit crimes in future – not whether you express remorse for something you didn't do.

Although it is very hard to overturn a wrongful conviction, it is not impossible. Over the last few years the list of prisoners wrongfully accused who have been released after having their convictions quashed is impressive: Sally Clark, the Birmingham Six, the Guildford Four, Judith Ward, the Tottenham Three, Mike Royle and Robert Hall, the Cardiff Three, Steve Davis, Adrian Maher, Kevin Callan, the Bridgewater Four and more besides. Many of these cases looked hopeless at first. **Conviction** supported many of them through to successful appeals. Successful campaigns such as those of the Birmingham Six and Tottenham Three have involved families and friends of the prisoners, who managed to link up with other sympathisers, and their combined efforts led to the prisoners' release. So encourage friends and relatives of the prisoner to join your fight.

Campaigning organisations

Action Against Injustice, PO Box 858, London E9 5HU, supports and co-ordinates campaigns against injustice.

Justice, 59 Carter Lane, London EC4V 5AQ, phone: 020 7329 5100/fax 020 7329 5055, will only consider a case once all routine appeals have been exhausted. They may be slow, but if they take on your case they are extremely thorough and they are well respected, so the chance of success is good. They have support from solicitors and other professionals. Justice publishes a guide to appeals – free to prisoners if they send a 6″ × 9″ addressed envelope with 31p stamp. The guide costs £2.50 to others.

Innocent, Dept 54, 255 Wilmslow Road, Manchester M14 5LW, campaigns with the families and friends of prisoners believe to have been framed, from the Greater Manchester area. Works closely with Conviction.

Conviction, PO Box 522, Sheffield S1 3FF, supports prisoners who are fighting their convictions. Because it is a small voluntary organisation, it restricts the cases it takes on to those who have long sentences (six years or more), and who it may be able to help. Can only take cases originating in Manchester or the East Midlands.

Liberty, 21 Tabard Street, London SE1 4LA, phone: 020 7403 3888, supports only a very limited number of test cases, but can pass cases on to members of their network of sympathetic solicitors.

Liberty may have a local branch in your home town or where your friend or relative is in prison who will take up your case. There is a strong branch covering the West Midlands area, who helped to uncover police malpractice there, so if you are from the West Midlands write to Anita Richards, 27 Montague Road, Birmingham B21 9DF; otherwise, write to Liberty head office.

Release, 388 Old Street, London EC1V 9LT, phone: 020 7729 9904 10am–6pm, 020 7603 8654 for overnight help and 020 7729 5255 for admin, campaigns on drug law reform and advises on drug-related matters.

Members of Parliament, House of Commons, London SW1A 0AA. Some MPs can be very helpful and some will support campaigns. They can be asked to extract responses from the Home Office.

Prison Reform Trust, 15 Northburgh Street, London EC1V 0AH, phone: 020 7251 5070. Ask them to send you their Information Pack, free to prisoners. Contains factsheets, including prisoners 'rights' (not many) and lists of organisations that help prisoners and their families.

National Prisoners' Movement, BM Prop, London WC1N 3XX, phone: 020 8542 3744.

Prison Watch, 24 Rochester Close, Derby DE24 0HS, phone: 0117 949 2883/01332 756158, fax: 01332 753515, a network of people concerned about prison conditions and how they affect prisoners and families. They support, advise and campaign. They can advise on how to get answers and results and where to get support, publicity and legal assistance concerning prison problems (but not fighting wrongful convictions).

Howard League for Penal Reform, 708 Holloway Road, London N19 3NL, phone: 020 7281 7722, produces a very useful information pack (including further list of support organisations), free to families of prisoners (£39 to anyone else).

Aftermath, PO Box 414, Sheffield S1 3UP, phone: 0114 232 6166, helps families and partners of offenders, especially of murderers and sex offenders. Has groups in other areas.

Prisoners' Advice Service, Unit 305, Hatton Square, 16/16a Baldwins Gardens, London EC1N 7RJ, provides prisoners with information and advice about their rights and takes up prisoners' complaints about their treatment within the prison system.

NACRO (National Association for the Care and Resettlement of Offenders), 169 Clapham Road, London SW9 0PU, phone: 020 7582 6500, administers a fund to help prisoners' families suffering hardship.

Women Prisoners' Resource Centre, 1 Thorpe Close, Ladbroke Grove, London W10 5XL, phone: 020 8986 3121 and at 567a Barlow Moor Road, Manchester M21 2AE, phone: 0161 861 9757, is part of NACRO.

NAPO (National Association of Probation Officers), 3/4 Chivalry Road, London SW11 1HT, phone: 020 7223 4887, campaigns against wrongful conviction in general.

Terry O'Hallaran Memorial Fund, BCM 5960, London WC1N 3XX, set up by the Revolutionary Communist Group and the National Union of Journalists, following the death of communist journalist, Terry O'Halloran, who campaigned for prisoners' rights. Provides books and magazines for prisoners.

Publicity

Publicity may be the factor that makes lawyers and courts take your case seriously – although they won't admit it. It may help to bring informa-tion to light, such as cases having important elements in common with yours. Take care to get the right publicity, and plenty of it. Do you think the Guildford Four and Birmingham Six would be free now, if it weren't for the publicity and the campaigns that generated it?

Whatever you send out to the media or to campaigning organisations, assume they know nothing at all about the prisoner and his or her case, and include all basic information, including (if possible):

- their full name;
- their age;
- date + place of crime;
- date + place of arrest;
- police force and squad;
- what they were charged with;
- date of trial;
- sentence received;
- how far appeal has progressed;
- names of all the lawyers involved;
- documents available (trial depositions, transcripts, advice on appeal);
- who is supporting the case (local MP, campaigning organisations, etc.);
- contact for further information – name, address, phone no.

Most important, the letter you send out should summarise the case in such a way that the interest of the reader is caught: what happened (briefly); the essential points of the prosecution case; the basis of the defence; and what went wrong for the convicted person. Tell the readers why they should be concerned about this case; how they can help – what help is needed (if you know). Remember: reporters and campaigning organisations are overloaded with work – send out a brief, clear letter which makes it easy for them to respond and deprives of them any excuse to put it to one side: grab their attention! Do not send large quantities of paperwork relating to the case until it's asked for.

Local papers will take an interest and print something about the convicted person and their case, but it may not be favourable (they depend on the police for much of their news, and won't want to offend them). Look at what they've printed in the past, and assess which reporters are likely to be sympathetic – then address your letters to them. The same applies to local radio and tv. Get friends and relatives to suss them out and talk to them.

The following journalists and publications have covered miscarriages of justice in the recent past:

- Duncan Campbell, *The Guardian.*
- Heather Mills and Adam Sage, *The Independent.*
- Dennis Campbell, *Time Out,* for London cases.
- Olwen Dudgeon, *Yorkshire Post.*
- *Caribbean Times/Asian Times,* 139–149 Fonthill Road, London N4 3HF. Good coverage of cases involving prisoners describing themselves as black British, Afro-Caribbean or Asian.

- *The Voice*, 370 Coldharbour Lane, London SW9 8PL, weekly journal, phone: 020 7738 5500.
- *Irish in Britain News,* Canal House, Catherine Wheel Road, Brentford, Middlesex TW8 8BD.
- *The Irish World,* 307a High Road, London NW10 2JR.
- *The Irish Post,* Uxbridge House, 464 Uxbridge Road, Hayes, Middlesex. UB1 0SP, phone: 020 8561 0059.

If you believe a friend or relative has been wrongly convicted, you should check that their appeal is progressing as it should. The family and supporters should know enough about the process and the time limits, so that they can check that the lawyers are doing what they should. The booklet, *A Guide to Proceedings in the Court of Appeal Criminal Division* is available but hard to come by.

A new organisation, **Criminal Appeal Lawyers Association**, has recently been set up and can be contacted through the chairman, Campbell Malone (Stephensons, 230 Chapel Street, Salford, Greater Manchester M3 5LE, phone: 0161 832 8844) or secretary, Jane Hickman (Hickman & Rose, Maple Business Centre, 144 Liverpool Road, London N1 1LA, phone: 020 7700 2211).

Necessary disclaimer: You should take legal advice at all stages in the development of your case.

Good luck!

Appendix 5

Recommended additional reading

Adam, L., *Marketing Your Law Firm: A Solicitor's Manual* (Law Society, 2002) (this comes complete with a resource CD and a short section on public relations and the news media)

Ali, M., *The DIY Guide to Marketing* (Directory of Social Change, 1995)

Ali, M., *The DIY Guide to Public Relations* (2nd edn., Directory of Social Change, 1999)

Arlidge, Eady and Smith on Contempt (2nd edn, Sweet & Maxwell, 1999)

Barker, A. and Marji, F. (Fahamu) *Writing for Change*: An Interactive Guide to Effective Writing, Writing for Science, Writing for Advocacy CD-Rom and User's Guide (Stylus Publishing, 2001) (a CD-Rom-based course in writing skills, including sections on writing for advocacy)

Crone, T. *et al.*, *Law and the Media* (Focal Press, 2002)

Cutts, M., *Plain English Guide: How to Write Clearly and Communicate Better* (Oxford University Press, 1999)

Doughty, K., *Business Continuity Planning: Protecting Your Organisation's Life* (Auerback, 2000)

Haggerty, J.F., *In the Court of Public Opinion* (John Wiley, 2003)

Kober-Smith, M., *Legal Lobbying: How to Make Your Voice Heard* (Cavenish, 2000) (this is mainly one lawyer's experience of achieving a minor change in the law as it affects notaries, but contains some useful guidance)

The Plain English Campaign, *Language on Trial: The Plain English Guide to Legal Writing* (Robson Books, 1996)

McNae, L.C.J., *McNae's Essential Law for Journalists* (Butterworths, 2001)

Lowe, N., and Sufrin, B., *Borrie and Lowe: The Law of Contempt* (3rd edn, Butterworths, 1996)

Miller, C.J., *Contempt of Court* (3rd edn, OUP, 2000)

Mitroff, I.I., *Managing Crises Before They Happen: What Every Executive and Manager Needs to Know About Crisis Management* (Amacom, 2000)

Nelson, V., *The Law of Entertainment and Broadcasting* (Sweet & Maxwell, 1995)

Newman, G., *Online Marketing Strategies* (Law Back Publishing, 2002)

Nicol, A., Millar, G. and Sharland, A., *Media Law and Human Rights* (Blackstone Press, 2001)

Phillips, D., *Managing Your Reputation in Cyberspace* (Thorogood, 1999)

Phillips, D., *On-Line Public Relations* (Institute of Public Relations, 2001)

Regester, M. and Larkin, J., *Risk Issues and Crisis Management (PR in Practice)* (Kogan Page, 2001)

Riskin, G. and McKenna, P., *Practice Development: Creating the Marketing Mindset* (Butterworths, 1989) (despite its age, this is still a valuable primer to help produce a business development strategy)

Robertson, G. and Nicol, A., *Media Law* (4th edn, Sweet & Maxwell, 1999)

Schlesinger, P. and Tumber, H., *Reporting Crime: The Media Politics of Criminal Justice* (Clarendon Press, 1994) (dated now but interesting)

Spillane, M., *Branding Yourself: How to Look, Sound and Behave Your Way to Success* (Pan, 2000)

Spillane, M., *Colour Me Beautiful: Looking Your Best* (Madison Books, USA, 2002)

Wacks, R., *Privacy and Press Freedom: Rights in Conflict* (Blackstone Press, 1995)

Witmer, D.F., *Spinning the Web: A Handbook for PR on the Internet* (Allyn & Bacon, 1999)

Internet sources

There is more information than you could possibly want or need. Try the following:

Media Trust (www.mediatrust.org/online_guides) which has online guidelines that are sensible and clear

JustDoSomething (www.justdosomething.net), the site set up by Common Purpose, which provides various professionals' advice under 'Handling the Media'.

Index

Accountancy Age 81
A'Court, Chris 56
Action Against Injustice 268
active media relations 76
Adam, Lucy 8
advertising
　'advertorials' 83
　naming clients 20
　public relations distinguished 78
　regional newspapers 83
　regulatory bodies 29
After Dark 173
Aftermath 269
anti-social behaviour orders 44–5
Any Questions 147
Archers, the 56–7
'as for live' interviews 160
Ashdown, Paddy 118, 232
Athens News Agency 75
Attorney-General 3–4, 38, 40, 41, 219

Baldry, Tony 162
Bar Mutual Insurance Fund (BMIF) 27
Bar News 25–27
barristers
　insurance 27–28
　rules for 25–27
Bawdon, Fiona 103, 114, 115–16, 246
Benn, Tony 99
Benn's Media Directory 72
Berlins, Marcel 34, 51, 56, 77, 122, 126
Bing, Steve 9, 16
Birmingham Post 83
Blake, Sue 28
blasphemy 29
Bloomberg 75
Blue Book of British Broadcasting 72
book reviews 125
BRAD Monthly 72
Brandman, Henri 185–6
Brass Eye 31
breach of confidence 30
British Rates and Data (BRAD) 72
broadcasting see radio; television
Broadcasting Standards Commission
　32
Burrell, Paul 2, 50
business cards 74
Butterick, Stephen 56

Camden Journal 53
Campaign for Press and Broadcasting
　Freedom 73
campaigning 11–12, 37, 58, 219
　Conviction, advice of 267–71
　Internet, on 63–4, 65
Campbell, Nicky 158
Carter, Stephen 41
Chambers 3, 20, 201
Chaplin, Richard 209
charges
　media handling, for 23–25
　time recording 25
　see also fees
'cheque book journalism' 15, 38
children
　reporting restrictions 43–5, 47
Chisholm, Scott 154–5
Clark, Sally 24–25, 95, 141, 227–9
　media campaign 9, 37, 63–4, 116,
　　129, 219–20
　second appeal 33–34, 64
　skeleton argument 47, 109
　statistical evidence 16, 34–35, 228
　website 63–4
clients
　introductions and referrals 18
　loyalty of 6
　naming 20
　perceptions of firm 7
　relationship with 5
Clifford, Max 98
Commedia 59
Commerce and Industry (C&I) Group
　80
　media relations guidelines 28, 266
Commercial Lawyer 80
committals
　reporting restrictions 41–42
Community Media Association 59
competitive tendering 6
complex prosecutions
　reporting restrictions 42–43
conditional fees 2
consultants
　'beauty parade'/'pitch' 210–11,
　　215–17
　brief to 212–15
　finding 208–9

recruitment process 209–12
sole practitioners and agencies
  compared 215
contact database 73, 74, 102
contact lenses 168–9
contempt of court
  'active' period 39
  admissions 37
  anti-prosecution commentaries 36
  anticipating course of trial 36
  character of defendant 37
  criticising decision to prosecute 36
  definition 33–5
  generally 29, 33–35, 54, 224
  impediment or prejudice 34–5
  jury trial 39–40
  magistrates' court 40
  payment into court, revealing 39
  payments to witnesses 38
  photographs of defendant 37–8
  predicting outcome of trial 36
  previous convictions 37
  risk of 36–39
  'serious prejudice' 35
  sub judice period 39
  'substantial risk' 35
  talking to media before trial 36–7
  tape-recording proceedings 39
  television coverage of criminal trials 39
  witnesses 37, 38–39
contingency fees 2
conveyancing
  contractual referrals for 17
Conviction 267–71
Cook, Alistair 142
Coronation Street 58
Corporate Finance 81
Cosmopolitan 81
Cotton, Louise 56
Counsel 80
court artists 32, 39
court restraints *see* legal and court
  restraints
'court steps' interviews 181–3
Coventry Evening Telegraph 53
Creative Butcher 81, 192
Crime Watch 2, 10
Criminal Appeal Lawyers Association
  271
crisis management
  active media management 244
  avoidance and limitation 13
  competent 232
  crisis communication 234–6

crisis plan 13
examples of legal crises 247–52
first reaction 233–4
immediate communications 234–6
incompetent 233
intentional lack of communication
  236
maintaining communications 245
merger communications 252–7
negative principles 237–9
phrases to avoid 243–4
planning 231–3
preparing by questioning 241–2
press centre 237
press releases 121–2
professional help 239–40
risk analysis 13, 231
rules of 236–7
spokesperson 236, 242–3, 246
toolkit 240–1
written communications strategy 236,
  240
Crossman, Richard 30
CSV Action Desks 73
Cunningham, Nick 225–7
cuttings 75–6, 91, 199, 200
cybercast seminars 200
Czech Happenings 75

D-notice system 31
Daily Express 50
Daily Mail 50
Daily Mirror 2, 35, 50
Daily Record 50
Daily Star 50
Daily Telegraph 50, 77, 79, 129, 248
database of contacts 73, 74, 102
Dean, John 74
defamation 30, 54, 128, 225
defensive medicine 2
diary columns 126
Dimbleby, Jonathan 147
Director 81, 192
directories 72
Document Exchange 121
Douglas, Michael 129
down-the-line interviews 132, 148,
  152, 183
Dudgeon, Olwen 83
Durrants 75, 76
Dyer, Clare 51, 77

e-briefings 3, 60
e-mail 3, 7, 60, 85

e-mail (*cont.*)
  dictating 3, 60
  disclaimers 109
  media lists 73
  press releases 102, 103, 109, 119,
    205–6
Eaglesham, Jean 101
Echo Research Ltd 111–12
electronic news gathering 57
embargoes 108–9, 110, 130
European Convention on Human
    Rights 29, 32
European Lawyer 80
European Legal Business 80
European legislation 32–3
exclusive interviews 93–4
expertise
  claims of 20
  recognition for 8

fax 74
  press releases 7, 101, 109, 119–20
fees
  clients' stories, for 23–5
  interviews, for 23–5, 93–4
  see also charges
Fenell, Edward 126
Financial Times 50, 79, 101, 248
'fishing expeditions' 97–8
fraud trials 43
  reporting restrictions 42
freedom of expression 29–33
Freedom of Information Act 2000 32
Freeman, Tom 205–7

Geldof, Bob 9
Gentleman, Fenella 217–18
Gibb, Frances 66–70, 85, 101
Global Counsel 80
Global Journalism Review 73
Gloucester Citizen 42
Google News 76
gossip columns 126
Guardian Media Guide 2003 72
Guardian, The 50, 77, 126
Guide to the Professional Conduct of
    Solicitors 1999, The 16–17, 20

hair 166–7
Harman, Harriet 224
Harpers & Queen 81
Harvey, Graham 56
Heaney, Mary 85
Hinze, Chris 91–2

Hitbox 64
Hollis Directories 208
Hollis UK Press and PR Annual 72
Howard League for Penal Reform
    269
Howe, Sir Geoffrey 167
Human Rights Act 1998 30, 32, 33
Hurley, Elizabeth 9, 16

In Brief 80
In House Lawyer 80
indemnity insurance
  barristers 27
  solicitors 22–3
Independent Lawyer 3, 103, 114, 115,
    246
Independent News Collective 59
Independent on Sunday 51
Independent, The 50, 77, 93, 224
Indymedia UK 59
information technology 3, 32–3
injunctions 34, 46, 223–4
INK 59
Innocent 268
Institute of Legal Executives (ILEX)
  guidance notes for branches of 28,
    262–5
Institute of Public Relations 208
insurance
  barristers 27
  solicitors 22–3
International Press Cuttings Bureau
    75
Internet
  accessibility 60
  audience range 63
  BBC News homepage 57–8
  campaigning on 63–4, 65
  chat 65
  constituents 65
  discussion lists 65
  e-mail *see* e-mail
  empathy 66
  generally 2, 7, 49, 58, 59–66
  keyboard skills 60
  message control, lack of 60, 61
  online media data 73
  online press conferences 201
  online transactions 59
  photographs 117
  porous nature of 60
  reach 60, 63, 64–5, 113
  richness 61–2
  search engines 7, 61, 62, 65, 72

speed 60
tracking services 64–5
transparency 60
updating 66
Virtual Press Office 62, 64
websites 3, 10, 59–66, 149, 151
interviews
'as for live' 160
conflict with interviewer 136
'court steps' interviews 181–3
critical interviews 134–6
current affairs programmes 137–47
down-the-line 132, 148, 152, 183
'dries' 147, 151–2, 159, 161
end of the interview 153–4
exclusive 93–4
fees for 23–5, 93–4
'fluffs' 151–2, 159
informative interviews 134
'interviewer's nerve' 135
name of firm, mentioning 18–19,
    94–5
news programmes 137–47
'no comment' 8, 181, 237
not answering the question 136
notes, using 152, 176
pre-recorded 147, 151–2, 159, 160–1
press interviews 96–9
profile pieces 113–15
radio interviews 132–55
reference to other lawyers 20–1
starting the interview 142–3
tape-recording 77, 97, 99
telephone interviews 97, 132, 152–3
workplace interviews 180–1
introductions and referrals 19

Jackson, Richard 56
Jaffa, Paul 95
Jeremy Vine Programme 56, 141
Jimmy Young Programme 23, 56, 141,
    150, 154
John, Elton 24
Jones, Rosamund 56
journalists
building relationships with 100–1,
    192–3, 199
checking copy 95–6
checking credentials 90, 91, 99
contacting 84–7
dealing with 71
exclusive interviews 93–4
'fishing expeditions' 97–8
generally 76–7

interviews 93–4, 96–9
leader columns 115
on and off the record 91–3, 97, 130
'op ed' pieces 115
opinion columnists 115
praising 100–1
quotes, attributing 94–5
reasons for contacting 84
rivalry between 101, 185
selling stories to 88–90, 198
unexpected approach from 90–1, 99
see also newspapers; radio; reporting
    restrictions; television
journals 79–80
jury trial 39–40, 222–4
Justice 268

Kay, Lord Justice 33
Kelly, Matthew 45, 223
keyboard skills 60
Kilroy 158, 179
Klein, Martha Sellers 101–2, 202–3

Lake, Julie 86
laptops 74
Law in Action 56
Law Society
Clients' Charter 5, 88
Commerce and Industry (C&I) Group
    28, 80, 266
external advisers 12
'Make A Will' campaign 56, 83, 88,
    154
motto 12
Parliamentary Officer 12
press relations advice 18
press releases 18
Law Society's Gazette 27, 80, 93, 100,
    126
Lawley, Sue 165
Lawrence, Philip 44
Lawyer, the 80, 94, 114, 126
'Lawyers for Business' 83
leader columns 115
league tables 3
Legal 500 3, 20, 102, 201, 202
legal aid 81, 83
Legal Business 80, 101, 113, 201, 202,
    205, 206
legal and court restraints
freedom of expression 29–33
generally 28–29
Legal Director 80
Legal Executive 80

legal executives
  guidance notes for branches of ILEX
    28, 262–5
legal journals 79–80
legal marketplace 1, 6–7
Legal Week 80, 85
Legal Week Global 80
Leslie, John 9–10, 223
Less, Michael 59
'letter before action' 32
letterheads 259, 261
Levick, Richard 66, 100, 224
  cybercast seminars 200
  inaccurate reporting 99–100
  marketing 184, 185
  myths of law firm PR 77–8
  name-checks 95
  online press conferences 201
  press releases 103
  trade press 81
LexisNexis 76
Liberty 268
litigation support 3, 219–29
  client's perspective 227–9
  guiding principle 221–2
  high court cases 229
  identifying newsworthy cases 220–1
  media as litigation tool 224–5
  partner's experience 225–7
  practicalities 222
  trial by jury 222–4
lobbying 12, 219
Local Independent Television Network
  (LiTN) 59
local media *see* regional media
Logan, Alistair 25
Lord Chancellor 4, 12, 38
Lovells 180, 217
lunches 124

McAllister, Samantha 56
McDonalds 3, 63
MacKay, David 63
McLeod, Jon 28
Macleod, Sandra 111–12
magazines 50, 81, 192
  see also print media
magistrates' court
  contempt 40
  reporting restrictions 41–3
Mail on Sunday 51
'Make A Will' campaign 56, 83, 88,
  154
make-up 166, 167, 169–70

Manchester Evening News 52, 83
marketing
  award-winning 201–3
  brochures 3, 59–60
  building relationships 193
  consultants *see* consultants
  follow-ups 199–200
  generally 5, 6
  identifying stories 194–5
  media relations 8
  packaging stories 195–6
  placing articles 196–7
  placing opinion pieces 197
  planned media relations 194
  principles 184–5
  professional guidance 185–7
  regional media 191–2
  research 196
  role of media relations in 188–91
  selling stories 198
  strategy 187–8
  unsolicited visits or calls 258
Marsh, Kevin 56
May, Teresa 162
Media Disk 73, 192
Media Law (Robertson and Nicol) 28–30,
  31, 32–3, 34, 41, 46, 222, 223
media list 73
  see also contact database
media lunches 124
Media Manager 73
media monitoring 75–6
media relations policy 13–14
Media UK 73
Mellor, David 98
merger communications 252–7
miscarriages of justice 37, 117, 219–20
  campaigns 11–12, 63–4, 65, 219, 275–9
  see also Clark, Sally
Mobile Commerce World 60
mobile phone 74
Moneybox 56, 192
Montgomery, Clare 47, 109
Moore, Matthew 8
'Moors Murders' case 41
Morgan, Piers 2, 50
Murray, Jenni 141

name of firm
  use in interviews 18–19, 94–5
naming clients 20
National Association for the Care and
  Resettlement of Offenders
  (NACRO) 269

National Association of Probation
   Officers (NAPO) 269
National Prisoners' Movement 268
Netgenesis 64
New Jour 73
New Law Journal 80
New York Times 78
news agencies 74–5
news releases *see* press releases
news stream 78
news wires 113, 119
   photographs 117
News of the World 51
Newsnight 179
Newspaper Society 83
newspapers
   advertising 83
   'advertorials' 83
   articles 126, 196–7
   'background' 92
   book reviews 125
   broadsheets 50, 51, 99
   checking copy 95–6
   'cheque book journalism' 15, 38
   circulation figures 50, 51
   contempt *see* contempt of court
   copytakers 120
   dealings with 66–70, 77–8
   defamation 54
   diary columns 126
   disclaimers 125
   evening papers 52, 53
   exclusive interviews 93–4
   fear, greed and sex 88
   freesheets 52
   generally 49–50
   gossip columns 126
   inaccuracies in 99–100
   interviews 93–4, 96–9
   leader columns 115
   legal columns 125
   local papers 12, 24, 52–3, 82–4, 98,
      115, 125, 192
   national 50–2, 79
   'night lawyers' 23, 32, 54
   'not attributable'/'not for attribution'
      92
   on and off the record 91–3, 97, 130
   online 50, 51
   'op ed' pieces 115
   opinion columns 115
   opinion pieces 197
   payments to witnesses 39
   photographs 115–18, 176, 199, 264

pre-publication legal advice 54
press briefings 124
press conferences 122–3, 232
press releases *see* press releases
profile pieces 113–15
quotes, attributing 94–5
regional papers 12, 23, 52–3, 82–4,
   98, 115, 125, 192
regular legal columns 125
research-based stories 127–8
restrictions *see* reporting restrictions
selling stories 88–90, 198
special supplements 83
Sunday papers 51, 52
tabloids 50, 51, 98, 115, 228
uncommissioned articles 196
unexpected approach from 90–1, 99
weekly papers 52–3
Newspoint 75
Nice Work 56
Nicholson, Emma 162
Nicol, Andrew, *Media Law* 28–30, 31,
   32–3, 34, 41, 46, 222, 223
'night lawyers' 23, 30, 54
'no comment' 8, 181, 237
'no win, no fee' 2
Norton Rose 18
'not attributable'/'not for attribution'
   92
notes, use in interviews 152, 176

Observer, The 51
OFCOM 41
official secrecy 30
on and off the record 91–3, 97, 130
online media *see* Internet
'op ed' pieces 115
opinion columns 115
opinion pieces 197
opinion polls 127
Osborne Clarke 86, 203–5, 252

packaging stories 195–6
panel discussions 147–8, 178–9
passive media relations 76
PDAs 74
People, the 51
Periodical Publishers' Association 73
Perrin, Leslie 203–5, 252
personal indemnity insurance 24
Personnel Today 81
Phillips, Andrew 56
Phillips, David 61
phone-in programmes 22, 149–51

photographs 115–18, 176, 199, 264
    defendant, of 37–38
PIMS 73–4, 119
Pims UK Media Directory 72
Pink Pages 81
police 2, 219
Ponting, Clive 223
popbitch 10
portable laptop and printer 74
PR consultants *see* consultants
PR Planner 72
PR Week 208–9
Practice Management for the Bar
    186–7
pre-publication legal advice 54
    'night lawyers' 23, 30, 54
preparatory hearings
    reporting restrictions 42
Press Association 74
    news wire 113, 119
Press Association Library 76
press briefings 124
Press Complaints Commission (PCC)
    32, 38, 100, 108
press conferences 122–3, 232
    online 201
press cuttings 75, 91, 199, 200
press cuttings bureaux 75–6
press releases
    addressing 121
    checking 107–8
    contact database 73, 74, 102
    contact details 107, 111
    content 105–7
    crisis management 121–2
    distribution 7, 73–4, 101–3, 112,
        118–21
    e-mail 102, 103, 109, 119, 205–6
    embargoes 108–9, 110, 130
    evaluating 111–12
    fax 7, 101, 109, 119–20
    figures in 111
    generally 69, 78, 101–3, 190–1
    Golden Shredder Award 102
    ILEX, guidance notes for 263–4
    Law Society 19
    layout 105–7, 110, 263
    media list 73
    news wires 113, 117, 119
    notes for editors 107
    objectives 104
    photographs 115–18, 176, 199, 264
    presentation 109
    punctuation 110

    reasons for 105
    research findings 118
    stylistic conventions 109–11
    supporting documents 118
    surveys 118
    targetting 112
    timing 105, 129–30
print media
    legal journals 79–80
    magazines 50, 81, 192
    pre-publication legal advice 54
    press briefings 124
    trade press 79–82
    see also newspapers
Prison Reform Trust 268
Prison Watch 269
Prisoners' Advice Service 269
Private Eye 126
Pro Bono Awards 2–3
proactive media relations 76
professional indemnity insurance
    barristers 27
    solicitors 22–3
Professional Marking Forum 209
Professional Services Marketing Group
    209
profile pieces 113–15
Public Relations Consultants
    Association 208
Publicity Code *see* Solicitors' Publicity
    Code
Pullen, Chris 92
punctuation 110

Question Time 31, 160, 161, 163, 167,
    172, 176, 179
quotes, attributing 94–5

radical lawyers 10, 12, 58
radio
    audience 55, 56, 138–9, 144, 148
    critical interviews 134–6
    cult personalities 148
    current affairs programmes 137–47
    digital 55
    discussions 147–8
    down-the-line interviews 132, 148,
        152
    'dries' 147, 151–2
    end of the interview 153–4
    'fluffs' 151–2
    follow-up calls or correspondence 154
    generally 55–7, 132
    independent stations 55

informative interviews 134
the interview 143–7
local radio 52, 144, 148, 192
national radio 55
news programmes 137–47
notes, using 152
panel discussions 147–8
phone-in programmes 22, 149–51
pre-recorded interviews 147, 151–2
preparations 132, 133–40
regional accents 140
remote studies 148–9
specialist stations 55
split frequency 55
starting the interview 142–3
studio 141–2
telephone interviews 132, 152–3
voice 139–40
rape
reporting restrictions 45
reactive media relations 76
Redhead, Brian 152
Reed, Oliver 173
referrals and introductions 19
regional media
marketing, and 191–2
newspapers 12, 23, 52–3, 82–4, 98,
115, 125, 192
radio 52, 144, 148, 192
regulatory bodies 29, 31, 32
Release 268
releases *see* press releases
reporting restrictions
breach of 42
children 43–5, 46
complex prosecutions 43
family cases 46
fraud trials 43
generally 41
lifting 42–3
magistrates' court 41–3
rape and sexual offences 45
remands and committals 41–2
transfers and preparatory hearings
43
witnesses 45
youth courts 44–5
research findings, presenting 118
research-based stories 127–8
Reuters 74
risk analysis 13, 231
Robertson, Geoffrey, *Media Law* 28–30,
31, 32–3, 34, 41, 46, 222, 223
Romeike and Curtice 75

Rose, Neil 100
Roskill Committee 43
Ross, Nick 10–11
Rozenberg, Joshua 51, 77, 91, 129–30

Sanderson, Kate 158
'Save Legal Aid' campaign 83
scanners 115, 117
Schachter, Jim 78
SchNews 58
search engines 7, 61, 62, 65, 72
sedition 30
self-regulation 12
serious fraud cases 43
sexual offences
reporting restrictions 45
Shop Talk 56
Sigler, Charlie 56
skeleton arguments 47–48, 109
Sky News 35
Smerin, Jessica 100–1
Smith, Andrew 54, 83–4
software 72–3, 192
Soham enquiry 35
solicitors
attitudes to 1
insurance 22–3
rules for 16–25
Solicitors' Advocacy Code 21
Solicitors' Introduction and Referral
Code 1990 17–18
Solicitors' Journal 80, 102
Solicitors' Publicity Code 258–61
claims of specialism or expertise
20
general principles 18
name of firm, mentioning 18–19
naming clients 20
professional stationery 259–60, 261
reference to other lawyers 19
rudeness 21
success rate, reference to 20–21
unadmitted staff 21–22
Special Professional Indemnity
Insurance Scheme 22–3
specialism, claims of 20
spectacles, wearing of 168–9
Spillane, Mary 166
Spycatcher 224
Squal 58
Starr, Freddie 98
stationery 259–60, 261
Stattrax 65
Stephens, Mark 70, 116

stipendiary magistrates 40
Stobbs, Mark 27, 28
Stuperstats 64
sub judice 34–5, 39, 137, 249
success fees 2
success rate, reference to 20–1
Sun, the 2, 50, 79
Sunday Express 51
Sunday Mail 51
Sunday Mirror 51
Sunday Telegraph 51
Sunday Times 51
support staff 21–2
survey findings 118
Sutcliffe, Peter 35
Swallow, Matt 94
Sweeney, John 37

tape-recording
   court proceedings 47
   interviews 77, 97, 99
Tasso, Kim 14
telephone interviews 97, 132, 152–3
television
   on air 175–6
   alcohol consumption 172–3
   appearance 162–70
   'as for live' interviews 160
   audience 179
   clothes 162–6
   contact lenses 168–9
   'court steps' interviews 181–3
   criminal trials, coverage of 40
   discussion programmes 178–9
   down-the-line interviews 183
   dressing for 162–6
   'dries' 159, 161
   electronic news gathering 57
   evaluating your performance 178
   first contact 156–7
   floor manager 174
   'fluffs' 159
   generally 57–8, 59, 156
   hair 166–7
   language 177–8
   live interviews 160
   make-up 166, 167, 169–70
   microphones 173–4
   nerves 170–2
   notes, using 176
   panel programmes 178–9
   pictorial material, using 176
   posture 171, 176–7
   pre-recorded interviews 159, 160–1
      preparations 157, 158–9
      press conferences 122–3, 232
      refusing to appear 157–8
      regulatory bodies 29, 31
      'snatched' interviews 181–3
      spectacles, wearing of 168–9
      studio 174–5
      voice 170–1, 173, 174
      workplace interviews 180–1
Terry O'Hallaran Memorial Fund 269
text messaging 60
Thatcher, Margaret 166
Thomas, Bill 56
Times, The 50, 56, 69, 79, 85, 101, 248
   Law Supplement 66, 67, 69, 113, 126
Today 8, 56, 152
tongue twisters 170–1
trade press
   legal journals 79–80
   non-legal 81–2
transcripts 47
transfers
   reporting restrictions 43
trial
   jury trial 39–40, 222–4
   magistrates' court 40, 41–3
   prejudicial media coverage, and 2, 3
   see also reporting restrictions
'trial by media' 3, 16, 35, 40–1
typing skills 60

unadmitted staff 21–2
Undercurrents 58
Universal Declaration of Human
   Rights 32–3
unqualified operators 2, 12

V Graham Norton 179
Verkaik, Robert 51, 77, 93
Vine, Jeremy 56, 141
Virtual Press Office 62, 64
voice 139–40, 170–1, 173, 174

Wade, Rebekah 2
Wall Street Journal Europe 79
Watchdog 158
websites 3, 10, 59–66, 149, 151
   see also Internet
Weekend News 56, 149
West, Fred 42
Wheeler, Peter 99, 138
Whitburn, Vanessa 56
Willings Press Guide 72
Withers 180

witnesses
  'cheque book journalism' 15, 38
  contempt, and 37, 38–39
  payments to 38
  reporting restrictions 45
Woman's Own 81
Women Prisoners' Resource Centre
  269
Writers' and Artists' Yearbook 2003 72

Xtreme Information 76

Yates, Paula 9
Yorkshire Post 83
Young, Jimmy 23, 56, 141, 150, 154
youth courts
  reporting restrictions 44–5

Zilkha, John 56